American Magdalene

American Magdalene

The Life Behind the Scandalous Book
Madeleine: An Autobiography

BRENDA S. TOLIAN

McFarland & Company, Inc., Publishers
Jefferson, North Carolina

ISBN (print) 978-1-4766-9801-4
ISBN (ebook) 978-1-4766-5792-9

LIBRARY OF CONGRESS CATALOGING DATA ARE AVAILABLE

Library of Congress Control Number 2025039249

© 2025 Brenda S. Tolian. All rights reserved

No part of this book may be reproduced or transmitted in any form or by any means, electronic or mechanical, including photocopying or recording, or by any information storage and retrieval system, without permission in writing from the publisher.

Front cover image: courtesy of photographer Jay Halsey.

Printed in the United States of America

*McFarland & Company, Inc., Publishers
Box 611, Jefferson, North Carolina 28640
www.mcfarlandpub.com*

To all the Magdalenes

Acknowledgments

THIS BOOK AND THE RESEARCH that shaped it would not have been possible without Kevin Binfield's instruction, guidance, and encouragement at Murray State University. His dedication to teaching and creating an environment that encouraged questioning, curiosity, and critical thinking gave me the tools needed to pull at the aged book threads of historical life-writing through attribution studies and textual bibliography. I am grateful for his patience, humor, wisdom, and belief in my work. I will always be thankful to Dr. Binfield for allowing his doctoral students to "chase squirrels" because, sometimes, the far-out questions return the most interesting results.

To my twins, who have supported me through this project for years, thank you for your patience and willingness to help with edits and citations. Thank you for listening to me ramble about the next new find in some odd archive or slamming into dreaded dead ends. To my mother, who listened as I worked out thoughts with her on the phone at 6:00 a.m., believing in me every step of the way. To my grandparents, whose support never wavered throughout my life and who showed me the importance of history and books. To Hillary Leftwich, who first showed me that a woman could fight for agency through the power of written words and the importance of a sisterhood of like-minded writers.

This book about women—their voices, struggles, and resilience, mirrors the trauma and tribulations of our time in many ways. I extend my deepest gratitude to the women who have supported me, whether through encouragement, listening, or simply reminding me why this work matters. Our agency is not a right we are born with—it is a right we fight for every day of our lives.

Finally, I want to acknowledge the countless women—past, present, and future—whose labor, in all its forms, has shaped families, communities, and this nation, often without recognition or thanks and frequently alone. This book is, in many ways, for them.

Table of Contents

Acknowledgments — vii

Preface — 1

Introduction: A Most Dangerous Book — 7

1. The Flames in the Background — 21
2. Demons in the Details — 28
3. Madeleine Blair — 37
4. Judge Ben Lindsey (1869–1943) — 42
5. Mary Agnes Regan—Child of God — 48
6. Mary Becomes the Madeleine: Saint Louis and Kansas City — 61
7. The Chicago Working Years — 76
8. Magdalene as Mother — 90
9. Living Picture of Sorrow — 103
10. Mount Sinai — 111
11. Greatest Mining Camp on Earth — 113
12. Mountains and Valleys — 119
13. Northwest Canada — 127
14. Somewhere Beyond Redemption — 136
15. Resurrection — 145

Table of Contents

16. The Well-Defended Barrier 154
17. American Magdalene 160

Appendix: Transcribed Epilogue from Madeleine: An Autobiography, *the Discovered 1924 Edition* 169

Chapter Notes 177

Bibliography 185

Index 191

Preface

WHEN YOUR RESEARCH FOCUS IS American literature, numbers and scientific analysis are not the methods that come to mind. Yet, they became my primary tools in investigating a literary mystery more than a century old. The mystery of the pseudonymized Madeleine Blair, the anonymous author of *Madeleine: An Autobiography*, has remained intact since the book's banning in 1919. I am not a "numbers person," but through textual bibliography and stylometry—a linguistic analysis technique—I began to uncover the hidden patterns within the text of *Madeleine: An Autobiography*. Stylometry, often used to identify anonymous authorship, has been employed in high-profile cases, such as confirming JK Rowling's authorship of a crime novel and exploring questions surrounding Shakespeare's works. Under the guidance of Kevin Binfield at Murray State University, I learned through trial and error how to use the tools of this often tricky analytical method.

As I began to apply these methods to my research, it felt like I was, as Dr. Binfield frequently called it, "chasing squirrels." Sometimes, the research and academic investigation led to dead ends and, other times, to remarkable treasure troves of information that had remained hidden for a century. You see, history and literature are frequently controlled, and the information we receive is fed to us. We often don't ask the hard questions, and usually, we don't know how or what to ask for or if we are even allowed. I was taught to ask questions and, in doing so, chased down one of the most remarkable American authors we have never really known.

Research, especially in literary attribution, is personal and often challenging. It is easy to develop myopia and unconsciously force a narrative that may not hold up under scrutiny. We seek absolutes in a discipline that contains many fuzzy details. This struggle was ever present during my work on *Madeleine*. It's important to remember that just because we want a research narrative to be true, it doesn't mean that it is. The research techniques I used were new to me, and much of my journey was about learning how to conduct research itself—something academia often assumes graduate students already know. We present our papers as if they emerged fully formed, but the process is far from magical. It's rigorous and often frustrating, but the reward of discovery makes it worthwhile.

My first significant breakthrough came when I turned to the power of AI and its ability to analyze huge amounts of style and language data. To solve the mystery of *Madeleine*'s authorship, I used comparison analysis. One of the tools I employed was something readily available to digital humanities scholars, Voyant Tools, a web-based text analysis program. Voyant allowed me to compare *Madeleine*'s linguistic patterns with other texts from the same period. I ran countless comparisons, wanting to replicate my findings scientifically and ensure the reliability of the results. I also employed various aspects of ChatGPT in building an application called the Clifton Method to examine multiple patterns in a specific way.

I began like many before me, doubting a woman had written the book. The narrative focuses on the struggles and perspectives of a woman involved in prostitution, but it would not be the first time outside motives would drive the creation of fiction posing as a true story. The author's anonymity raised many questions about authenticity. The available documentation, though limited, fueled my curiosity: Who authored *Madeleine: An Autobiography* and why? Could we trust the author's stated purpose—to help women in similar situations—when the author chose to remain anonymous? With no personal records or clear author to study, I was left with only the text and the data I could extract from its pages.

Stylometry, the technique I employed, analyzes writing patterns through metrics like word variety, word count, and sentence length. These metrics provide what is known as a lexiconic fingerprint—a unique signature for each writer. I began to wonder what insights the linguistic patterns of *Madeleine* could offer. The task was intimidating, and I often doubted my capabilities. Yet, holding a rare first edition of the book—a 1919 copy that survived the banning and subsequent destruction of almost all others—and later discovering an unknown 1924 edition felt like I was touching something sacred. In today's world, where book banning is a persistent threat, the physical artifact of *Madeleine* and the story of its survival reminded me of the power of suppressed voices, marginalized experiences, and culture.

As my stylometric analysis progressed, I found remarkable similarities between the writing of *Madeleine* and the prolific Colorado judge

Ben Lindsey, who wrote the book's introduction. I compared *Madeleine* with Lindsey's works—*The Beast*, *The Revolt of Modern Youth*, and *The Dangerous Life*. The results showed that Lindsey's writing style was incredibly close to *Madeleine*'s. I also compared texts by female authors from the same era, including Madeleine Doty's *Society's Misfits*, Elizabeth Cady Stanton's *Eighty Years or More*, Edith Wharton's *The Custom of the Country*, and Jane Addams' *Newer Ideals of Peace*. Interestingly, *Madeleine*'s linguistic fingerprint aligned more with Lindsey's and Addams' than with other women authors who wrote about social justice issues of the time.

The word "social," for example, appeared 132 times in the combined works of *Madeleine* and Lindsey's texts. It was used in terms related to social justice, social reform, and social class—a pattern not found to the same extent in the works of other suffragettes. Although suffragettes used "social" to describe class and social upheaval, they did not employ the term in the same broad or frequent way that *Madeleine* or Judge Lindsey did in regard to the plight of women and children. Jane Addams came closest, unsurprisingly, given her role as a social worker and head of Hull House in Chicago.

Another term that emerged was "white slavery," a phrase used in connection with prostitution within the national discourse of the 1890s. The societal fears of "white slavery" were fed due to the social discourse of purity, religious organizations, and social-concerned groups raising their voices to illuminate the problem. This idea was that young "white" women and girls, due to their innocence and inexperience, became easy prey to those who would take them by dubious means, subjecting them to sexual exploitation. This belief that they "didn't know better" was widespread and led to laws regulating women's bodies and sexuality. Many laws are still on the books today, and others are experiencing a resurrection in the 21st century. The term "white slavery" arises often in the text of *Madeleine: An Autobiography*, encountered first in the introduction written by Judge Ben Lindsey. The author of *Madeleine* states that they did not believe in the concept of "white slavery." Through such unique terms and their usage, clues arose in the search for the author's attribution.

Like many researchers before me, I had many doubts and ideas about the author. I wondered whether Judge Ben Lindsey could have been the author or at least heavily involved in the writing of *Madeleine*. Judge Lindsey was a well-known social justice crusader who advocated for women's rights, setting up the first juvenile court in Denver. He had remarkable progressive beliefs around women and marriage that differed from many of his friends and colleagues, and he often rubbed against the grain of society, pushing for modern marriage and family planning reforms. He, like others, would have had reasons to write or edit a book such as *Madeleine*. His controversial stance on topics like abortion and contraception certainly reflected the same radical thinking found in *Madeleine*.

I also considered Lindsey's wife Henrietta Brevoort Lindsey as a possible author. She was a fascinating figure, a radical socialist, and a supporter of women's issues. There were striking similarities between her life and the protagonist's, including their age, involvement in social justice, and concerns regarding issues affecting women and the marginalized.

Henrietta coauthored several plays with her husband, focusing on social issues like vice, crime, and unwed mothers—topics central to *Madeleine*. Like her husband, she had close connections with suffragettes, especially Jane Addams, who, as it turned out, was one of three early reviewers of *Madeleine*. Yet, despite the tantalizing connections, the evidence did not lead to a satisfactory conclusion.

My stylometric analysis of Henrietta's plays didn't match *Madeleine*'s text data closely enough to attribute authorship. I do believe that Henrietta, like her husband, was an important figure to the author; however, I do not think either was a primary author of *Madeleine*. Later, this belief seemed valid when the author thanked a "Man and Wife" in an unknown and unreported 1924 edition. In the acknowledgments, the author thanks the "Man and Wife" for mentoring her during the difficult writing process.

The turning point came after spending months attempting to find elusive copyright entries for the book, hoping it would appear as a renewal by family or some other agent. The only entries I came across in the records were attributed to Lindsey—until I discovered a 1947 copyright renewal filed under Agnes R. Sears. This was a name that had not appeared in any previous research. Who was Agnes R. Sears? The copyright renewal occurred 28 years after the book's initial publication in 1919, following the rules of the 1909 Copyright Act. At this point, I had to consider that Sears could be the actual author—or, at the very least, someone directly connected (perhaps through family) to the work. Further digging revealed that Agnes R. Sears was listed as a writer in San Francisco voting records from 1919, but other biographical details were scarce.

Could Agnes R. Sears be Madeleine? The timeline fit. Sears would have been in her sixties or seventies when the copyright was renewed, which aligned with Madeleine's claim to be 34 years old in 1919. Despite the fact that I found no direct evidence linking her to the narrative at

```
v. 1.
Scoutmastership
  see Baden-Powell, Robert.
SCOVILLE, SAMUEL. The out-of-doors
  club. © 26Apr19, A561206.
  R17851, 17Apr47; Samuel Scoville,
  Jr. (A) Philadelphia.
SCULPTOR'S angel. R25639.
  SEE Corelli, Marie.
The search
  see Lutz, G. L. H.
SEARS, AGNES R. Madeleine, an
  autobiography. With an introd.
  by Judge Ben. B. Lindsey.
  © 15Oct19, A535347. R14418,
  2Jan47; Harper & brothers
  (PCB) New York.
SEASHORE, CARL EMIL. The psychology
  of musical talent. (Beverly
  educational series) © 13Dec19,
  A559080. R15583, 6Mar47;
  author, Iowa City, Iowa.
Seattle, the seaport of success
  see Thomas, L. M.
```

This Sears, Agnes R., 1947 copyright entry is the first clue of the authentic author of *Madeleine: An Autobiography* (Catalogue of Title-entries of Books and Other Articles Entered in the Office of the Librarian of Congress, at Washington, 1947.45).

first, Sears' name continued to surface in my research. Finally, after exhaustive research that revealed remarkable details of a life and countless dead ends, I concluded that *Madeleine: An Autobiography* was authored by Mary Agnes Regan Sears, also known as Madeleine Blair, among other pseudonyms. Throughout this book, her legal name, Mary, replaces the pseudonym Madeleine, affording her authenticity, attribution, humanity, and agency as never before.

The book has always been clear in its purpose: to communicate to society the struggles of women caught in the complicated situation of prostitution, societal expectations, and the dream of personal redemption and agency. It was also intended as a message of hope for women like Mary who sought to change their lives. Although Sears was self-educated, her voice emerged then as it does now as a voice for the marginalized, ignored, and silenced.

The following pages detail Mary's life using her name and words. This book refers to the 1919 and the 1924 long-lost second edition, combined with years of research findings, weaving her narrative and the hidden truth that has finally come to light. Due to the often unreliable and subjective nature of memory, autobiography, and narration, the dates presented are as close as possible to those found in *Madeleine: An Autobiography* and the various records that have since come to light. Even newspaper entries and census and other records sometimes conflict, and when this occurs, I try to highlight this information and suggest why the discrepancies might have happened. Some sources and the text occasionally conflict by a year or two, mirroring how our memories shift over time, making absolutes elusive.

Mary Agnes Regan Sears was much more than a prostitute and the author of *Madeleine: An Autobiography*—she was an example of resilience, intellect, and transformation. A poet, essayist, mission worker, and fierce advocate for social justice, she defied the societal constraints of her time with tenacity and determination. She was a daughter, a mother, a wife, and, above all, a woman who refused to be defined by the heartless and inhumane judgments of her time.

Introduction:
A Most Dangerous Book

PROSTITUTION IS OFTEN CALLED THE oldest profession in the world, but this phrase understates all the reasons women engage in the work. Mary Regan Sears, in her book *Madeleine: An Autobiography*, published in 1919, pseudonymized as the writer Madeleine Blair, noted that women have always had to trade parts of themselves to survive in a male-dominated world. Women have traded their bodies for food, shelter, money, clothing, education, and medical care. They have traded their bodies to feed their children and care for their extended family. For some, it was a choice, though a dangerous one and often a life-or-death gamble. Prostitution is hard labor that takes an emotional and physical toll on countless women and girls of all ethnic and cultural backgrounds. Emma Goldman asked in her essay "The Traffic in Women," "What is the cause of the trade of women? Not merely white women but yellow and black women as well? Exploitation, of course; the merciless Moloch of capitalism that fattens on underpaid labor."[1] Prostitution emerges wherever women face economic hardship, social exclusion, or a lack of viable means to earn a living to support the needs of daily living and survival.

The women of the scarlet sisterhood are known by many names: soiled dove, scarlet woman, woman of ill repute, harlot, mistress, and whore. The labels placed upon their persons and their bodies have set them apart and marginalized them beyond the borders of society. They have been immortalized by their bodies and the supposed "sin" they commit without a complete understanding of their humanity and contributions to the society they serve. Under the burden of timeless and deeply rooted inequalities, women have labored their bodies, seen as transactional with or without their consent in prostitution and marriage. The prostitution problem is, at its root, a women's issue that reaches beyond categories of cultural, religious, and political spheres and has proven resistant to eradication. The continued issues of societal problems and imbalances in power and opportunity remain unresolved in the 21st century as they were in the 19th century, resisting any easy solution.

Prostitution is not an issue that exists alone. The work is intertwined with systems of patriarchy, misogyny, power, and exploitation, functioning in ways analogous to industrialization and trade. The sex trade, when considered as a means of living and labor, is no different from women's labor in other areas, in factories, fields, and domestic settings. The prostitute's labor, though not given the same credit, is equally significant in the economic and social development of nations. Despite their contributions, sex workers are often demonized, forgotten, or sensationalized. They are judged under the focused lens of sex. They are not remembered for their labor under frequently harsh working conditions, physical and emotional abuse, societal judgment, and little to no legal or medical protection. Many faced grueling hours, meager earnings, and the constant threat of arrest, violence, or disease, making survival short-lived or difficult at best.

For many women, entering prostitution was a decision born of desperation within complex life situations that warranted the choice when no other choices were offered. This choice, however, often became a life sentence, permanently stigmatizing women in the eyes of society. The scarlet brand of prostitution burned no matter how far one might go to escape their past, and it followed them throughout their lives, irrespective of the circumstances that led them into the trade. Poverty, lack of education, gender inequality, and rigid social structures left many women with few alternatives, forcing them into the vilified yet high-demand profession.

Prostitution exists on the coattails of the movements of men, whether it be colonialism, war, or industrialization. The effects are especially apparent in situations where economic upheaval and displacement disproportionately affect women. Brothels have always thrived near military encampments, ports, and industrial centers, catering to men in transient or exploitative occupations. Laws and policies have often sought to control or regulate prostitution. Frequently, those in powerful positions bent societal rules to profit off the labor of prostitutes through complicity and corruption and through "illegal protection." The laws built to control frequently failed to address the underlying economic and social conditions that perpetuated sex work. Instead, they served to criminalize and marginalize the very individuals most vulnerable to exploitation.

Prostitution, then, becomes something more, and in a way, it becomes a metaphor for the inequalities and power dynamics embedded in societies throughout history. Yet, it is a metaphor that is often unobserved. So what does an absence of firsthand narratives of prostitutes say about a nation that owes some of its success to their labor? The narratives of a prostitute could have been insightful, full of firsthand accounts of resilience, autonomy, agency, survival, exploitation, systemic failure, and brazen success. Unfortunately, the voices of prostitutes, especially in the 19th and 20th centuries, mostly remained suppressed or were not deemed worthy enough of recording or saving. Yet, sex work, despite efforts to suppress and reform, persists, raising critical questions about justice, gender, power distribution, and resources in human societies.

Dominant society throughout history has tolerated prostitution and decreed the labor as a necessary evil. Early on, with the growth of the United States, prostitutes were viewed as sinful saviors of the home and commerce. Due to beliefs connected to the physical needs of men and the sheer numbers of men required for industrialization and expansion into the West with the propagation of military and mining camps, prostitution became a lucrative and reliable source of income for women. The big, industrialized cities and the call of the West provided work opportunities and an environment ripe for commerce in sex work, ranging from brothels and cribs to part-time clandestine engagements and street work. Mary would eventually work in many of these environments. For many women, this work equated to opportunity; for others, it was damnation. Women like Mary felt they made the choice, though her autobiography suggests it was made because she was robbed of all others.

Mary was born and raised, came of age, and worked during three transitional periods. The first was the aftermath of the Civil War, and the second was the approach of the new century. The last was just after World War I. In each, the moral and social norms shifted. For women, no matter their circumstances or the period, it was a time marked by rapid change and uncertainty. Within the text *Madeleine*, Mary chronicles her life from childhood (though briefly) through her thirties, including a decade she spent as a sex worker. Her motivation for writing her autobiography was rooted in a desire to guide other women and girls like herself toward making different life choices. At the same time, her writing sought to challenge prevailing narratives about "white slavery," prostitution, and single motherhood. By sharing her story, Mary tried to shed light on the many issues affecting women in her position and to provide a voice for those whose voices were absent in the narratives.

Despite frequently feeling alone and isolated for much of her life, Mary understood she was far from unique. She was one of countless women struggling to survive in a rapidly changing societal landscape. Her story, therefore, was not just personal—it was symbolic of a broader struggle faced by many women during this chaotic period in U.S. history.

Mary understood through experience and observation that many women had, though not often recognized, shared realities, both negative and positive, as wives, mothers, and prostitutes, carefully navigating a society in flux. Her honesty in sharing her struggles and choices reflects her desire to fracture the silence around issues like prostitution and single motherhood placed on women. She rejected popular social notions of sex work and concepts of "white slavery" at a time when such topics were often touted in moralistic concern, often cloaked in shame and judgment. Mary's book called for empathy, understanding, and reform before she was silenced in a court case that would obliterate her book and voice. Or this is what was commonly believed.

The narratives of women like Mary were often subverted by others who did not have direct experience. Most of the books written about prostitution from this period were written by men such as Reverend Frank Goodchild and William W. Sanger. Female social workers and writers such as Jane Addams, Victoria Woodhull, and Tennessee Claflin, the last two of whom ran a reform paper called *Woodhull & Claflin*, shared experiences as they were shared with them. Almost all of the views were secondhand and exterior to the prostitute's experience. The narratives were often seeded with moralistic, medical, and sociological leanings, helpful to the social reformer but not to prostitutes or women who were on the cusp of taking on the work.

There were few true memoirs of direct experience from prostitutes, and the few that existed in book form were later proven to have been written by men. That is why Mary's book remains a valuable testimony to the experience of women like her. The importance of *Madeleine: An Autobiography* as a primary document, though held in high regard by a handful of scholars, was always at odds with its unknown author and questions about its validity. Yet the author's purpose differed from that of the scholar, whose primary purpose is to investigate. Mary's only desire was to humanize and rescue.

It was with this intent to rescue and in the stormy climate of the early 20th century that Mary Regan Sears completed her book, which would become the most quoted and, though it could not be confirmed until now, reliable account of prostitution in the 18th century to this day. For two years, Mary wrote and explored her life, revisiting memories and trauma that she mostly locked away and certainly didn't share more publicly in her mission work. She examined her choices with a critical eye, etching her words carefully, humanizing women of her experience and class—prostitutes, laboring women, and poverty-stricken mothers and daughters who struggled in a rapidly changing world that ignored them.

When the book approached its publishing debut, women's roles were shifting again during and after World War I. By December 1919, the world was still coming to terms with the aftermath of the war, its long-term effects just beginning to surface. With the passage of the 18th Amendment and the onset of Prohibition, society, as it had done after the Civil War, embarked on another moral rehabilitation campaign that targeted not only alcohol but also issues like prostitution, contraception, and abortion. Fears of radicalism—fueled by the Red Scare and anxieties over Bolshevism and anarchism—ignited concerns about radical, moral, and political agitation, which exploded into the public and political forum.

Into this storm, Mary Regan Sears offered her story, a candid memoir about the life of a prostitute. Her book became a lightning rod for controversy, kicking off one of U.S. history's most notorious book-banning cases that has faded into obscurity. John Sumner, head of the New York Society for the Suppression of Vice (NYSSV), declared the book "one of the worst and most dangerous books of the day."[2] Clinton T. Brainard, president of Harper & Brothers, publishers of Mary's book, found himself in the eye of a political, moral, and literary storm. This "dangerous" book, *Madeleine: An Autobiography*, captured the attention of a nation and set off a legal battle that would create a ripple effect in the modern era.[3] Even over a century later, the case serves as a reminder of how such laws continue to shape discussions about women concerning their bodies, freedom, agency, morality, and control.

The contentious winds of outrage initially fell upon Clinton T. Brainard, president of Harper & Brothers, who faced charges of offering for sale what the *New York Post* called an "indecent, vile" book. The book and the subsequent sensationalism were sparked by John Sumner, the figurehead of the NYSSV.[4] As a New York State institution, the society operated as a strong arm for censorship and the recommendation of works, primarily published texts for prosecution. Like so many books before and since, *Madeleine: An Autobiography* became a target for censorship. The NYSSV went after the publisher and its president, offering them up to the courts for conviction and imprisonment. *Madeleine* was "dangerous" enough to be suppressed into obscurity and forgotten, or so it was understood, until a new edition resurfaced in 1986 with an academic introduction by Marcia Carlisle published by Persea Books of New York.[5] Carlisle pulled from various threads of known research in writing the new introduction, offering the most comprehensive profile of the court case and author profile of the time. This edition garnered some attention, but like the first edition, it faded into obscurity.

The book and moral societies were born of an era in which moral panic and pervasive concerns focused on women's purity alleged that white women were coerced or kidnapped into prostitution. This led to the concept of "white slavery." The *Washington Times* in 1919 reported through various opinions and reviews that the supposed female sex worker who wrote the "obscene" text denied "white slavery" existed, a point that would remain an unwavering belief of the author. The news organizations also made much of the author's life choices presented in the book, such as when the author writes about her abortion. She noted in the book that she told the doctor who attended to her that she "fooled God." She also wrote that men know nothing "but sexual gratification" while women pay the price for the results that come after.[6] Her words were quoted in the papers and used to sway popular opinion to the cause of morality. It became apparent through investigation that many of the reviewers either did not read the book (almost all of the first editions were burned) or decided to use their interpretation based on rumor, hearsay, and gossip to promote the NYSSV's cause.

Interestingly, not every reviewer was unkind, especially those who worked to end the trade of female bodies and what they called "white slavery." While most critics focused on sensationalism, others wrote, "Even in her most degraded moments, Madeleine remains a proper person."[7] This was also the view shared by the widely popular judge Ben Lindsey, who committed to writing the book's introduction. The judge, not known to mince words, wrote in the introduction, "I have an intense appreciation of *Madeleine*. It ought to be read and pondered over. It is *true*. The Madeleines are right in your midst."[8] In our current era, we picture the feathered, scantily dressed saloon girl to epitomize the experience and persona of the working prostitute. However, this does not correctly capture the experience of women laborers of the 19th and early 20th centuries. Many, like Mary, could fly under the radar in the world outside of the brothel. She could be Madeleine within the brothel walls but step out as Mary, a handsome but plain-dressed woman. Some, as Mary noted in her book, worked in factories or supplemented family income with prostitution on the side with no one, especially society, the wiser.

The many problems that arose from the clandestine commerce, as pointed out by Judge Lindsey and Mary, included diseases, sexual crimes, and the exploitation of women. The sex trade penetrated other aspects of society, with results such as unwed mothers and underage children being subjected to the sex trade or crime. Orphaned children were also an added burden and stigmatized through no fault of their own, often assumed to be the result of prostitution and loose morality of women causing single motherhood and unwanted children. Other societal issues placed on prostitutes were the social ills of abortion and drug and alcohol abuse. Society always made a scapegoat of the prostitute, whose prevalence was a by-product of a nation's growth and male appetites. Rather than looking at the wider problems within society, reformers projected many of the social ills on the bodies of the women engaged in the work rather than acknowledging their role in perpetuating it.

Judge Ben Lindsey, the father of the Colorado juvenile court, was no stranger to the heartache of prostitutes. In the introduction of *Madeline: An Autobiography*, Lindsey speaks to the many interactions with women in his Denver court caught within the predatory sex trade. He writes that he chose early on not to "hate the sinner but the sin," explaining that adults are "just children grown-up."[9] The previous abolitionist movement used this framing successfully concerning the enslaved, and new social justice groups hoped to apply this "need to rescue" viewpoint of fallen women as children for a similar outcome. The Progressives of the era borrowed from the tried-and-true linguistics of the last social war to build momentum for the new one. Purity societies, suffragettes, and newly framed social movements took up the next crusade to rescue "good" families, especially impressionable girls, ushering salvation in on the coattails of the Progressive era.

Most believed that prostitutes were beyond redemption, but not all. New voices on the social reform front thought various forms of rehabilitation could restore some women to Christian society. Lindsey writes of Madeleine Blair in his introduction in biblical terms, attempting to guide the reader toward an impassioned contemplation of Mary Magdalene, assumed by many Christians to be the prostitute who washed Jesus' feet with oil and was the first to see him when he rose from the grave. Magdalene, who in Christian dogma is described as a sinful woman and a working prostitute, is transformed into a forgiven woman by Christ. Lindsey, who gives Mary authenticity without giving away her identity, writes in the introduction, "Not that I may not have some criticisms and that I may not differ in some conclusions.... But the author has told us the facts—as fine, as splendid, and as sordid and as human as some of them are."[10] For Judge Lindsey, the book symbolized humanity rising from impossible lows, and for Mary, his approval provided a seal of authenticity that, from its publishing date, resisted questions of attribution.

Scholarship on the book has remained elusive until now. Most topics centered on prostitution or referenced research on women's suffrage, immigration, sex, sex work, women's studies, and social commentary. However, no comprehensive analysis of the book's textual or bibliographic relevance has been conducted. Historically, scholarship has not questioned Mary's pseudonym, Madeleine Blair.

The research reveals more than a life of prostitution, uncovering facets of Mary's life that had never been exposed before—elements she only hinted at in the epilogue. Mary, affectionately called Minnie by her parents, adopted working names like Madeleine Blair, Mary Fiske, Agnes Fiske, and Anita Gordon, not only to shield herself and her family from the stigma of prostitution but also for reasons far beyond its shadow. Her life was far more complex than the image of the prostitute she is associated with. Yet upon rediscovering Mary's story and her quest for happiness and redemption, there are truths to be revealed and learned from. She struggled with agency, which remains elusive for women in the United States today, highlighting her message's timelessness. The issues she faced often parallel with women's experiences of the past, present, and most likely, the future, anchored in social unrest, selective rights, and shifting moral perceptions surrounding women and their bodies. Her story is often unsettling because it resonates with tangible truths.

Madeleine: An Autobiography was published in an era when modern ideas of social justice regarding humanitarian issues were in their earliest development. For many, the realization of the effects of industrialization came too late, leaving its victims caught in a daily struggle for survival. Mary grew up during a period of leftover trauma from the Civil War, yet her book was published just after World War I. The pains of loss and growth suffered by the United States would forever dominate Mary's life through her experiences, choices, and relationships with men within her family, social circles, and working life.

During World War I, the country saw dramatic social shifts. Women entered the workforce in greater numbers, requiring greater independence. They also became aware of their growing power and were often active in the women's suffrage movement. The aftermath of the war fueled the Progressive movement, which sought to address new concepts of social justice, labor rights, and government corruption. The younger generation was irrevocably changed by the horrific realities of modern warfare. They clashed with what they perceived as the dated cultural perspectives of previous generations, challenging traditional values and moral sensibilities. The early opinions, reviews, and editorials surrounding the book capture the clash of divided national ideals.

Some questioned the author's motives at the time of publishing and during the often-dramatic court proceedings. The *Washington Times* reported various opinions from the public, reviewers, and critics. One such critic wrote, "The anonymous author asserts that the book is a true story of her life, and Judge Lindsey, in his commendatory, sentimental introduction, says that it is true. He could only have the word of the unknown writer as to its disclosures of her past."[11] One critic, F.M. O'B in the *New York Herald*, wrote, "This is one anonymous book over which there will be no quarrel: at least no lady in this century will rise and claim that it is her story."[12] In the *Battle Creek Enquirer*, the book is suggested as a "record of an actual experience" and ends with the assertion that "librarians, social workers, and ministers have given this book their endorsement. It is, first of all, a great human document."[13] While in Tennessee, critics accused the book of French morality writing: "It is a notorious fact that since the beginning of the world war, the European book stalls have been flooded with indecent works of the lowest type." The *Tennessean* also asserts *Madeline* "to be more lascivious that anything Paul de Kock ever wrote when in an absinthe dream."[14] The wide range of opinions moved from endorsing its authenticity and societal value to outrage and condemnation of its content and moral worth, highlighting the cultural tension and significant moral and religious transition within the United States.

Opinions about the book continued, morphed, and disappeared, but the author's mystery remained unsolved. Scholars accepted the mystery, focusing on prostitution and its conditions rather than attribution. Even today, the book is studied through the lens of the female body and the male gaze, often with feminist questions of agency. This approach misses the interesting and humanitarian connections this book seeks to illuminate. The original text, especially in its original epilogue, hints at a new life Mary assumed after she left prostitution, but research will uncover a later life lived in devotion to others.

Since 1919, it has been widely accepted that *Madeleine: An Autobiography* was authored by an anonymous woman whose life, as depicted in the book, spanned the years of prostitution and brothel ownership across various cities, including Chicago, Saint Louis, Kansas City, the mining towns of Montana, and eventually Canada. The author wrote about global travel, stops at San Francisco and New Orleans, and living in Helena, Montana. Mary's life spanned a period of monumental change, wars, and shifts in attitudes regarding sex and women. She bore witness to prostitution on a global scale as a traveler, an experience often barred to women unless they were monied. During this time, she witnessed the conditions working women experienced, from the most respected bawdy houses to the lowest cribs, wondering how she could change her life and find the strength to help others. It was within her desire for redemption that the book found life, and her courage found support in the likes of Jane Addams and Judge Ben Lindsey.

Judge Ben Lindsey described Mary's work as "a book that may be misunderstood by many, and it deserves to be read without prejudice—with an open mind. And I commend warmly the courageous frankness of the author in writing it and of the publishers in bringing it out."[15] Ben B. Lindsey used his platform as judge of the juvenile court of Denver in September 1919 to endorse *Madeleine: An Autobiography* with his official signature. Known for challenging the era's social mores, Lindsey often found himself at war with powerful entities like the Ku Klux Klan (KKK) and various social vice groups. His public introduction to a book so candidly detailing the realities of a prostitute's life and covering topics like sexually transmitted diseases (STDs), abortion, and client interactions highlights his devotion as a champion for social change. This courage to stand up in his personal and public work in his writing and courtroom was lifelong and audacious. Lindsey, who liked a good fight with the vice and moral societies as much as the KKK and later the Nazis, likely anticipated the sensationalism and public outcry his endorsement of *Madeleine* would provoke. The opposition mirrored the controversies he faced in his Denver courtroom over his unique ideas and publications. His stance was a testament to his fearlessness in opposing societal norms, which he observed only worked for a small segment of society. Lindsey lived and followed a vision of educating and eventually producing a more socially aware and conscious society. Yet even he couldn't have anticipated the controversy over the book.

Outrage over *Madeleine* was palpable and reported on the front pages of national and international newspapers. The *Washington Times* reported that the publisher, Clinton T. Brainard, "was arrested and found guilty of publishing, possessing and selling obscene literature, fingerprinted like any other common lawbreaker."[16] During the court proceedings, Brainard wavered, at first denying knowledge of the book's publication. Later, he too fought back. As reported by the *Washington Times*, he repeatedly drew comparisons between the narrative of "Madeleine's" career as a prostitute and the stories in the Bible. Once, when the magistrate McGrath read an exceptionally detailed part of the book, he asked if Brainard considered it proper to publish it as "uplift" material. He answered, "I'd hate to say that about every book of the Bible."[17] The questioning continued with the prosecutor reading another section and asking Brainard's opinion, to which he answered, "If I were to edit the Bible—."[18] Brainard's defense begged their client to stop referencing the Bible in every answer during this interaction.

Brainard thought the court case was ridiculous and often gave comical but sobering answers. However, he understood the dark underpinnings that propelled the book into front-page sensationalism. The case revolved around the book's validity and the political agendas behind the scenes, which began in the New York mayor's office and swept through the halls of William Randolph Hearst's expansive corporate kingdom.

Records of the court case support that Judge Ben Lindsey and the famous social worker Jane Addams reviewed the book before its publication but were never called to testify. Clinton T. Brainard was never compelled to reveal the author's identity. Lindsey's name appeared only in quotes from his introduction, and in the present digital age, his name supplanted Madeleine Blair as the author.

Even as a text mostly known for the author remaining anonymous, it cannot be denied that the narrative pulsates with universal themes and truths, sharing the often familiar traumas of poverty and the female struggle for agency. Mary writes about the harsh realities faced by women amid factory labor, domestic violence, the challenges of single parenthood, and child loss. She also candidly noted the ravages of substance abuse and the hopeless reality of women, choice or not, resorting to their bodies for transactional survival. When considering the author of *Madeleine*, researchers Julia Watson and Sidonie Smith noted in their work *Before They Could Vote: American Women's Autobiographical Writing, 1819–1919*, that "her tentative and mobile subjectivity shifts with the various social worlds she encounters, but her confessional narrative refuses any easy resolution."[19] It is true that Mary shows herself to be a woman of complex contrasts. She could nurture as a mother but also could take full possession of her agency and body by inducing an abortion. Although uneducated, she was knowledgeable and wise. She was both a victim of abuse and capable of inflicting it. She could be pious, sober, and controlled yet easily fall into alcoholism's clutches. She could be both Mary Agnes Regan Sears and Madeleine.

Many academic and commercial nonfiction books have focused on prostitution and women. These books often included *Madeleine: An Autobiography* and the pseudonymized author Madeleine Blair as an anonymous authority on the subject. Mary's book has been quoted in articles and journals and invoked in blogs and fiction. Yet, trust in her writing has always been questionable due to the writer's ambiguity.

Although her writing was compelling, researchers had to ask if her story was true. Some questioned if *Madeleine* might be based on composites of other young women who faced life and its bitter terms or social workers trying to raise awareness of the plight of sex workers. In her book *We Don't Talk About Those Women*, Belinda Crowson asked these same questions, writing, "How accurate was the story told by Madeleine? Who was the anonymous author? Was it actually written by an ex-madame and ex-prostitute? It was impossible to find the identity of the writer."[20] Uncovering Mary's story was a complicated endeavor requiring a key that did not seem to exist.

Anonymity within the textual study is often regarded as unreliable or dangerous. However, in the 19th and 20th centuries, it was frequently an avenue for writers, particularly female writers, to express themselves, choosing to conceal their identity without othering themselves within society. This necessary "hiddenness" removes the societal danger and pitfalls that could be inflicted on the author in their engagement with readers and therefore their engagement with the text. The decision to remain anonymous allows for a certain freedom of creation and writing, especially on subjects that might be distasteful to society, such as prostitution, substance abuse, or mental illness.

There is a specific patriarchal component to a female writer retaining anonymity, which may pertain to writing beyond the boundaries of social expectations that are hung around the neck of women. There is also power in "hiddenness" for the author to disassociate past reality from a present lived reality, especially if the past is considered transgressive.

The process of finding Mary was a journey through the necessary research steps, using textual bibliographical means and historical and genealogical digging for attribution—the mystery needed resolution—a name tied to its universal truths. The research involved countless hours of reading archived newspapers, searching files, and writing to archivists at the University of California, Los Angeles, who kindly found odd-numbered files in dusty boxes. Genealogies were searched, and books from the same era were fed into programs for stylometric data comparisons. Months were spent poring over New York Supreme Court case transcripts, and years were dedicated to combing through primary documents and records to attribute authorship as accurately as possible.

Unexpected figures often emerged—senators, members of the Church of Jesus Christ of Latter-day Saints familial hierarchy, social justice leaders, and some of New York's most prominent political figures. As the research progressed, intrigue and mysteries paralleled the book, with startling revelations continually reshaping the direction of the investigation. It became clear that this was not just about the author's identity but a wider cast of characters involved in a national drama.

Madeleine Blair was well hidden, obscured below the narrative she chose to tell and others who used it for their ends. What follows is the remarkable true story of Mary Agnes Regan Sears—the American Magdalene.

1

The Flames in the Background

THE NYSSV WAS A DIRECT response to the explosive changes brought about by many complex societal changes. The most notable changes followed in the painful wake of the Civil War, Reconstruction, and the Industrial Revolution, leading to the expansion of U.S. territory in manifest destiny ideals. The culminating economic growth and greed both helped and endangered women. What all these events had in common was the rapid transformation of the economy, which in turn affected the labor force. More people were working and moving nationally, and many others immigrated to the country. Therefore, more people navigated into urban areas seeking jobs and hoping for better wages. As a result of this movement, an increasing number of laborers, including women, left rural farming communities and their former countries to follow their American dream in urban centers.

This movement caused nervousness among those in society who historically held power and control. Not surprisingly, topics surrounding the female body, family planning, and vices became hot-button issues, especially around those who sought reform and called for a return to white Christian ideals and purity. In many ways, a working woman was a free and thinking woman who might begin to question systems of power, especially concerning the self and body.

In 1873, legislative action was taken. Anthony Comstock, a prominent lobbyist of the time and head of the NYSSV, hammered out the federal anti-obscenity postal statutes. The Comstock Act of 1873 was a federal law that sought to regulate moral standards through the U.S. postal system. The law targeted and criminalized the circulation of materials of immorality, pornography, contraceptives, sex education literature, personal letters and pamphlets, and books that discussed sex in any manner. Comstock, a rabid moral crusader and lobbyist, felt it was his Christian duty to look out for the morals of a nation. Comstock was instrumental in deciding what constituted pornography, hardly drawing a line between porn, art, and health. He is central to the criminalization of abortion and, during Mary's time, contraception and censoring literature that contained instructions for family planning. Emma Goldman wrote that Comstock "is the autocrat of American morals; he dictates the standards of good and evil, of purity and vice. Like a thief in the night, he sneaks into the private lives of the people, into their most intimate relations."[1] Comstock, through his moral obsession, perfected entrapment to catch those selling questionable books, pamphlets, pictures, or contraception sent through the post. He also used violence when the need supported the cause. Through his efforts, the NYSSV was created, quickly gaining power and prominence in New York and the nation, becoming its national moral conscience.

The NYSSV emerged directly from the nation's head-spinning chaos just after the Civil War. Industrial capitalism drove the shift with the nation's rapidly changing economic dimensions, necessitating an increased workforce. This workforce would include formerly rural workers, homesteaders, immigrants, and the formerly enslaved. This workforce would comprise not just men but women and children as well. The growing presence of these perceived outsiders within the public sphere, filling needed spaces in the workforce, also expanded into education and activism, threatening Victorian beliefs surrounding proper society, class, domesticity, and the built-in nature of dependence on men within marriage and families. In simple terms, these outsiders, by culture, race, age, and gender, were a threat to the ideals of a patriarchal society—a threat that required a solution.

Those in power were afraid of losing their hold over society. Workers were needed to supply the demands of the young, growing nation. Still, fears began to grow around controlling the numbers required to uphold the capitalistic fever that swept over the country. The moralistic concerns during the period following the war were partly due to the broadening of Victorian values emphasizing sexual purity, modesty, and strict adherence to Christian morality. It was during this time that temperance and purity movements rose to prominence. The unknowns of rapid industrialization and urbanization fed the moral concerns of reformers who saw change as the harbinger of eroding social values in the face of increased immigration and the inclusion of women in the workforce. The face of the United States was changing, and the reformers did not like what they saw.

Comstock, often described as a heroic figure in American history, used any means to disrupt what the dominant society saw as contraband, "swooping down on the dealers of illegal literature and

1. The Flames in the Background

The seal of the New York Society for the Suppression of Vice, founded in 1873. On the left, the purveyor of obscenity is being thrust into a cell, while on the right, a Christian layman consigns infamous volumes to the flames (Wikipedia).

contraband pictures, consigning tons of these mind-poisoning productions to the purifying action of the flames."[2] Comstock, in his book *Frauds Exposed*, compared his work to the terrible battle of Gettysburg in terms of national and moral importance. He wrote, "The conflict was to be a determined one. It was to be bitter and relentless. It was to be a Gettysburg."[3] He thought of his work as having a primary objective to "arouse a public sentiment against the vampires who are casting deadly poison into the fountain of moral purity."[4] It is claimed in the *Grand Island Independent* newspaper that Comstock was responsible for the arrest of 2,970 people; the confiscation of 93,000 tons of bookplates, printed matter, and pictures; and the suppression of 316 book titles from publication.[5] NYSSV agents obtained broad powers under

New York Penal Law article 106-1147 in 1919. Agents for the society, after designation by a sheriff of "any county" in the state of New York, could make arrests and "bring the court or magistrate under their jurisdiction offenders before found violating the provisions of any law of the trade-in and circulation of obscene literature, illustrations, advertisements and articles of immoral use."[6] The society operated within vague, unregulated government oversight and well-placed, robust support from New York City's upper and middle class. Some noteworthy wins for the NYSSV after the banning of *Madeleine: An Autobiography* were the suppression and banning of *Ulysses* by James Joyce in 1920 and *Lady Chatterley's Lover* by D.H. Lawrence in 1929. These were only two texts among the countless books banned. The society used well-honed tactics of arrests and lengthy court battles to accomplish their archaic aims, using the courtroom and news syndicates to arouse public opinion against various books, authors, and publishers they deemed obscene.

Anthony Comstock was a social justice crusader and creator of the New York Society for the Suppression of Vice. Photographer unknown (from Charles Gallaudet Trumbull, *Anthony Comstock, Fighter: Some Impressions of a Lifetime Adventure in Conflict with the Powers of Evil* [New York: Fleming H. Revell Company, 1913]).

Yet it was not Anthony Comstock who would lead the sting and prosecution of the book *Madeleine: An Autobiography* but his appointed successor, John Saxton Sumner. Sumner, unlike Comstock, was quieter in the ways he went after vice, preferring undercover stings and the courts to bravado and violence. Before succeeding Comstock, Sumner worked in banking and law. Jay A. Gertzman, in his 1994 article "John Saxton Sumner of the New York Society for the Suppression of Vice: A Chief Smut-Eradicator" in the *Journal of American Culture*, summarized Sumner's tactics and reception by the public as extraordinary. Gertzman described the support, noting, "the support he [Sumner] received from clerical and secular authorities and the way he stigmatized not only the publishers and booksellers he prosecuted but also the lawyers and civil libertarians who defended them as un–American and un–Christian tell us much about the way eroticism and moral subversion shared for many Americans a thick and foggy borderline—and why they still do."[7] Sumner was double deputized and could work with the same lawful authority as Comstock as an agent/detective. Sumner embraced this authority to its full extent and beyond, utilizing agents who worked under him in the never-ending search for devious materials. This deputized moral police's mission was to choke off the proliferation of articles, art, and literature that induced socially immoral behavior, such as gambling and prostitution, including secular materials, which could be as innocent as pamphlets for family planning, contraception, and STDs. The society carried out investigations, which primarily focused on the lower class. The target was often the immigrant, particularly the Jewish and European immigrant sectors, people of color, perceived political disruptors, and the labor class, especially working women, who demanded more independence under the new working environment.

During the industrialization era, technological innovations made employing children and young women profitable without regard to long working hours, low wages, or working conditions. Immigrants and their families were particularly at risk for exploitation, as were Black families who moved after the Civil War. Mary's family were immigrants from Ireland and Canada and faced economic hardship when they came to the United States. Although Mary writes that the Regan family was comfortable before and just after the Civil War, they, like many families, fell on hard times, and it was not easy to get ahead under

John S. Sumner took the helm after Anthony Comstock at the New York Society for the Suppression of Vice, banning and burning *Madeleine: An Autobiography* (Bain News Service, George Grantham Bain Collection, Library of Congress).

such conditions. Mary, though not a fresh-off-the-boat immigrant, faced similar harsh realities of female life in America, making factory work and eventually prostitution a choice for survival.

Women, especially young and unmarried, who through circumstances had to enter the working world, faced harsh scrutiny. The number of women employed saw a sharp increase in 1900, and according to S.J. Kleinberg, they were "72 percent more likely to have jobs than males of the time."[8] The 1910 census noted that race, sex, and ethnicity also contributed to the rising employment of children 10–15 years old. Although numbers for Black females were the highest for children 10–13 years old, European (immigrant) workers rose to almost equal numbers at 15 years of age compared to their Black counterparts.[9] This means that younger women of diverse backgrounds were entering the workforce without rights or protections to keep them safe. Yet, for low-income families, there was little choice due to the social and domestic conditions of the time. Survival depended on the contribution of all within the family group, and in many instances, this meant any work from the factory to the brothel.

Education was not considered a need for people experiencing poverty, especially girls, and school often covered only the elementary years. Mary tells us that she only made it through grammar school, and her testimony reflects the shared experience of the poor in America beyond the topic of prostitution for which the book is known. Education is one theme that is often ignored and traverses throughout the book. The author expresses a longing for knowledge and understands that her lack of education held her back and kept her locked into the caste in which she found herself.

Wages of the time were deplorable, and it took the whole family and even children to sustain enough for basic needs. S.J. Kleinberg notes that these "circumstances led the Massachusetts commissioner of labor to complain that the low wages paid to the male worker forced him to overwork his wife and deprive his children of education 'so that he may supply by their labor their cries for bread.'"[10] This shared fate of many Americans would prove a grim reality for Mary and her family. Poverty was a recursive situation that caused hardship and gave it few viable options to change one's circumstances.

Due to the rapid changes that Reconstruction and industrialization brought, the role previously held by women inevitably changed. During the 1880s and 1890s, women challenged long-held domestic expectations of femininity. Loralee MacPike noted that "the debate about women's nature and women's place in society intensified because of real changes in women's lives, and the New Woman who embodied these changes became the focus of a battle to control cultural change, a battle that is still going on."[11] Women's roles were changing as they filled a gap in the working world. Styles of dress were altered to accommodate factory conditions, and bikes were utilized for women to get to work independently. Women lived away from their families, living alone or sharing housing as Mary did when she first left. This new independence also allowed women to live beyond the typical constructs of femininity, and sexuality was sometimes more freely explored. A concern held by those in power was that if women grew accustomed to independence, they might choose how to live their lives and even decide to live without men, children, or marriage. The concept of female agency in the early modern era was beginning to emerge, and the dominant society sought to control or suppress it. Societal concerns grew out of fears of the disintegration of the Christian nuclear family, which was centered on patriarchy.

Marriage, fertility, and domestic responsibilities had long been the center structure of society, and women were subjected to unyielding cages into which they were born. A woman's work and responsibilities were a moral and domestic duty to which they were bonded their entire life. Breaking free from these constraints was considered a dangerous, radical act. A woman who chose not to marry or had a child out of wedlock was shunned. Women who sought higher education suffered ostracization. Their exile from society was a punishment uniquely reserved for women. Engaging in sexual relationships outside of marriage, especially if it resulted in pregnancy, often led to banishment from the family, forced marriages, or a lifetime of living in mental and moral institutions. While the ideals of the era of the "New Woman" were beginning to challenge traditional views, the stigma of single motherhood remained deeply entrenched. For Mary, despite facing abuse (both sexual and physical), child labor, and poverty, it was her unexpected pregnancy in her teenage years that would ultimately alter the course of her life. Without support from her family, the church, or other adults, she was forced to walk an often lonely, lifelong path. She learned, however, to reckon with the world on her terms and, because of this, found an alternative way to live and reclaim some of her agency. Mary represented in life, as much as in the pages of her book, everything society was afraid of—power, tenacity, and unequaled motivation to live and prosper.

≋ 2 ≈

Demons in the Details

THE DEMONIZATION OF THE BOOK may have only happened because of the polarizing political climate into which it was born. As an anonymous author, Mary understood that her vulnerability would lead to exposure, sparking flames around the written body and experience of both women and the sex worker. Without the political climate and tumultuous drama of the upper crust of society, *Madeleine: An Autobiography* might have gone on to sell with only reviews, both good and bad, to worry about. Initially, the advance copies sent out garnered such reviews. One such review, before John Saxton Sumner of the NYSSV got his hands on the book, called *Madeleine* interesting and informative writing: "Even in her most degraded and sinful moments, Madeline remains a proper person." The reviewer even suggests, "Perhaps there are problems in the world which are beyond solution, but at least there is a certain satisfaction in having an author suggest a remedy."[1] Reviews before the undercover sting on Harper & Brothers ran the gamut of opinion. Still, none found in the archives so far accused the book of outright obscenity. Yet the flames, once sparked, could not be held back, racing just ahead of the book's debut.

The book was immediately challenged despite the author's ambiguity and the fact that it had yet to be published. The general public did not know about the book before it was sensationalized in the newspapers and courts. The outcry over Mary's book came about because of a staged purchase by the NYSSV and the innocent delivery of one copy thrusting Harper & Brothers into the crosshairs of John Saxton Sumner and District Attorney Edward Swann. It was alleged in opening court documents by District Attorney Swann that

> The said defendants (said defendant Harper & Brothers being a corporation), on the 24th day of October 1919, at the city of New York, in the county of New York, unlawfully did possess, with intent to sell and show, a certain lewd, lascivious, indecent, obscene, filthy and disgusting book entitled "Madeleine an Autobiography," whereof a more particular description

would be offensive to this court and improper to be spread upon the records thereof, wherefore such description is not here given—[2]

Clinton T. Brainard personally and Harper & Brothers as a corporation were brought up on charges concerning the book by the state of New York.

Brainard and Harper & Brothers were placed on trial in the Special Sessions of New York court on January 23, 1920. They were duly accused of violating Section 114 of the state's Penal Law and found guilty. Sumner of the NYSSV called *Madeleine* "one of the worst and most dangerous books that has come to our attention in a long time."[3] According to records, the publisher and Brainard were fined $1,000 each and paid under extreme protest. Brainard, publicly shamed and fingerprinted, was jailed until he could pay the fine.[4] His name was on the front page of every prominent newspaper of the time, especially those owned by William Randolph Hearst, who had a personal interest in crucifying Brainard in the national popular opinion.

So it was no coincidence that Brainard was targeted for prosecution and public humiliation. He served as secretary to an extraordinary grand jury charged with investigating a scandal in New York involving

John Francis Hylan, the embattled mayor of New York, 1917 (Bain News Service, George Grantham Bain Collection, Library of Congress).

District Attorney Swann's offices and the Hylan city administration. Oddly enough, the investigation began at the request of Mayor John Hylan, who wanted to highlight corruption intertwined with a strike by subway employees. However, the investigation quickly broadened in scope, and the grand jury shifted away from the strike to uncovering potential trails of corruption that led directly to the offices of Mayor Hylan and the district attorney.

The extraordinary grand jury investigated whether public officials had engaged in unlawful activities or improperly handled labor disputes, particularly those related to the transit strike. As the investigation deepened, suspicions of misconduct, mismanagement, and possible collusion between the mayor's office and the district attorney emerged, raising serious concerns about the integrity of the city leadership. Outcries arose from those who supported Hylan, and one of his biggest supporters, William Randolph Hearst, was ready to go to war.

The powerful and wealthy William Randolph Hearst was a fascinating and formidable national figure. He was a giant in the publishing industry and political circles for most of his life. His influence on Mayor Hylan's career was undeniable. Hearst not only backed Hylan's run for office but also played a huge role in securing his win. As one of the most powerful media moguls of his time, Hearst's business priorities quickly became governmental priorities, solidifying his sway over New York's political landscape.

Hearst was calculating in the steps and positions he took in politics and business, always looking to build his empire to feed his political ambitions. Hearst's reach extended far beyond typical media influence—he commanded his empire with an unparalleled talent to capture public attention, both locally and nationally. His strategic use of yellow journalism showcased his ability to shape the public's perception and drive the narrative to his advantage, bolstering his agenda and empire.

Yellow journalism, popular during the 1890s and into the early 1900s, utilized sensationalism over facts, not unlike the dissemination of sensational loose fact-based reporting of today. According to the U.S. Office of the Historian, yellow journalism was a significant factor in fanning the flames between the United States and Spain until the Spanish-American War broke out.[5] Hearst and his rival Joseph Pulitzer often used yellow journalism to drive profits, even if the truth of the reporting was murky. Hearst frequently said, "You furnish the pictures, I'll provide the war!"[6] This mode of using journalism to direct public opinion is a weapon that Hearst, Hyland, and the NYSSV reverted to in their fight against the extraordinary grand jury's secretary, Clinton T. Brainard. Hearst used his publication, *New York American*, to "break"

2. Demons in the Details

Newspaper tycoon William Randolph Hearst used his newspaper syndicate to humiliate Clinton T. Brainard publicly (Bain News Service, George Grantham Bain Collection, Library of Congress).

the story and launch a campaign against *Madeleine: An Autobiography*. He used Brainard's name in a focused smear campaign in every article covering the court proceedings, shifting attention from the corruption of government offices to that of perceived social evils in publishing.[7] Hearst's focus on Brainard, however, went beyond the political extraordinary grand jury's issues; his angst was also tied into a very personal slight that had come years earlier.

In many ways, the sensation was never about the book *Madeleine: An Autobiography*. The battle began much earlier and came to a head during the New York extraordinary grand jury with many of the same characters who would play a part in the case of *Madeleine*. Some of the biggest names in New York and the country would be connected between vastly different cases, such as Clinton T. Brainard, New York mayor John Hylan, William Randolph Hearst, and District Attorney Edward Swann.

William R. Hearst was interested in locking down the grand jury investigating the mostly Hearst-controlled city administration, including Mayor Hylan. Hearst was not a man to be ignored or refused, especially at the cost of business. Early on, Hearst positioned his then young protégé Clinton T. Brainard as the editor for the *New York World* and the *Washington Herald*. Eventually, Brainard left Hearst's employment to take over Samuel McClure's publishing syndicate around 1914. The McClure syndicate was a competitor of Hearst, and although no documentation seems to prove one way or the other, it can be assumed that Hearst was not pleased that his protégé became a competitor. Brainard later expanded his publishing holdings by becoming the president of Harper's Publishing Company. Clinton T. Brainard, by daring to distance himself from Hearst's influence and refusing to conform to his demands, triggered what Hearst saw as a deep betrayal. In retaliation, Hearst leveraged his syndicate and newspaper, the *New York American*, to launch an aggressive campaign against Brainard and the book *Madeleine: An Autobiography*.

On the front pages of those newspapers, Hearst featured explosive and damaging leads about *Madeleine*, Brainard, and Harper's Publishing. Hurst went further, offering damning opinions and sensational reporting, especially emphasizing Brainard as a peddler of obscene books. John Sumner was often quoted, and since its beginning the NYSSV and Hearst worked well together. Although their ideals differed somewhat, they sought to retain dominant social, moral, and political control. Whereas a misplaced moral superiority drove John Sumner, Hearst was driven by what appeared to be a personal vendetta. Paul S. Boyer explored connections between print and vice in his 2002 *Purity in Print*. He wrote, "Charges of collusion between Hearst and the Vice Society were widespread, but Sumner stoutly maintained that he had actuated solely by considerations of public welfare." Privately, it is said that Sumner expressed irritation at the fact that Hearst had exploited the prosecution for his purposes.[8] Some saw weakness in Sumner's character, who preferred to operate in the shadows, unlike his predecessor Comstock's combative moral warrior character. Instead of strengthening the Penal Section 1141, Sumner's attack on *Madeleine* was the beginning of the end of Comstock's vision of a purity crusade. Henry F. Pringle, in *The American Mercury* in 1922, wrote a lengthy essay titled, "Comstock the Less," noting, "strangely enough, the cunning agents of Hell used Mr. Sumner himself as the instrument of their work." He goes on to note Sumner's loyalty to William Randolph Hearst and Hylan, and their loyalty to each other, as a factor in the ultimate loss of the case against Brainard and Harper & Brothers.[9] Could it be that corruption of another kind seemingly entered the arena, or was it just as easily understood that times were changing in the era just after World War I?

Harper & Brothers and their president Clinton T. Brainard understood the political and economic underpinnings of the charges. After losing in court, the defendants filed a notice of appeal on January 30,

2. Demons in the Details

1920. Edward Swann, the state prosecutor writing the back information on the case, wrote:

> Be it remembered that I, Edward Swann, the District Attorney of the County of New York, by this information, accuse the defendants mentioned earlier of the crime of unlawfully possessing an indecent book, with intent to sell and show the same, committed as follows: The said defendants (said defendant Harper & Brothers being a corporation), on the 24th day of October 1919, at the City of New York, in the County of New York, unlawfully did possess, with intent to sell and show, ascertain lewd, lascivious, indecent, obscene filthy and disgusting book entitled "Madeleine, an Autobiography," of which a more detailed description would be offensive to this court and improper to be spread upon the records thereof, wherefore such description is not here given; against the form of the statute in such case made and provided and against the peace of the People of the State of New York and their dignity.[10]

Edward Swann suggests that *Madeline: An Autobiography* was so vile that a proper description could not be suitable, even for court. The public, unable to read the book due to its banning and later its supposed destruction, would only be guided by the language of the vice societies, newspapers, and the court. The book, as described, would become sensational by this subjective description alone.

The court case stems from the previously mentioned well-planned trap set by the NYSSV, who arranged to buy and deliver the book to one of their employees, Emily Pfanschmid, a stenographer, on October 24, 1919.[11] The trap was set, and upon delivery, Sumner and the law were ready to launch charges.

The Penal Code section supposedly violated was Section 114, stating that a "person who sells, loans, or gives away or offers to sell, loan or give away any obscene, lewd or lascivious book, magazine, pamphlet, newspaper, etc., shall be guilty of a misdemeanor."[12] The defense argued that Mr. Brainard

District attorney Edward Swann (shown here in 1917) was tasked with prosecuting Clinton T. Brainard and Harper and Sons for lewd publishing concerning the book *Madeleine: An Autobiography* (Bain News Service, George Grantham Bain Collection, Library of Congress).

had no connection to the book and wasn't even aware that the board and Literary Conference of Harper & Brothers had decided to publish it. During the case, it became known that the popular Judge Ben Lindsey of Colorado and the well-known Jane Addams, an activist and social worker, and the *Boston Transcript* newspaper all acted as early peer reviewers of the book and approved its contents. Brainard himself stated he didn't care who supported it. He did not so much argue about the book's contents but noted that the "fact was that this girl could have got out of that life if she wanted to, and it did not have uplift for that reason."[13] Previously, Brainard was challenged for publishing *Oriental Tales and Arabian Nights* in a different company he worked at, which had "not for prudes, children or young ladies" printed across the front and was presented as People's Exhibit 3 so that the prosecutor could establish a history of illicit publishing practices. Paul de Knocks, the author of the book, was convicted on a complaint from the NYSSV.[14] Brainard testified that they used questionable advertising to sell the books quickly. Brainard was no fool. Before his publishing career, he was a working lawyer and understood the forces awakened and the political underpinnings of why he was under attack.

During the appeal, certain points arose and were filed under a request to review or reverse the prior court decisions. The defense brought up various points in their bid to have the charges against Brainard and Harper & Brothers dismissed. During the appeal, under Point I, the defense stated, "This book is not fiction and is not produced under any theories of art. It is an autobiography and is a 'human document." Point II affirmed that "its price, style of publication, total lack of

(From left) John Saxton Sumner, Grant Showerman, and Clinton T. Brainard. The court case over *Madeleine* was not the end of Brainard and Sumner's sparring over morality, art, and books. *The New York Herald*, January 15, 1922.

illustrations, and all the other circumstances of its issue, to wit, elimination of original title, submission to representative persons and publications for opinions, all show the serious purpose of the publisher."[15] Both points reiterated the book's purpose of testimony of a life of prostitution onward to reclamation without any illicit or pleasurable words or pictures. The book was to be read in seriousness, not for entertainment. The defense goes on to list two cases, *People v. Eastman*, 188 N.Y. 478, 480 and *People v. Muller*, 96 N.Y. 408, as precedent. Both of the cases argue that simply being or suggesting nakedness is not obscenity and question if it's the artist's fault it induces impure thoughts. The defense appeal makes an impassioned argument for autobiography, stating that

> The book is a plain unvarnished story of fact and not of fiction, and as an autobiography should be published and read. If enough autobiographies were written by successful as well as unsuccessful men and women, by degraded as well as by the high-minded, by the noble as well as by the ignoble, some genius or some group of men would be able to discern the laws which make for success or failure and apply them to the individual as the scientist discovers the laws of nature and applies them to the benefit of mankind.[16]

The defense argument continues, describing 11 points for dismissal and asks that the judgment of conviction be reversed.

In the end, the sentence was reversed but not before 900 copies of *Madeleine* were ordered destroyed; the plates were reportedly destroyed or never found (variations of this story persisted in the papers and documents). While Clinton T. Brainard and Harper & Brothers were absolved of wrongdoing, the book remained banned. In the subsequent years, the book's sensationalism burned and faded into memory, which was the understanding of scholars. Supposedly, only four known copies of the original first edition remained.

Clinton T. Brainard pictured in *The Editor and Publisher and Journalist*, Vol. 13, No. 18 (New York: October 18, 1913).

During and after the trial, the author was never revealed, and neither the prosecution nor the defense engaged in trying to unmask the writer in any of the court proceedings. Letters between the author and publisher were shown to have been passed back and forth, but not once during the trial were the letters subpoenaed or entered into evidence. Jane Addams was mentioned a time or two, and Judge Lindsey was mentioned three times in all of the hundreds of pages of court documents and, even then, briefly as a reviewing reader, not as the writer of the introduction. It seemed that the Madeleine's secrets were hers to keep.

≈ 3 ≈

Madeleine Blair

ACADEMICS AND READERS HAVE COME to know Madeleine Blair as a self-reflective, startlingly honest narrator through her prose. As the pseudonymous author Madeleine Blair, Mary always hid in the writing, using the text to protect herself, her family, and her reformed life after. In writing under a pseudonym, she was able to write with candor, portraying prostitution not as a desired life choice but as an imperfect form of independence. She contrasts this with the only other choices left to women, which were hardly choices at all: marriage and motherhood and job opportunities with low wages. Mary's viewpoint was radical in an era where women had few rights over their bodies, children, and households.

The details of a prostitute's life were mysterious to most of polite society, hence the rise of the term "white slavery" and the slanted understanding of how a woman would enter the profession. Few questioned the male-dominated world and a woman's place within it. Women's suffrage was in its early days when Mary's life of early childhood abuse and the following years of sex work began. The movement's concerns pushed for purity and, in their way, control, especially regarding women of lower social status, race, and ethnicity. Upper-class women could not fathom the lower laboring-class women's need to provide for their families, though every bit of lower-class women's labor supported the women of the upper class. Even more remote was the understanding of the higher social class of how a woman could fall into such a deplorable situation that she would seek to make a living through sex work.

Prostitutes, one of the world's most notorious working groups, were not often the subject of literature or reliable study at the time. From the mid–1880s into the new century, there was a push for reform and an even louder cry for the incarceration of sex workers. The social purity crusade was in many ways a reaction to modernization, industrialization, the suffrage movement, and the vocalization of silent abuses of women in work and domestic settings. David Levy, in a review, ascertained, "The purity movement originated in the antebellum struggle against prostitution. That effort, born in romantic perfectionism and closely allied to both antislavery and temperance, sent dozens of well-meaning urban reformers scurrying through unpleasant neighborhoods, trying to 'rescue' fallen women."[1] During the Civil War, prostitutes were sometimes the only comfort to be found in the hotbed of the battleground. Prostitutes also served in other capacities, often as spies, nurses, and laundresses. After the war, weary American society sought to rein in the women's seeming independence during the period. Levy tells us that the act of reining in was called "reglementation—a series of schemes for licensing and registering prostitutes, segregating them to specified areas, and supervising health examinations."[2]

Reglementation sought to corral the prostitutes away from the pure women of society. Levy writes, "The reglementationists were practical men who understood lust and wanted to contain it so that pure women might go unmolested and venereal disease be checked."[3] For those who sought purification, only absolute eradication would suffice. Levy contrasts the opposing views as a schism between ideologies, writing, "To the purifiers (now reinforced by the leadership of former abolitionists looking for something else to reform), this attitude was a disgusting surrender to evil and a betrayal of a noble vision of what America might be."[4] This did not sit well with the social purists or other interested groups, who had differing visions of addressing the problem. The problem of prostitution was timeless and pervasive, but it was quickly reaching a boiling point with the changes directly influenced by the fallout of the war and the building lust of industrialization. The country was raw with the damages and societal fractures of the Civil War, and on top of the bloody ground, people began a mass migration driven by work needs that would only be fulfilled in the rebuilding of a nation and fueling the industrial machine.

The mass movement of people covered the whole of the country. People poured into urban areas to claim jobs in manufacturing and service. Still, others went west following railroads, gold strikes, farms, and ranching. Jobs became plentiful in ever-expanding urban environments, and those in power sought to retain control over the working masses, which increasingly included women to fill those positions. Madeleine would eventually step into this role, trying to navigate an ever-changing world. But this world was not friendly to women who were paid lower wages under often terrible conditions. Social expectations remained relatively high for women, but the means and understanding to navigate this new world were woefully nonexistent, especially for young women.

Single women comprised 75 percent of the female workforce from 1870 to 1920.[5] Wages were not totaled in a certain amount per hour but were often determined by a finished piece. Claudia Goldin, who studied the conditions of single women during the 1870s–1920s, wrote, "Earnings rose steeply with experience and peaked early; learning was mainly on the job."[6] In the 1880s–1890s, women often entered the workforce with hopes of supporting families back home and a small measure of independence. Still, factory jobs rarely offered fair pay or safe conditions, especially for young women. Factory work and prostitution were surprisingly connected: low wages, harsh treatment, and exploitative bosses made it easy for women to slip from one to the other. As factory wages stagnated and debt to employers became almost inevitable, some women found prostitution a viable means to survive, where madam or pimp replaced the factory boss. This shift may have felt less like a choice and more like an escape from one form of exploitation to another. For many, labor in either world with similar rules was endured solely to survive, without hope of bettering their lot—until, like Mary, they found a small measure of agency within the constraints of sex work. Her journey, however, starts like many young girls and women of the time, leaving their rural homes to seek work in a big city.

When a teenage Mary arrives in Saint Louis, she lives with a former servant Mrs. James and her family. Her mother did not send her with at least some protection from a familiar family friend. Mary came to Saint Louis, hoping to send money back home to her mother and siblings, whom her father had again abandoned. Mary and her mother also hoped that she could carve out a life for herself away from the dangers of their small community. Saint Louis offered an ability to contribute to the family, but to a single young woman, it also meant entering a bustling city for which she was woefully unprepared. Mary writes, "I was only a little girl, and I did not in the least want to work in a factory, nor live with our former servant, nor leave my home and my little brothers and sisters, nor the cuddling baby brother who was my especial care."[7] Yet her father's absence, his struggles with addiction, and the fracture of her family contributed to her lost innocence. She tells the reader that she would make $5 a week at the factory, two of which would go to room and board. Her job, working as a "check-girl, whose duties consist of checking out bundles of work to the machine-workers and checking in the finished product,"[8] wasn't glamorous but a step toward a sliver of independence and helping to provide for her mother and siblings who lived in extreme poverty.

Poverty was a shared curse suffered by an overwhelming majority of Americans at the time, and conditions persisted despite the rise in manufacturing due to low wages and increasing rents. As a result, poverty became more challenging to ignore, and with this came an undercurrent of fear fed by the anti-vice campaigns, especially when young women like Mary entered the workforce. Emma Liggins noted that "this tendency betrayed a wider desire in society to police the dangerous classes and fear of uncontrolled working-class sexuality."[9] Distress bordering on panic drove the monied classes into "Christian" concern for the urban poor, influencing the developing social attitudes toward poor women. It was thought that without the protective walls of their familial home and paternal figure, young women were like sheep exposed to demonic forces waiting to feed on their innocence. Poor women, in particular, suffered society's attacks under the assumption that their exposure to the working world rendered them impure. Liggins writes that "the working-class girls are always already fallen, given that they have a 'familiarity' with and completer knowledge of sexual matters than middle-class girls."[10] Society often grouped working-class women and girls as just above the prostitutes in the social hierarchy, even if they didn't sell their bodies on the street. This reflects the prevailing anxiety over the sexual knowledge of working-class women and girls, which purity figures sought to change, heal, and even control in various ways.

The army of virtue, purity, social, temperance, and various other popular moral societies mobilized after the Civil War when vices, especially drunkenness and its far-reaching social consequences, were seen as an invasive disease within the family and society—the inclusion of the Comstock laws upholding their views as firmly as the Bible only gave them more moral standing with which to fight their new war. The moral societies believed that the country's social ills were connected, and their focus was on the lower working and poverty-stricken classes. Alcohol was often blamed as the first rip in the seam of proper society. Burns and Novic suggest that "among urban factory workers, this level of intoxication created unreliability in the labor force, dismaying employers. At home, women and children often suffered, for they had few legal rights and were utterly dependent on husbands and fathers for support."[11] Who, then, would protect the innocents if not the army of Christ working in conjunction with the political arms of the government?

The moral societies believed that low wages and narrow economic opportunities were often brought on by the breakdown of families through alcohol and poverty. Although their concerns and efforts were not without justification, Mary felt that their focus was misplaced. In her book, Mary deconstructs this idea that the issue of destitution only occurs within the lower classes of society and the morally damaged. In

Madeleine, Mary presents the reader with a beginning that contradicts the widespread perception that her family life and early childhood were not destitute but well-off, comfortable, and respected in their community. Mary does, however, acknowledge the devastation brought on by alcohol and, in this way, seeks to show that no tier in society is immune.

From the introduction to the first chapter, the book gives a sense of being specifically written for the social institutions that already held negative beliefs about working women, poverty, race, contraception, and abortion. The same societies clung to impossible ideals of purity conjoined to the principle of a white woman's value and self-respect as solidified within the Christian movements of the 19th and 20th centuries. The author breaks out of the definition of the fallen women who succumbed to the trade due to lifelong poverty or religious and familial neglect. Although these conditions eventually affected her family, they were not the foundation on which her choices were constructed.

4

Judge Ben Lindsey
(1869–1943)

AT FIRST, IT MIGHT SEEM strange that a judge penned the introduction to such a controversial text and did not suffer any personal repercussions for doing so. The court proceedings and fallout hardly mention Judge Ben Lindsey in connection with it. Judge Lindsey's history is peculiar, and his stance on women's and adolescents' rights was far ahead of his time. His beliefs were so aligned with those shared in *Madeleine: An Autobiography* that questions arose around how much influence he may have had in the writing of the book. Similarities arise between his story and Mary's that show how a connection may have been created in friendship, mentorship, or even within a writer-editor relationship.

Although small in stature and thin, he more than compensated with his vocal desire for social justice reform and his surprising views on children, women, and marriage. When he developed an idea or theory or found fault in the world, he would speak out on it, never worried about how it might affect his status or social standing, especially when children were part of that concern. In his autobiography *The Beast*, he wrote that he had "one ambition—to be a lawyer" and had an "unusual curiosity about politics."[1] In 1901, at 31, Ben Lindsey became a judge. He asked that all juvenile issues be "remaindered" to his courtroom, establishing the first juvenile court in Colorado. Within his court, he worked to effect change by passing child labor laws and child conviction laws that "prevented the conviction of any person under the age of eighteen except in cases of a capital offense."[2] His care and mission on behalf of children continued all of his life.

Lindsey, the oldest of four children, recorded sudden hardship after moving from the Deep South to Denver, Colorado, when he was 11. As told in his autobiography, the hard years read similar to Mary's. He writes of poverty after an early childhood of comfort, stating that

4. Judge Ben Lindsey (1869–1943)

"poverty was fraying us all out. It was not exactly brutalizing us, it was warping us, breaking our health, and ruining our dispositions."[3] He describes his mother as a beautiful Southern belle who used to have Black servants, and with the loss of their wealth, she slowly declines into a shadow of her former self, not unlike the situation and decline described by Mary of her mother.

M. Susan Yetter of the Colorado Historical Society recorded the inventory of Benjamin Barr Lindsey within collection No. 389, from which valuable information was gathered. The record noted the location of his birth as Jackson, Tennessee, on November 25, 1869. He writes of his father moving to Denver in 1878, while the rest of the family moved to join him a year later. Lindsey was sent to the University of Notre Dame in Indiana in 1881 and won prizes for public speaking. Unhappy there, he went to Tennessee to live with his grandfather, a Confederate veteran, and then attended Southwestern University in Jackson. He was admitted to the Colorado Bar in 1894 and began practicing law.[4] Although the record with the Colorado Historical Society includes his writing and judgments, the holdings also included correspondence, biographical material, writing, speeches, magazine articles, political articles, books, and court records. The collection did not appear to include notes or his introduction to *Madeleine*. There are, however, strong statements recorded from articles contained within magazines such as *Redbook* that feature some radical ideas, such as his stance

Judge Ben Lindsey was a social reformer who established the first juvenile court in Denver, Colorado. He supported *Madeleine: An Autobiography*, including writing the introduction to the book (Los Angeles Daily News Negatives Collection, 1935 [UCLA Library Digital Collections, CC BY 4.0]).

against prohibition, stating that "I think it is up to the human race to behave in a way that will intelligently make for the happiness and welfare of the greatest number of persons."[5] His views always seemed to elicit a reaction from one group or another, but as radical as they were, they helped to shift national thoughts regarding crime, children, and women. Unlike those who only knew privilege, he understood the absolute lows of poverty and hunger and the desperation and hopelessness that often parallel the conditions of the destitute.

Lindsey was very open about his views on marriage, particularly companionate marriage. The topic became a highly debated book with his suggestion of a trial year for marriage that included birth control. Also recorded is an article on "Why Girls Go Wrong" in the *Ladies' Home Journal*, where he writes, "Girls often get into trouble due to the carelessness and inattentiveness of their parents. Parents are also remiss in not adequately instructing daughters about sex."[6] Lindsey believed that society as a whole needed to find a way to instruct female youth about sex, contraception, and family planning. His views in this era were considered too progressive and dangerous, and he faced the anger of various purity societies, religious groups, and churches in his time.

Lindsey, in his youth, was sent away to school in Indiana. In his book *The Beast*, he recalled his father's failing health. At 18, after his father died, Lindsey was thrust into the role of head of household. The family was destitute, with only $150 Lindsey had saved from his job writing proofs. Their furniture was mortgaged, and his father's life insurance, which the family thought was paid, had lapsed entirely the day before his death. Lindsey noted that they were forced to move into a tiny cottage on lower West Colfax Avenue in their deplorable state.

Lindsey supported his mother and siblings with $10 a month as an office boy in a real estate office, later earning $25 a month working for a mining company. During this time, he describes a suicide attempt in his misery. Lindsey wrote with straightforward, startling language,

> I got a revolver and cartridges, locked myself in my room, confronted myself desperately in the mirror, put the muzzle of the loaded pistol to my temple, and pulled the trigger. The hammer snapped sharply on the cartridge; a great wave of horror and revulsion swept over me in a rush of blood to my head, and I dropped the revolver on the floor and threw myself. By some miracle, the cartridge had not exploded, but the nervous shock of that instant when I felt the trigger yield and the muzzle rap against my forehead with the impact of the hammer that shock was almost as great as a very bullet in the brain. I realized my folly, my weakness, and I went back to my life with something of a man's determination to crush the circumstances that had almost crushed me.[7]

4. Judge Ben Lindsey (1869–1943)

His candid, self-reflective writing shared many qualities with Mary's. He frequently spoke of his shortcomings, not to belittle himself but to reveal his humanity. Through his struggles, he developed a deep empathy for societies marginalized and unwanted. Lindsey was a man shaped by his experiences, which truly connected him to the people. He believed this gave him insight into the misunderstandings the poor and working class suffered. He thought society could do more and empathize with those in need. In *The Beast*, he addresses this problem by writing,

> Why do I tell that? Because so many believe poverty is not sensitive, the ill-fed, overworked boy of the slums is as callous as he seems dull. Because so many people believe that the weak and desperate boy can never be anything but a weak and vicious man. Because I came out of that morbid period of adolescence with sympathy for children that helped to make possible one of the first courts established in America for the protection as well as the correction of children.[8]

To Lindsey's way of thinking, something could be done about the assumed "lost causes." He was not, however, naive due to his observance within his courtroom. Lindsey understood that some could not be reformed and that others functioned as predators and saw the weak as easy prey. He feared the threat of moral suicide for himself and those he considered innocents in a society set up to consume the weak, poor, and oppressed. This moral imperative was not empty political speech but a lifelong war he fought until his last breath.

At the beginning of his autobiography, Lindsey included a poem called "The Brute" by William Vaughn Moody that outlined those he believed were the beasts that consumed and those he desired to save:

> And they fling him, hour by hour,
> Limbs of men to give him power;
> Brains of men to give him cunning; and
> For dainties to devour
> Children's souls, the little worth; hearts
> Of women, cheaply bought:
> He takes them and breaks them, but
> He gives them scanty thought.[9]

Lindsey believed that the destitution of children who came into his juvenile court were products of a cycle, recalling that

> the dependent and delinquent children who came into my court came almost wholly from homes of dependent and delinquent parents who were made such by hopeless economic conditions of their lives, and those conditions were made hopeless by the remorseless tyranny of wealthy men who used their lawless power to enslave and brutalize and kill workmen.[10]

Lindsey felt strongly that the government was corrupted by corporate wealth and that parents could not care for their children morally or physically due to long hours at low-paying jobs. He was concerned that widows went unsupported and that saloons protected by corporations lent to the destruction of families. He also fought for women's rights and bonded with the suffragettes. His wide-ranging concerns were set with a particular focus on child welfare, child labor laws, penal reform, birth control, marriage and divorce, sex education and hygiene, and the Women's Protective League. His ultra-progressive views often had Lindsey at odds with politicians, political forces, and even the KKK.

In 1924, the Democratic Party in Colorado was under the spell of the powerful KKK, which opposed Lindsey. His life, public or private, was never easy, and his beliefs and outspokenness ensured his position was never secure. "During his entire career, his conduct was scrutinized closely by those whose enmity he had incurred and who would plot his downfall."[11] Lindsey wrote of his experience of always being watched in his book: "My private life has been gone over with a microscope.... I have been followed by detectives ... my chambers in the court have been broken into, my desk drawers forced open, and my letter files searched."[12]

The Survey reported that Judge Lindsey faced the KKK as they tried to legislate his juvenile court "out of existence, then ran a candidate against him in the elections."[13] The KKK and the KKK-affiliated mayor Benjamin F. Stapleton hotly contested his win in the judicial election, seeking to overturn the election and even took it to court and the Supreme Court. Lindsey won in that instance, but the same KKK forces managed to see him disbarred for a time, ushering in years of depression and battles to get reinstated and even forcing a move from Denver to California.

Linsey was a unique persona within the country, and his writing was "fiery and pungent with vitriolic language to attack the establishment and its leaders."[14] The judge who later inherited his court called Lindsey "absolutely fearless, flamboyant and irrepressible."[15] Lindsey published *The Beast* in 1910, *The Revolt of Modern Youth* in 1925, and *The Companionate Marriage* in 1928. The same man who went toe to toe with the KKK and, later, Nazis did not consider writing an introduction for *Madeleine* as something shameful; in fact, he thought it was necessary to support the message of the book. In the introduction, he writes, "I have an intense appreciation of *Madeleine*. It ought to be read and pondered over. It is *true*. The Madeleines are right in your midst."[16] He goes still further, suggesting that society is responsible for the "sins they denounce" and that the social welfare workers lack real humanity, offering that they would agree and support the book if they truly invested time, energy, and extended empathy to the fallen woman. He wrote that society encourages "sin" and punishes its "own victims" with ostracism and jail. He recommends that society should want to "fight evil more and women less." In defending *Madeleine*'s pages that include sex, STDs, unmarried pregnancy, miscarriage, and abortion, he writes,

> During this time as judge, I have dealt mostly with human problems that some people look upon altogether as moral problems. For seven or eight years, I tried most of the divorce cases in such a city, with a record of having divorced some five thousand people in that time. And then, for many years, it has become my duty to preside in those delicate affairs known to the officers as "sex cases." At first, they were primarily concerned with protecting society against prostitution. Then they turned gradually to the *protection of women against society*. These cases are often conducted regardless of the technicalities of law. We cease to be a court; we become, instead, a place of adjustment of human frailties and difficulties.
>
> In a word, we now deal with people and the causes of bad things. We no longer deal merely with the things. We no longer use vengeance, violence, stupidity, and ignorance as the only remedy for these things. In this experience, I was forced to the conclusion that there are no good people and no bad people—only good things and bad things. It gives me a great charity and a great sympathy—not for sin, but for sinners. It teaches me that while it is difficult at times to know how to fight sin without fighting sinners, in the end, it is the better policy to conquer sin and save the people. For sinners are only people. We do not fight sick children—we fight the *disease*. People are only children grown up.[17]

Lindsey's remarkable empathy is recorded time and again, as well as his unmoving stance on social justice for women and children. His most startling suggestion in the introduction was his analysis that the book's themes were comparable to the universal themes found within Shakespeare or the Bible, indicating it would be a good book for "girls reaching reasonable maturity to know more about our Madeleines."[18] His introduction goes further than any writing of the time on the subject of prostitution. Yet, when the book and publisher were dragged into court and jailed, his name was rarely mentioned or denounced through the many newspaper articles and court arguments. No record seems to support that he gave any interviews or opinions on the book beyond the introduction. How much assistance he may have offered Mary remains unclear. Stylometric data suggest their writing was similar, hinting that he may have helped with editing or revision. What is clear is that he supported the book and did so publicly, giving weight to Mary's already powerful narrative.

5

Mary Agnes Regan— Child of God

Mary Agnes Regan, later known to the world as the pseudonymized Madeleine Blair, was born to Patrick Regan and Mary Coughlin Regan in 1872 under the wide blue skies of Iowa. Soon after, the family settled farther south in Missouri. Her story begins in Unionville, Missouri, as recorded in the 1880 state census, and belies the sensational chapters that would later define her life as an author and figure in the world of prostitution. She writes of her early years as pleasant, her childhood and family normal for their status. Her family was initially comfortable, if not well-to-do, with a house, servants, and other properties.

Her parents' families originated in Ireland. Patrick's father—Mary's grandfather, Cornelius Regan—was born in Cork, Ireland, in 1804 and immigrated to Canada in 1834, settling in Westminster. It is unclear why Mary's family initially left Ireland. However, in 1834, a Catholic Irish family's decision to emigrate from Ireland to Canada was likely driven by a combination of economic hardship and political oppression.

Perhaps the Regans were driven by the prospect of a new life and opportunities in a land that seemed large enough to offer such possibilities. Their Irish homeland was marked by severe poverty due to frequent crop failures and limited agricultural opportunities, which made survival challenging for the working class and impossible for those experiencing poverty. Although the Great Famine had not yet struck, food insecurity and economic instability pushed families that could manage it to seek livelihoods abroad. Canada actively encouraged immigration, offering land grants to settlers and presenting a rare chance for Irish Catholics to own and cultivate land—a significant draw given the dominance of British landlords in Ireland. Canada also had a long history of Irish migration, going back to the French-dominated 17th century, as mariners and fishermen.

5. Mary Agnes Regan—Child of God

It could be that Mary's Regan ancestors faced religious discrimination as Catholics under British rule, which restricted Catholic participation in politics, education, and other aspects of public life. Ever since Mary's grandfather, the Regans were devout. Even when she worked in the sex trade, Mary's faith was a raft she clung to, a commitment that endured despite the challenges imposed by her circumstances. Throughout her book, she often exemplifies the Christian struggle of faith and belief in a God whom she felt loved her even at her lowest. She starts the book with her grandfather's story to highlight an internal source of strength and a reminder of her family's values, allowing her to connect to her heritage and maintain hope, even in the most difficult times.

Cornelius Regan, who may have come to Canada for religious and economic reasons, might have relied on family or community support in the early days of their new life. The *Catholic Record* suggests that he and his family came over from Ireland "in company with several others, neighbors, and relatives."[1] For many generations, networks were established by earlier Irish settlers in Canada, which often provided financial support and a community to ease the transition. It was initially unclear if the early Regans had family already living and working in Canada or what circumstances would have instigated Cornelius Regan to leave Ireland with his young family and make Canada his home, but what is clear is that he built a life and had children, one of which was Patrick, Mary's father, who would also have this pioneering spirit.

Cornelius died in April 1879, and obituary notes from the *Catholic Record* recorded that he was a highly respected citizen with Christian fortitude and was admired for his exemplary piety.[2] A similar obituary is mentioned in the first pages of *Madeleine*, where Mary wrote lovingly about the family patriarch:

> When I read in a very old newspaper, a cherished possession of my mother's, an account of the death of my great-grandfather, together with an account of his life, his virtues, and his piety, I retained a clear recollection of one paragraph because there were many new words in it that fell musically upon my ear. It read: "He represented the highest type of a Christian gentleman, this venerable citizen, this grand old patriarch, who as a young man left his native land to found a home on the virgin soil of free America that he might worship God according to the dictates of his own conscience."
>
> My mother had a portrait of him which showed a benignant-looking old gentleman, clothed in the stately garments of his day; and he was to me a very real person, though he had died many years before I was born. My mother often spoke of him in terms of great reverence, referring especially to his piety and his kindliness. He was often quick to anger, she said, but he was also quick to repentance, and if he had offended relative or friend, he asked his pardon and the pardon of God before he slept.[3]

Mary held her grandfather in the highest esteem, especially growing up and watching the pitiful demise of her father Patrick due to alcohol addiction. Perhaps this is another reason she writes of her grandfather so early in the book, contrasting the Christian devotion of family ancestry with the fallen status of herself and her father. She may have had another reason, especially concerning her motives for writing *Madeleine*, which was to combat the pervasive myth that only godless poor families produce children capable of falling so far into the vices of alcohol addiction, abuse, and prostitution. If vice could touch her family, then no one was safe, not even the dominant privileged class.

This early passage in the book is crucial for another reason: Mary withholds her grandfather's name, recording it as "Great-grandfather C—," and positions him as a great-grandfather instead of a grandfather. She also writes that he died before her birth, a claim contradicted by historical records. This is one of her earliest decisions to weave fact and fiction together in a deliberate effort to protect her identity and that of her family. Not every word in *Madeleine* could be accepted at face value; details that seemed inconsistent required careful comparison with available records.

Mary does not write about her grandmother or the family in Canada beyond her grandfather. However, research revealed exciting details hinting at some of the family's early history through the obituary of her grandmother, Mary Crowley, in the Canadian *Catholic Record*. Her grandmother was born at Enniskeane near the Bandon River in the Irish county of Cork. She and Cornelius left Ireland with their first child, a daughter:

> In search of homes where industry would receive its just reward. The hard lot of early pioneer and first settler (Cornelius), "deep in the Canadian woods." Mrs. Regan shared resignfully and cheerfully with her husband and children until prosperity smiled and independence with competency crowned all their efforts. To untiring industry was added faith sublime. Religion lent her charm and helping hand to every work untaken.[4]

The obituary reports that their home was happy and pious and that she, like her husband, was a devoted Catholic, never missing mass and raising "bright, righteous, talented, above the ordinary children."[5] Mary's grandparents produced two daughters and two granddaughters who became nuns in the order of Saint Joseph. The rest of their progeny are reported as all married and successful. Mary Crowley Regan died in 1898, quite alive when her granddaughter was actively working as a prostitute.

In many ways, these omissions and discrepancies were the keys to unlocking parts of Mary's story that she chose not to reveal in the book.

5. Mary Agnes Regan—Child of God 51

Her subtle adjustments became more apparent—telling her story in a way that protected her name and mission work while safeguarding her family and, later, her husbands.

Mary moves from her brief reflections on her grandfather and turns her attention to her parents and their journey to the "Middle West," which was not a journey from the eastern states of the United States but from Canada. Mary writes, "A few years after the Civil War, my parents came from their birthplace near the Atlantic seaboard and settled in a thriving town of the Middle West. I was born in this place and grew into young womanhood without ever having been more than twenty-five miles from my native town."[6] This was more fact-wrapped in fiction. America, as described, is the continent, but again, it was Canada where her family first planted roots in the New World, where her parents met and married in 1868. Her omissions and ambiguity offer if not direct clues and hints in the direction in which to direct research. Not much is known about her parents' early life before moving to the United States. Her mother Mary Coughlin was born in Canada in 1841 to Irish immigrants, according to the 1880 U.S. census.[7] Before coming to the United States, Patrick was active in sports such as rowing and community politics.

Her brother John is her parents' first child, born in Canada before they immigrated to Iowa, where Mary was born. Patrick had a brother, Cornelius, living in Iowa, and it seems this was the first stop before moving to Missouri. It is unclear when they moved to Unionville, Missouri, but it was most likely between 1872 and 1873. It seems that Patrick Regan found monetary and commercial success as a butcher.[8] Eventually, he opened a storefront that sold meat, had taxidermy services, and operated as a grocery and drug compounding establishment.[9] The evidence even points to Patrick's involvement in early governmental positions. Patrick, like his father Cornelius, found prosperity in Missouri, quickly buying up land and farms in addition to the fine home where Mary's earliest memories of her childhood begin. This aligns with the narrative of Mary's childhood recollection, which mentions their home and servants and brings to light the devastation of losing such status. Mary writes of her parents,

> My parents had many traditions of the race, of class, of education, and of religion; they were looked upon as being rather peculiar in the principles which they sought to instill into the minds of their children. Even as a small child, I received much religious instruction, which, singularly enough, I wove around the personality of my great-grandfather. I had learned to read at an unusually early age and possessed rather a remarkable faculty for the English language. Sonorous words appealed to me and soon found a place in

my memory. The two questions most often found on my tongue were: "How do you pronounce this word, father?" and "What does it mean?"[10]

Mary continues rebuffing the purity critique and immediately tells the reader of a well-off household; they had education, servants, health, and a beautiful home. Mary describes her family's spiritual and intellectual attributes, writing, "Both of our parents possessed a high degree of intelligence and sane religious beliefs. No children could have begun life under more auspicious conditions."[11] She goes on as if solidifying this curious dynamic for the reader, stating,

> My mother seemed to have been created for the expressed purpose of being a mother, for poise and common sense were her distinguishing characteristics. My father was the mainspring of our pleasant home life. Mother was the balance wheel. We heard much of the beauties of literature and had access to many good books.[12]

The child Mary could not hope to understand her father's internal, mental, and physical struggles. Within the text, she does not attempt to understand why he makes choices that are detrimental to the family. At the beginning of the book, she remembers her father as the one she loved most in the world and was most proud of. However, this seems to change as his relationship with alcohol grows. Mary speaks to the terror and heartbreak of the beating she suffered at his hands around age 11. She then recounts the continued physical abuse that she experiences from her father, recalling that "when he was sober, I was his favorite child. When he was drunk, I was the one who suffered the most." Without any other firsthand accounts, it is hard to say how, once loving, Mary's father became such a monster. So what circumstances led to Patrick's moral degradation?

Research revealed some information that might describe variables that led Patrick Regan to lose almost everything. Before becoming a husband and father, Patrick Regan served the Union during the Civil War from 1861 to 1865. However, it is unclear if he came to the United States to fight in the war or enterprise on some other venture. Over 40,000 Canadians served in the Union armies. Records support his joining of the Union militia, but no records were found regarding Patrick's official citizenship at the time.[13] The volunteers signed for three years and saw considerable action during the war. Patrick would have been present for the siege of Corinth, the assault and capture of Fort Hindman, the Battle of Champions Hill, and the siege of Vicksburg, among others.

He entered as an 18-year-old private and exited as a 23-year-old sergeant in the Sixth Regiment of the Missouri Infantry, serving well beyond the three-year requirement. His regiment saw nonstop action in unbelievably harsh conditions. He would have been witness to the bloodshed and carnage of the war, and it is assured that he would have taken lives perhaps up close. The regiment lost 4 officers, and 80 enlisted men were killed and mortally wounded, while 182 enlisted men died of disease.[14] The traumas of war add up to an unspeakable burden. The daily fear and mental and physical hardship of the war are unmeasurable.

Serving in the Sixth Missouri Infantry Regiment throughout the Civil War would mean that Patrick faced many years of hardship in a stressful, demanding hellscape. The relentless marches and intense combat during his early formative years would have hardened him and possibly caused invisible mental damage due to the traumas of war. It is unknown what drove soldiers like Mary's father Patrick to sign up for a battle between a divided nation that was not his own. What is clear is that he joined the regiment in Saint Louis in 1861 of his own volition and fought the entirety of the war. For many, enlistment meant leaving their families, homes, and livelihoods, often unsure of when they would return or if they would survive the ordeal. It is unknown if Patrick's family in Canada knew he had signed up to fight in an American war or what Patrick may have left behind.

His early months must have been spent on guard duty and fighting minor skirmishes in Missouri, but soon, his regiment was drawn into some of the most significant campaigns of the war. The battles that the Sixth Missouri engaged in—from Corinth to Vicksburg to Atlanta—were key moments in the Union's strategy, and their involvement would have demanded incredible grit and stamina. Combat at Chickasaw Bayou, the siege at Vicksburg, and the capture of Fort Hindman at Arkansas Post must have subjected Patrick to grueling and dangerous conditions, where intense artillery and small-arms fire was constant, and every advance meant risking his life. The losses were significant, with many comrades wounded or killed in each engagement. Witnessing such devastation and knowing it was only a matter of time before the next battle must have weighed heavily on the soldiers, who dealt with both the physical dangers of combat and the psychological toll of war.

Life outside of battle was hardly easier. Soldiers endured long marches between engagements, sometimes covering hundreds of miles through rugged terrain, facing extreme weather, hunger, and disease. Illnesses such as dysentery, malaria, typhoid fever, smallpox, and tuberculosis claimed many lives, and the effects of camp diseases were as devastating as the battles themselves. Long periods of monotony, punctuated by bursts of intense, deadly action, characterized their service and most likely attributed to alcoholism. The infamous March to the Sea (November–December 1864) initiated General William Tecumseh Sherman's "scorched earth" policy, leaving destruction in its path as a way to demoralize the Confederacy. This included orders for soldiers like Patrick to seize or destroy anything that could support the Confederate cause, from railroads, plantations, and even homes. One wonders, knowing the Christian upbringing Patrick experienced, if the relentless atrocities of war began doing the work that would later allow him to unravel, abusing Mary and abandoning his family for months and years at a time. The rigors of these campaigns, the deprivations of supplies, and the weariness of years of marching and fighting tested every soldier's spirit, and Patrick most certainly would have felt the long-term effects.

Finally, after the surrender of Confederate general Joseph E. Johnston, the soldiers of the Sixth Missouri Infantry made their way to Washington, D.C. Patrick, having survived the war, might have participated in the Grand Review of the Armies—a massive parade celebrating Union victory. Following this final event, his regiment mustered out in August 1865. Patrick returned home to Canada with scars, memories, and an experience that transformed him. In Canada, he married but did not remain there long as the call to return to the United States grew. He finally packed up and took his new wife and year-old son to Iowa, intending to return to Missouri.

The early years in Iowa and then Missouri were productive, and Patrick's young family was growing, as were his monetary holdings and business affairs. However, it was not long before the peaceful existence of his family, as Mary remembers it, unraveled. Even though Patrick was raised as an upstanding Christian man, he fell into alcoholism. Many men suffered from mental, physical, and drug and alcohol conditions after the close of the Civil War. Post-traumatic stress disorder was not a diagnosis of the era, and even psychological trauma induced by war was not extensively studied until World War I. The National Museum of Civil War Medicine (NMCWM) suggests that there is abundant evidence that soldiers exhibited symptoms that today we ascribe to post-traumatic stress disorder. The NMCWM acknowledges that although weapons of mass destruction, as seen in World War I and World War II, were not as prevalent, other equally devastating horrors of war were. The NMCWM noted that "companies were formed locally. Company mates were likely relatives or men the soldiers had known for years. Thus, witnessing a soldier—maybe a neighbor or brother—horrifically killed had a more personal impact."[15] Drug addiction and alcoholism were so prevalent after the war that the term used for it was "army disease." Soldiers during the war had open access to alcohol, which was used as medicine and to numb the war's horrific and often tedious conditions. It took a decade before doctors would finally start to understand that the experiences of war were devastating to veterans and, by association, their families.

Joseph Parrish, a Quaker physician who served in the Sanitary Commission during the war, established in 1867 the Pennsylvania Sanatorium for the Cure of Inebriates to reclaim drunkards and opium eaters. In the decade that followed, Parrish became one of the leading drug experts in America. He was one of the first to identify similarities between drinking and drug habits, and in 1877, he warned against the lack of medical interest in the creeping menace of hidden addicts plaguing American society. However, when he first opened his sanatorium, the drug menace was not yet understood or in full swing. In 1868, he reported that only 2 out of his 26 patients were treated for the opium habit. The rest were "addicted to the excessive use of alcoholic stimulants."[16] Alcoholism during and after the war was a blight that overtook the nation as quickly as the war had done, and the effects of both would be keenly felt for generations.

What we know from Mary's accounts is that as a child, she was sheltered by her mother and a family servant from her father's alcoholism until the first beating. Patrick was 19 when he entered the service, and alcoholism historically was higher for the younger demographic. There are no records or primary sources other than the book to substantiate her claims, but it can be assumed that her family was not spared the mental fallout of the war and the failures that were a symptom of the addiction.

In the book, Mary often reflects on her childhood, nature, and the conditions that influenced her path. How could a family from such grace and proud ancestry create a woman capable of the choices she would eventually make? She writes about this in the beginning pages, reflecting, "If I dwell at some length on the story of my ancestry and my childhood, it is for the purpose of setting forth the elements of weakness and of strength which were inherent in my character and which, combined with the circumstance of my life, brought about my social bankruptcy and made possible my spiritual redintegration."[17] While she admits to her social downfall, she also reveals that she eventually reintegrated into society and attained spiritual redemption. This book serves as her declaration, detailing her journey as a prostitute who endured immense hardship and returned to society with her dignity and spirit preserved.

Research suggests Patrick was accused of assault with intent to kill in 1873.[18] Although no more information is available, this hinted at the earliest beginnings of his downfall and the real possibility of violence, especially combined with his failing monetary prospects and alcoholism. At some point, Patrick Regan sold his business and disappeared for several months, leaving the family alone. Mary tells of her father's long drinking binge and the wasting of money during this time. She also notes the difficulty of his return from sustained physical abuse she experienced at the hands of her father, recalling that "when he was sober, I was his favorite child. When he was drunk, I was the one who suffered the most." Patrick's return not only heralded abuse but also the swift decline of their comfortable financial situation.

On March 25, 1881, her father lost a lengthy legal battle with J.L. Taylor, J.A. Taylor, W.D. Elliot, and Ed. E. Bruce. The Putnam County, Missouri, circuit court ordered a sheriff's sale of land and their family home.[19] The property is sold, and although Mary writes in *Madeleine* that they are allowed to stay in the house for a time, her father eventually tells the family that they must move to a farm her father still owns in Saint Joseph. Although he tries to make it sound like a pastoral dream setting, this, too, is a lie. Mary writes, "Instead, the pledge was broken, the farm sold, the family never saw a dollar of the proceeds, and we went to live in a small house in a poor neighborhood. Father soon lost his position and went away to seek work."[20]

In Mary's vivid recounting, Saint Joseph, Missouri, is a stark contrast to the warm, servant-filled home her family left behind. Once, her family had some wealth and status; with the move, they sustained a loss of stability in impoverished surroundings. Mary describes the town's residents as less educated and worlds apart from her family's previous status. In their new neighborhood, the rules they understood changed, social morality was reduced, and Mary's spirit and body were in peril. The guardian of the family, her father, was frequently absent for long periods, and her mother, locked in the marriage both legally and mentally, may as well have been as absent as her husband.

Mary writes about her older brother taking over as head of the household, their hunger, and the periods that her father would return home to repent before falling again into the abyss of alcoholism and abandonment. That first winter was one of hunger. Her brother John was 15 and worked during the day, trying in the evenings to stay caught up in his education. Mary recounts that there was no work or school for her. Instead, she did what she could to help her mother. Her mother gave birth to another baby in an already large, hungry family. Mary remembered this era for her family as full of "black and bitter waters of hunger and humiliation, of shame and sorrow, of unmerited punishment and social injustice, of physical suffering and spiritual despair." Madeleine

5. Mary Agnes Regan—Child of God

keenly observed her parents' marriage and her mother's loyalty, even during the hardest times. She wrote of her mother's devotion in passionate terms:

> Mother never failed him. We, children, heard no word of reproach for the man who had wrecked her life and ours. She met poverty and shame, as she had met prosperity and honor, with a poise and a dignity that I have never seen equaled. She was powerless to change conditions. She was powerless to change him, but she could meet any fate with a calm exterior. This man had been the playmate of her childhood. He was the lover of her youth and the husband of her choice. She had not taken him for fair weather only; she had chosen him for life. It never entered her mind to abandon him.[21]

The ambiguous theme of "choice" is threaded throughout the book. However, in this instance, her mother "chooses" her husband even when their earlier life of ease is replaced by hardship and pain and even if it was not the best choice for her children.

Early on, Mary shows that her mother, like herself and other women in the text, made choices for survival, love, and independence but only in the most basic terms. There often were no choices for happiness during a woman's life. For women, especially wives and daughters, choices were almost nonexistent. Men mostly had command of a woman's life as father and husband. The laws favored the men, and women were trapped within the constraints of domestic expectations. Patrick could abandon his family and leave them starving. At the same time, he could also choose to drink away what money they had, and according to social and judicial understandings, it was perfectly legal for a man to do so.

In the spring of 1885, after the harsh winter, they moved again into what was known as the worst neighborhood in Saint Joseph. Her family's fall was insurmountable, with consequences that risked Mary's safety and opened the door further for abuse and starvation. This new home and community that surrounded her would be her first confrontation with prostitution. She describes the community as follows:

> On either side of us and across the street, the houses were occupied by prostitutes. All of them had other ostensible means of support. The attitude of the town was too puritanical to permit wide-open, publicly recognized houses of ill fame. They were boarding houses, dressmaking shops, hand-laundries, and the homes of workingmen whose wives added to the family finances by occasional prostitution. Thus disguised, these resorts flourished, and they were a far greater menace to the youth of the neighborhood than any wide-open places would have been. These women assumed the virtuous air that deceived none but the very young; even they heard whispers which aroused prurient curiosity and quickened the cosmic urge.[22]

At just 13, Mary begins to experience the full extent of the stigma accompanying her family's fall from grace and status. Her father was no longer a man of importance but known as a drunk who frequently disappeared. Her understanding of the world, her family, and her placement within it was confusing. The new neighborhood was even more dangerous, and Mary, an outsider, wrote of the ostracization that followed:

> One would have to live through it to realize the agony a high-spirited, sensitive girl may endure when she is the town drunkard's daughter, especially when that town drunkard had once been one of the leading citizens. I was never permitted to forget that this was my position. I had no girl companions—my sisters were too small. Instead of girlfriends, I made clandestine visits to ignorant, corrupt women who wore a scanty garb of respectability and whose influence was far more pernicious than public prostitutes would have been.[23]

From the outset, Mary's descent is marked by ostracization. In some ways, it was made more painful because of how far the family had fallen, especially her father. At the beginning of her teenage years, Mary is cut off from her peers and isolated, only finding comfort in the women of the scarlet sisterhood even before she understands what this association might mean for her reputation. Mary, so young, was already experiencing gender disparities, without understanding that a woman's fate was inexorably tied to the male head of the household, leaving them voiceless and vulnerable.

Mary calls the surrounding houses "resorts" in that they functioned covertly as houses of prostitution. It is assumed that the family moved to the area of North Main Street, where bawdy houses operated openly with an unspoken agreement with the police.[24] The public bawdy houses were only a small percentage of boarding houses, assignation houses, and regular single-family houses that advertised laundry or dressmaking in the front and prostitution in the back.[25] In 1880, the U.S. federal census factored the population of Saint Joseph, Missouri, cataloging the names of 20 prostitutes, their madams, and in some cases, their children listed as illegitimate. Most resided on Main Street, though some were also listed on South Street, and of those listed, most were born in the Midwest and were between 16 and 20 years old.[26] The ages of the girls and women were close to that of Mary, and during a time when she considered herself friendless, it would be plausible that connections might arise.

Mary first noticed that these houses had "good meals served on nice china. They had clean tablecloths. Their houses were palaces compared with the wretched place that I called home." Mary could borrow books from these neighbors, and although she says she could not make

5. Mary Agnes Regan—Child of God

friends of better status, it is implied that among these neighbors, she made instead "forbidden companions." Mary, throughout *Madeleine*, speaks to her love of reading and the knowledge imparted by the written word. The environment she grew up in had good and bad influences that eventually became tools for her physical and mental survival.

Mary tells of the "dirt and squalor, ignorance, vitiated standards, and sin" as the environment that impacted her future. She further solidifies this argument by stating that the failure of both her parents and their mental and physical absence removed all protection. Madeleine insists that the "mating instinct" was "developing strongly," and without school, her old amusements, friends (implied status), or recreation, she finally "lost the battle."[27] This suggests that she is becoming sexually active, and when her mother attempts to tell her about "secret things," Madeleine feels shame that she "knows more than her mother."[28]

In his book *Companionate Marriage*, Judge Ben Lindsey agrees with Mary's experience, writing that "we have a social order which deferring marriage till the twenties or later, takes no account of the fact that sexual maturity a terrific force arrives in the teens."[29] In the book, Mary does not tell the reader of her first sexual experience; instead, she suggests that although she tried to "keep above the level" of the new destitute environment, she "lost the battle." It seems that without her father present, she was left unprotected from the abuse of men, even men who knew Patrick. She describes this as a result of the loss of her father's protection: "Men who had been my father's friends made open or tentative advances to me." In one instance, when a man went too far, she claimed that her father would do something about it. She writes, "He laughed contemptuously and answered, 'That would not help you. He would only get drunk and beat you.'" At that moment, she realized that her father could not and would not do anything to help. Mary tells the reader, "I had not only lost my father's support in material matters, I had lost his protection as well. My mother was tied hand and foot by ill health, poverty, a sickly baby, and the care of a large family. I needed both my parents; I had neither."[30] Although it is not described, it is inferred that some of her father's friends had sexually harassed, if not assaulted, her. Yet, still a child, she couldn't have given consent and had no one to whom to turn for protection.

Even if Mary reported the assault to her mother, most likely nothing would have come of it as many families would rather hide the crime that happened to their child than endure the lifelong notoriety that came with reporting. Rape was punishable by death in Saint Joseph; however, the bar to prove assault was high and remains high to this day. The Regan family living in an impoverished part of town known for prostitution would have made the chances of winning such a case near impossible. Mary did not fully understand what happened to her, and she couldn't have anticipated or understood the consequences. Patrick, her father, was gone a year and would not return before Mary left to seek out work to support her family.

≋ 6 ≋

Mary Becomes the Madeleine: Saint Louis and Kansas City

EVENTUALLY, IT WAS DECIDED BETWEEN Mary and her mother that she would answer a letter sent by a former family servant to work in the factories of Saint Louis. Mary felt that by leaving the family home, she would be easing the strain on the family. Mary also knew this was a chance to help her mother financially, which for now fell on the shoulders of her older brother. Mary also wanted to distance herself from the sexual sin she felt she had caused. The book does not go into detail about her earliest sexual encounter. It does not clarify if she had prostituted herself, believed she was in love and might marry the man, or if she had been raped. She noted, however, that it had been "several months" since the act. At this time, Mary does not appear to suspect she is pregnant or is in denial. It could be assumed that she would know some of the signs, having watched her mother go through the experience with her younger siblings, but denial or not understanding the changes that occur in the body, especially firsthand if the act itself was wrapped in trauma, is understandable.

Mary's life thus far is filled with jarring traumatic experiences. Each succeeding year seemed to reduce her self-worth as her status diminished. Virginity was so prized in the era that even as a young woman, she would have understood the price women paid for its loss. To have sex outside of marriage was a detrimental undoing of the promise of a stable home and family initially hoped for. Her father Patrick ironically placed a high value on her chastity but not enough to remain sober or in the home. Nor did he provide a safe environment for his wife or children. Later, he would cut her from the family tree, never taking any of the blame for her downfall.

Mary does not have control over being born into a male-dominated society; even if she gave consent to the act, she was far too young to understand the full ramifications. Women of this era were still not considered adults below the age of eighteen and, therefore, fell under the control of their parents, particularly their fathers. Regardless of law, consent, or situation, Mary, during this time, is but a child.

Mary describes her mother as the ideal of womanhood in her earliest memories. This vision of the ideal woman was shared across society. Women before marriage were held to a high moral standard; women after marriage were equated the same with the addition of the traits of blessed motherhood. Carroll Smith-Rosenburg writes, "The American girl was taught at home, at school, and in the literature of the period that aggression, independence, self-assertion, and curiosity were inappropriate for the weaker sex and her limited sphere."[1] All of the traits listed would eventually be the tools that allow Mary to grow, survive, and prosper. They are also the traits that, in her teenage years in Saint Joseph, were allowed to grow unchecked without familial stability, housing, or food security. Although her early experiences allowed her to survive in Saint Joseph, they could not prepare her for life in an urban environment, especially with the repercussions of past sexual activity.

In 1888, as a girl of just 16, Mary's arrival in Saint Louis at eleven o'clock at night was a startling experience. Never in her life had she beheld such a large metropolis. She writes she was "bewildered by the clamor and the crowd."[2] But the old family friend Mrs. James finds and comforts her. Mr. James says she looks like her mother, and Mrs. James denies it, hoping to impede Mary's thoughts of beauty and therefore sex. This feeds into Mary's sense of self, which is notable throughout the book. If she does not resemble her mother, she must be more like her father. This must have led to questioning how much she shared with her father regarding temperament. Mary never describes herself as beautiful. Instead, she uses words like "handsome" in the description. Her most notable attribute is her thick, long hair.

Although she went to bed late that first night, she was awakened to her new reality at four-thirty in the morning. Her new job was two miles away, and the factory was filled with the loud shriek and spin of 80 power machines stitching cloth. Her pay would be $5 a week, and her rent $2.

Mary found it challenging to befriend Mrs. James' daughters or their friends, possibly due to prolonged social isolation stemming from her family's fall from society. This difficulty might have also come from Mrs. James, who had been a longtime servant of her family; class roles within society were hard to erase even when her family had fallen into dire circumstances. Mrs. James monitored her with maternal vigilance,

6. Mary Becomes the Madeleine

restricting her activities to work and church to safeguard her. Although Mary's parents had instilled a sense of higher social status, reflected in her refined language skills, this distinction alienated her from peers, who perceived her "aristocratic" English as snobbery. Consequently, Mary attributed her social struggles to what seemed like speaking "a foreign language" when her elevated diction set her apart.

Three months into her new life, she began to grow ill. Unfortunately, Mary could no longer ignore the signs. Her mother had given birth to many children, probably in the home, and Mary often looked after her mother and the children during and after birth. So when she began to have hormonal outbursts, growing nauseated and vomiting often at work, she suspected her worst fears had come about. She was pregnant.

Mrs. James remarked that the sin would have never happened had Mary's father been half the man he was 10 years prior. Mrs. James refused to tell her daughters, but Mary understood that girls of the new industrial age understood her condition too well. Mary wrote, "The conviction that finally penetrated to my consciousness was that the girls must know." Until now, she still retained the idea that although her family had fallen on hard times, her class was still superior. The foolishness of her supposition and the reality of how it would change her life are reflected in her thoughts. She tells the reader, "Who in my secret heart had felt so superior to these illiterate working girls, must become a byword to them, because, despite my better birth and breeding, I had lost that jewel of virtue which they still retained."[3] Mary was keenly aware of the shame it brought on her and her family, but she was also aware of the shame it brought to her family friend's house.

Mrs. James remembers, as Mary does, a time before when her family had status and resources. The only thing from the previous life she still had of value was her virginity, and now even this was gone. Her marital value was destroyed in the eyes of society, and if her family found out, she would be cut off completely. Mary explains that at 16, motherhood meant nothing to her but disgrace. It also meant "the penalty of separation from my loved ones and disability for the work which would enable me to sustain life."[4] A child would also mean poverty, hunger, and diminished working value. No one would hire an unwed mother, and she knew with a certainty that whereas her mother might take her in, her father, if he returned, would cast her out.

A pregnancy outside of marriage meant social separation for women. Even in the case of rape, women were often forced to marry the person who violated them. It also caused a spiritual separation between Mary and God, which parallels the separation from her parents. Frequently, the solution was spiritual and physical reform. She knew that women and girls were sent away to places to cause repentance. Mary was afraid of being forced into a reform institution:

> Visions of the reform school, of the House of the Good Shepherd—places that I had heard the girls at the factory refer to as punitive refuges for wicked young girls—swam before my tortured imagination. Public disgrace; my proud father's daughter, my beautiful mother's little girl, my splendid brother's sister in one of these institutions with a public brand of infamy upon her. It was too much; my soul rose in revolt against a punishment that was out of all proportion to my offense.[5]

Her fears were not unfounded. The Convent of the House of Good Shepherd, a Catholic enterprise, was part of the Magdalene Laundries. It operated as a prison where infants were separated from their mothers and adopted out. The women would then remain hidden behind tall walls to work the laundry and other domestic labor. Often, their names were changed, stripping them of any former agency. It was the norm in these systems to suffer physical and mental abuse, starvation, and often worse. Many of the women who entered never left except in death. James Smith, in his scholarship of Irish and, by extension, American homes for wayward and unwed mothers, titled *Ireland's Magdalene Laundries*, suggested that women who were outside of societal norms of the day because of their occupations as prostitutes or escorts, or who were considered at risk because they were unruly, or sometimes merely because they were too pretty, or for the simple crime of being born out of wedlock could be sent to a Magdalene Laundry. Although they could enter a laundry on their own, more commonly, they were placed there by their families, priests, or courts. Once there, many were held for life, enslaved, abused, and unpaid as workers in the laundry.[6] Mary would have known of the institution through her familial connection to the Catholic Church. The compound was well known in the city, easily identifiable by its imposing building and 12-foot walls in Saint Louis. The women of the factory spoke of the "punitive refuges for wicked girls," details that frightened Mary as her situation became more real.

The Sisters of the Good Shepherd was a Roman Catholic order that, according to Elizabeth V. Cardinal, "began in France in 1835. The sisters take the usual three vows of charity, chastity, and poverty, and an additional fourth vow, binding themselves to the labor for the conversion of fallen women and girls needing refuge from the temptations of the world."[7] There are many accounts of parents committing their daughters, ages 10–19, to the convent for rehabilitation. Various reasons were recorded, such as obstinate behavior, wanting to marry a man of their choice, pregnancy, running away, drunkenness, and sexuality and non-normative sexual practices. These reformatories were in every

6. Mary Becomes the Madeleine

major city nationally, including New Orleans, Chicago, New York City, Louisville, Philadelphia, Boston, Saint Paul, and Saint Louis. The Homes of the Good Shepherd were established wherever major vice and fallen women were considered endemic. No matter if they were reformatories or named refuges, for most women, they were prisons.

Although she did not want the shame of unwed motherhood, Mary did not want to give up her freedom, agency, or life because of it. Girls were committed to the House of Good Shepherd through courts, the health department, or their families. If Mary returned home in her condition, the court or her parents would most likely, in conjunction with the Church, have her committed. If she stayed, Mrs. James might do the same under her parents' direction. Nowhere felt safe, and Mary felt cornered.

Throughout the book, Mary often speaks of choices; even though women had so few, she was determined to make her own. At the time, Mary felt that she "took advantage of her father's disability by striking him in his most vulnerable spot, the last remnants of his honor concerning womankind." She goes on in the text to speak to how her father did not "impugn the character of a woman" and looked down on men who spoke lightly of feminine virtue. Yet, she is left alone to navigate early womanhood. She is too young and of an era that held virginity higher than character and physical and mental health. If Patrick had been the father Mary needed, would life have been different? It is perhaps the question every child of an alcoholic might ask but for which they will never find the answer. It also serves to show the trauma of childhood with an alcoholic and physically abusive parent, the heart and mind fluctuating between genuine love for the parent and continued desire for love to be returned amid parental abandonment.

Mary, however, is a survivor and decides to strike out on her own. With $12 to her name, she, a 16-year-old girl, decides to face her shame alone and somehow still protect her family in sharing it. She says, "Although I was not at the time aware of it, it was from myself that I was trying to hide." Mary took nothing except the clothing she had on and a picture of her mother and left in the late afternoon with no direction, plan, or protection into the urban environment of Saint Louis.

Eventually, she takes up with a man for a night in exhaustion and suffering pangs of hunger. She has sex with him, hoping for money, but is left with nothing. She wanders the city and stops in one of the large department stores to write letters assuring Mrs. James that she found work, and to her mother, she writes as if she has not left Mrs. James' house. She waits in the small lunchroom of the store for the patrons to leave before digging in the trash to find whatever scraps of food she can find.

Later that night, an older man saves her from a dangerous situation in which pimps tried to kidnap her on the street. This second man of the city treats her more as a courtesan, buying her clothing and fancy dinners and providing her with a place to stay. She speaks of this time as her learning process for the world's oldest profession. Ultimately, she contracts a venereal disease, most likely gonorrhea, from him, but he provides a doctor and care. Even at this early stage, Mary knows the risks that come with the profession. But she also learns that sex work can provide and offer her some of life's necessities and something else that women did not have an abundance of—control. There is no sense in the text of her hating this man or indication of being mistreated by this particular "John." She speaks of him with words of empathy and care. Even when he explains that he has a venereal disease, she still chooses to have sex with him, though in her early innocence, she does not fully understand what this would mean for her long term. What it did mean is that within days, she contracted her first STD, which threatened the life of her child. This "John" did not leave her but provided her with medical care for the illness. The doctor treats her and doesn't make an issue of the pregnancy.

At the hospital, she shares a room with Mamie, another sex worker, who explains the life and work of a woman of ill repute and warns as parting advice, "Don't ever be fool enough to go into the streets."[8] Mamie tried to get Mary to come to her keeper's house, who is described as a landlady named Miss Laura. Mamie understood the hardship of the pregnancy that was coming and knowing the hardship that awaited Mary offered the expectant mother a chance to get back on her feet. Mary resisted initially, but it was harder to say no as her pregnancy approached six months. She finally agreed, seeing no other plausible way to support herself and the coming child.

Miss Laura, called Madame Lovejoy during the time, was a relatively famous figure in Kansas City. As a madam, she was known not only for her business sense but also for her kindness. An offender notice from 1886 records her as being fined $29 for keeping a "ranch" of 11 inmates/prostitutes who worked in her house and were fined $9 each.[9] The research describes Laura Lovejoy's house as a 24-room house at 200 and 202 West Fourth Street. It was known as "the Old Ladies' Home" due to its draw of older clientele.[10] The house was richly decorated. Some even considered Miss Laura Lovejoy's house one of the gilded palaces of sin—plush, being both comfortable and clean. It sat in a trinity of the most high-class brothels of the time in Kansas City. Many academic works that look at this particular section of location, vocation, and history wrongly suggest that Mary was a crib girl. This assertion couldn't be further from the truth—the women who worked in these high-class houses did not operate out of cribs but instead richly appointed rooms, garbed in the highest of styles. This would be Mary's first bawdy house, and as a first-class establishment, enough comfort a woman like Mary could hope for under the circumstances.

Laura Lovejoy is described as kindhearted but has rules about how her girls present themselves. These women were not hanging about the balconies half-dressed in public, nor were their services cheap. Mary often spoke to a hierarchy among prostitutes, and the houses she worked in were at the top. Besides her first "John" in Saint Louis, she would never find herself in such dire straits. However, she needed to learn the trade and the expectations of working at the top. Madame Laura Lovejoy would be her first instructor in the craft of the working prostitute.

When Mary finally met Miss Laura, a person she imagined in fear, she found something different. Mary describes Miss Laura as "a woman comely and middle-aged, who bore no resemblance to the horrible creature of my imagination. She greeted me in a soft, well-bred voice, and everything about her so eloquently spoke of her potentialities for motherhood that instinctively, I looked around for the children who should have been clinging to her skirts."[11] In earlier parts of her autobiography, Mary expresses her longing for a mother figure who is healthy and loving and shows her care. In Miss Laura, though madam of a bawdy house, she felt she had found a figure of warm motherhood. She also found something else: her working name, Madeleine Blair.[12]

Other characters arise, and rules of the house and profession are uncovered unceremoniously. A "Jewess" called Bessie warns Mary about the short-lived profession, intoning her to change her mind and not follow the sex worker path. Bessie tells her,

> You are young now. Men will swarm about you if you learn how to please them. It lies with you whether they show you much consideration or not. It is in your power to make them do so. But as you grow older, you will find them losing consideration for you. Men who have known us for five years are always ready to swear that they have known us for ten. Those who have known us for ten years refer to us as "grandmothers," "old women," "has-beens," and call us other names even less complimentary. Most women who have been ten years in the business are still under thirty and retain much of their youthful charm; many of them have improved in appearance, but if they stay in the place where they are known, they become "old-timers" to the men and do not receive the consideration shown to younger women. The one consolation is that they usually make more money than beginners.[13]

This was a forewarning that the business, once entered, did not usually provide a way out. There was little hope for redemption for body, mind, or soul. Mary tells Bessie that she heard girls lived for only seven years. Bessie laughs at this belief, revealing that even Miss Laura has been around since the end of the Civil War 20 years ago. Due to societal problems, venereal disease, shame, and ostracization, women once caught in life had very few choices to get out. Some indeed chose the life, but more often, women and girls were coerced, unable to leave because of the shame and because they were deeply in debt to their madam. A return or dreamed of reunion to the family left behind was impossible and, even if attempted, would result in extreme punishment or forced placement in institutions like the Magdalene Laundries. Mary may not have fully understood the choice she was making, but even she knew that this was her best chance at life when faced with the road that women in her position usually walked. She would not be homeless or hungry.

The learning curve was difficult, but the environment of Madame Laura Lovejoy's was less harsh than other houses. Lara's house was known for first-class women. Mary would pay $5 a week for the board. She would need to make $10 or more to make a profit and save money, along with paying for necessities. Unlike other houses, Miss Laura did not add extra percentages except to pay half of all standard earnings. If they were given an amount over, they were allowed to keep it. This was not the norm for sex workers who, in other houses, were drawn into increasing debt to the house. The only fines that Miss Laura applied concerned missing "parlor hours," which were 8:00 p.m. to 4:00 a.m., and even then, Mary writes that Miss Laura was flexible unless the girl was drunk.[14] The men who visited were regulars referred to as "Oldtimers." Mary writes that Miss Laura smiled at the reference to her place as having an older crowd, stating that she would rather her girls feel the place was more a home than a place of work. To Mary, it was as close to a loving home as she had in many years despite the work she performed.

Miss Laura Lovejoy's remarkable story showed the grit necessary for survival, leading to her bawdy house. Her father, a slaveholder, was killed in Missouri during an early battle in the Civil War. Their family home was burned, and Laura was made to watch her pregnant mother tortured to get them to reveal where they had hidden their family valuables. Laura was 16 at the time. Her mother gave birth to twin boys soon after. Her mother died shortly after from the trauma of the torture and birth.

Laura, her twin brothers, and her sister were left alone. A Union general offered them safe passage to Saint Louis, but the sisters were sexually assaulted during the journey, and with no money and an abundance of trauma, they both entered a house of prostitution. Eventually,

6. Mary Becomes the Madeleine

Laura and her sister make their way to Kansas City, opening their own place. They hired some of their father's former slaves to work for them as freedmen. They bought a house where the sisters lived separately, caring for their twin brothers who were born "simple-minded," most likely due to the physical torture and resulting trauma their mother suffered during the war.[15] Mary reflects that every business portrays the "personality of the keeper," and at Miss Laura's, Mary finds kindness, tolerance, and fellowship that is "seldom seen elsewhere."

Miss Laura directed the house servants to see to it that the women were comfortable. The house was always heated, and food was freely given; the women were also allowed an abundance of time for rest, almost unheard of in the sex trade of the time. Mary grew close to the cook, a former enslaved woman who would tell stories of her experiences growing up in the chains of slavery. She arose early to breakfast to visit with the cook each morning.

Mary, during this time, faltered in learning the trade. She writes of stupid mistakes such as forgetting to collect payment. Having been so isolated most of her life, she struggled to talk with her clients, sometimes not talking and other times talking too much about how repugnant the work was. The results of her awkward approach meant that customers would rarely visit her a second time. She describes Miss Laura as patient with her failures, noting other madams wouldn't have kept her two weeks. Mary also struggled in selling drinks, a huge source of income for the house, due to her hatred of alcohol. Men would buy drinks for the women, and Mary would refuse to drink until it was explained that she did not have to consume them, merely to pretend.

Mary also refused to see a distinction between the blackguard, "a villain," and a gentleman. What she understood by now was that men could impregnate, give disease, abuse, and punish, and all of these distinctions were born from her short life experience. She told the housekeeper, who was to help her through the early days at Miss Laura's house, that she "didn't believe that gentlemen came into a 'sporting house.'"[16] She continues that "time proved me mistaken in this opinion."

Her education in the ways of sex work was a slow process, and she writes that she had two specific difficulties in doing the work. One was that the men who came wanted her to share her life and story. To Mary's mind, they were buying her body and nothing more. Her internal person was her own. The second was her repugnance to exhibit affection, especially during the act of sex itself. Here again, she felt they bought her body and that her love was not "for sale piecemeal to every man who had the price to pay for my body." She expressed her frustration and amazement that men expected more than a body, writing, "For the life of me, I could not see why they should want more." Of the sexual act itself, she writes, "I could make no pretense at a response I did not feel; on the contrary, I made little effort to conceal my repugnance."[17] Mary explains that the transition from virtue to vice is a personal experience for every woman in the business. Mary describes her experience as a stripping away of moral attrition. She also writes that almost any girl or woman who enters the profession is not worth any value initially. Like any business, the trade must be learned, the services advertised and sold, and the best business is a pleased customer. Mary notes that the men demanded top service, no different than they expected from a waitress at a top restaurant. Slowly, Mary developed not only survival skills but also business skills that would eventually make her successful.

In Madame Laura Lovejoy's house, she eventually met a man who did not require her to fake feelings during the transaction. He came for service only and was known to leave just as quickly as he entered the house. Laura explained to Mary, "You ought to suit him down to the ground. He dislikes having girls make a fuss over him, and if she tries to make love to him, he flatly tells her she can eliminate that part of it because she will not get anything extra for it." Mary was keen on this idea. She tells the reader, "I felt that I would be delighted to meet such a man, although I had by this time decided that there was no such animal as a man who did not also want to claim a woman's soul for the price he paid for her body."[18]

His name in the book is Paul Martin, and although he was never known to stick with a girl over the two years he visited Lovejoy's house, he and Mary would grow close in love and a devoted friendship. Much to Mary's surprise, she began to look forward to his visits. Paul returned every day for a week, and then suddenly, his visits ceased. Mary thought it was over, but then she received a letter from him explaining that he had business in Winnipeg, Manitoba, and even though he felt nothing good would come from their friendship, he did want to see her again.

Although it was a life of prostitution that Mary had entered, it was a stable, comfortable situation that saw to her needs. Even though not suited as other women with the life, Mary finds a kind of hope that she had lost long ago. She is not coerced into sex work and knows that she does have some choice on whether she will stay or not. This detailed description within the book of Laura Lovejoy's house that Mary writes of is at odds with the prevailing purity society theme of "white slavery," an anthem used to highlight further the condition of the body and soul of the "wretched prostitute." Mary seems to include such a detailed account to rebuff ideals around the term "white slavery" in a pointed manner. Much of the research leaned into the belief that this was not intended to indicate

6. Mary Becomes the Madeleine

race but referred to the practice of "organized coercion of unwilling persons" into prostitution. Any race could be forced into "white slavery," although of main concern was white women.[19] Any race could also be a "white slaver" (pimp, madam/bawdy house owner), yet this characterization was reserved for those who were not white or considered Christian. These notions were blatantly racist, often xenophobic and anti-Semitic. Social justice ideals and uplift overwhelmingly had concerns for white women much as they would in the suffrage movement. So, in this way, "white slavery," for all intents and purposes, was a fear dreamed up by whites as a crime perpetuated on the white female body.

Interestingly, "white slavery" was used to draw up images that white was usually attributed to, such as race, heaven, cleanliness, and purity. It is hard to imagine that it was not somehow tied up with race and the developing ideas in eugenics, social Darwinism, and purity of the "white" race. The term itself heightened racial insecurity and the need to "save" European immigrants who came to the country inexperienced, young, and often under questionable circumstances. The term was never intended to save the Asian, Indigenous, or those of African American ethnicity who were exploited at more significant numbers within the trade. This need to be "saved" by polite society was mostly extended to those who presented as white.

It was believed that young girls and women, the poor, immigrants, and those in the workforce were particularly in danger due to their lack of protection. It was also believed that these women, more than the privileged class, were impressionable to economic means of improvement and therefore vice. Mary thought that some were coerced or chosen, but she also believed that many women, though misguided or because of lack of choices, often chose the life over the alternatives. Mary, in the book and later in other documents and interviews, insisted that she time and again chose to remain. What may have horrified her in the beginning became tolerable if not stable. William A. Davis in "'Irréconciliables,' 'Reclaimables,' and 'First Falls': Lady Mary Jeune and the Fallen Woman in *Tess of the d'Urbervilles*" recounts a narrative as put forth by Lady Mary Jeune:

> The downward history of her career, the more abandoned and hardened woman would dwell on the fun, the excitement, the gaiety of its different phases, always keeping silent ... about the squalor, misery, and degradation of the other side of it. Foul, coarse language, oaths, and jests were used, and the darkest page of the woman's life discussed with such freedom and absence of shame that the least corrupted of women would become habituated to thoughts and aspects of vice from which they would have shrunk in horror a few weeks before.[20]

It was true that some were lured from Europe with a promise of ease and leisure. It may also be true that women were worn down by their keepers, locked in a life of vice from which they could not escape. However, although sharing many of these views, Mary's narrative also promotes freedom in the work and control over one's destiny. The bawdy house was a home where she felt safe even while her pregnancy progressed.

Mary, now 17, tells of leaving Miss Laura's house on Christmas Day for a walk. She goes to Union Cemetery and approaches a tall tombstone. On it is an inscription, "Leave hope and faith alike adieu—would I could add remembrance, too." She goes on philosophizing:

> I stood there speculating about the inscription, the monument, and the man underneath the stone until I was nearly frozen. Why should a dead man bid adieu to Faith, Hope, and Remembrance? What had the dead to do with these graces of the living? As I walked back to the car, I turned this over in my mind. I did not like him, this man who had bidden adieu to Faith and Hope. But he had reached out of the grave to befriend me; he had raised such a revolt in my soul by his pessimism that I vowed I should never bid adieu to either of these graces.[21]

Her resolve to do the opposite and hold on to memory, hope, and faith is striking. The inscription was not unique to the author; it was a poem crafted in the early 1800s by Lord Byron called "Remembrance."[22] The allusions (one of many) within the book show the reader that Mary is something else beyond a sex worker. Mary was literate and knowledgeable about great works of literature and the philosophy of the time. She is self-reflective and able to observe her actions and learn from them. Mary does not blame others for her sins. Instead, she says, "Knowing the difference between good and evil, I had deliberately chosen evil. The fault was entirely my own. This was the verdict I had passed upon myself, and I did not ask for a more charitable one from others." In some ways, no one could be harder on herself than she was; society, of course, would be brutal, but because of her lived experience, she would survive and go on to do the extraordinary.

It was with faith and hope that Mary had to mentally and physically prepare for the coming child. A child herself, she wanted her mother and family, even as the women of Miss Laura's house tried to fill in, buying gifts and small garments for the coming infant. The closer her time came, the more she felt apathetic, writing, "I did not want this child."[23] Miss Laura, trying to be realistic, suggested that the child couldn't be kept and that it would be best to find a good family.

Mary refused the house physician, and Miss Laura called in an old friend, a famous retired physician, to whom Mary quickly responded because of his kind character. Mary's growing illness and depression during the latter half of her pregnancy were partly due to the case of gonorrhea she had contracted and treated months before. Her illness, which was not cured, complicated the birth, making her labor long and dangerous. Over several days, it was unclear if Mary would live or not. When the danger passed, she was told her daughter did not survive. It is unknown if she saw the infant or a grave; no records of the child have been found, which is not uncommon. What seems to be clear in the text is that the emotional and mental pain, though not vocalized, remained with her for the rest of her life.

Society is preprogrammed to lessen the humanity of those of the outer edges. Prostitutes are reduced to the act they do in work rather than the whole of their humanity. Mary longed for her mother and a daughter she would never see grow, a child she had sacrificed everything for, including her body. Sorrow is often denied to these women; they were mothers, daughters, and sisters, and their pain was real and experienced in all the fullness of what it meant to be human. Yet, as so many like her, sorrows were bent inward due to her position. There was no room for mourning in the life of a soiled dove. Mary struggled with feelings of sorrow, relief, and shame, which tangled in her heart and mind with no relief.

Mary needed someone to care. The person who stepped up was her doctor. This doctor, who saw her through the delivery, loss, and recovery, became a good friend. Mary describes him as grandfatherly in his attention. He believed in "regeneration," or the ability to change one's life. Mary felt safe enough to share her life and choices with him, and he helped her plan her rehabilitation. He noted her artistic ability and intelligence, and Mary writes, "he believed that I had marked artistic talent and that I should not be forced to waste it in uncongenial work. He decided to pay for my education and to help me in the upward struggle."[24] The doctor would help her go home to her family for a month, and then she would return and go to school, leaving the life of prostitution behind.

Miss Laura Lovejoy also stepped up to help Mary, supporting her decision to leave the life. The women of the house helped her get ready, modifying her clothing for reentry to proper society. Miss Laura looked her over and declared that the life had left no outward stain. Mary told her, "Whenever I hear anyone denounce the women who lead this life, I shall think of the kindliness I have received from those I have met in it, and I shall defend them."[25] Miss Laura, however, knew that although Mary's heart was in the right place, she could never safely defend any woman caught in the life. Miss Laura tells her,

> You must do nothing of the kind. The more one knows of our life, the more one must denounce it, lest it be suspected that one has a personal motive in

defending it. When other women speak of us, you must assume an attitude of scorn, not only to protect yourself from suspicion but that you may also feel it for yourself and have no temptation to return. When you think of us, do not remember any small kindness that we may have shown you or that we show to one another. Remember only the things that have shocked you and outraged your traditions and your sense of decency. Remember your sufferings at the hands of beasts who are miscalled men. If you keep these things in view, you will never again fall into temptation.[26]

Mary kept this rule for a short time when she reentered society and remembered Laura's words much later in life when she finally turned away from prostitution. Her promise to defend prostitutes was more than words.

When Mary returned home, she found her family in the same state. Her father was somewhere in eastern Illinois and had not returned home. Before she arrived, her brother John set out to find or act on a job offer out west in North Dakota. Fessenden, North Dakota's historical record, titled *The Fessenden Diamond Jubilee 1893–1968*, noted J. Austin Regan as an important resident who arrived sometime in 1891.

In North Dakota, John went by his middle name, Austin, and became the first postmaster of Fessenden on November 23, 1893. After 1895, Austin managed a farm implement business and later became a partner before taking over the company. Austin also formed a business partnership with W.W. Lyness, building up the first grain elevator and then an entire chain of grain elevators serving the county and state and providing a much better life than the one he escaped.[27] He eventually married a Fessenden teacher named Grace Christie, and they had a son named Arthur. John Austin Regan later made a name for himself as a state senator and even had a town named after him.[28] It is unknown what made him decide to make such a bold move away from his family, but with her oldest brother gone and her father still absent after many months, Mary must have felt pressure to provide for her mother and remaining family.

It also seems clear that Mary, for a time, decided to turn her life around, hoping her past mistakes could be forgotten. She wanted an education and to live beyond the poverty and abuse to which her father had doomed the family. Perhaps in many ways, Mary and her brother John Austin were more similar in their means of escape, even if attaining that escape favored those of the male gender.

Mary brought with her trauma and pain that she could not put into words, and even if she had them, they were not to be spoken aloud. Not once did Mary tell her family about her troubles or mention the loss of her daughter, not even to her mother. Instead, she spoke passionately

6. Mary Becomes the Madeleine

The only known photograph of John Regan, Mary Agnes Regan Sears's brother. Date unknown, 1890s (courtesy Digital Horizons, North Dakota Histories Collection, ND State Library).

about going to school in Saint Louis. Her mother did not want her to leave and was upset with the doctor's offer. Not knowing what work Mary had been doing, her mother probably thought that the doctor was showing unbecoming attention to her daughter. Women were also not encouraged to seek an education, and this most likely added to Mary's discomfort. Not wanting to stay but not wanting to disappoint her mother, Mary changed her plans and decided to go to Chicago to work an honest job, send money back home, and live a rehabilitated life.

The Chicago Working Years

Mary first worked in a department store in Chicago, trying to turn her life around. She felt lost in the city, though she had the metropolitan experience of Saint Louis and Kansas City. The city, she writes, felt "boundless." She was 18 years old and settled in a boarding house on the south side of the city, gaining employment at one of the large department stores. She understood from her sex work at Miss Laura's the value of her looks, smile, precise English, and good manners. These assets worked well selling French undergarments at the store. She was a favorite with customers, none of whom knew of her work in the cities in the West. Here, women came to shop and often requested her to wait on them, earning her an increased salary.

From 1890 to 1891, she still enjoyed the letters from the doctor in Kansas City and Paul. She also dived into the study of literature and American history. She writes, "Every spare moment was devoted to this object. I had no teacher nor anyone with whom I could discuss my plans and efforts."[1] This was a brief time of happiness in Mary's life, when she finally did legitimate labor, had savings, and was independent. This happiness did not last.

A letter arrived from a family friend, alerting Mary that her family was in its most dire hour. Her father Patrick, the letter explained, was in trouble. His abuse of Mary growing up and continued alcoholism, as well as the loss of his land, farm, home, and social standing, meant that almost any crime was possible. In her book, Mary writes that he had, while drunk, gotten himself in a "row" and had been jailed under an assumed name. He contacted a lawyer friend back home, but the local sheriff had found out and made it a public spectacle. Her older brother John was already settled in North Dakota, taking up duties in a new job, but he suffered a sudden illness that had cut off the money he sent home.[2] With the money dried up and Mary's father in jail, her mother was threatened with the county poorhouse, and Mary's siblings were to be divided and sent out in "bondage" to whoever would take them in. Mary, in her book, rails against the "cold-hearted philanthropist" community and church members who would divide a family into poorhouses and bondage rather than help with food or money. Mary describes her view of this type of philanthropist born during the Progressive era, views she held until the end of her life: "To this day when I see 'kindly' philanthropists disposing of the bodies and souls of those whom poverty has delivered into their clutches, whenever I hear them suggesting the separation of children from a good mother, I feel the brand of a potential Cain upon my brow, for I must exert all the self-restraint of a lifetime of training if I would withhold my hand."[3] Her views extended from poor families to sex workers who had children. Mary felt that the world was set against the familial happiness of the poor, marginalized, and othered.

During the 1890s, as today, the poor were politicized. Poorhouses were a means to institutionalize those who suffered through the economic downturn of the 1890s. In Saint Joseph, Missouri, the mentally disabled were also housed in poorhouses after the nearest insane asylum burned down, with the general population causing conditions to deteriorate further.[4] Mary's mother and family, already living under the stigma of Patrick's alcoholism and loss of social standing, could not escape the magnifying glass of the relief societies. Children could be separated and forced into indentured bondage, made to work in homes or on farms. Poorhouses provided harsh environments seeking to deter poverty, and Mary knew that her mother, who was already sick, might die in such conditions.

To her mind, there was no other way but to sacrifice her new life in Chicago and reenter the one she had left behind. Mary's quick decision did not show a deficit of character but instead exhibited the great love and responsibility she felt for her family. This attribute of children acting in the place of an adult is a shared characteristic among many who grow up in a home of abuse and alcoholism. Mary, after reading the letter, spent the night pacing until the early morning hours reflecting:

> I went down into the depths with my mother, but I suffered no less with that proud man, my father, lying in a prison cell. For I was heart of his heart and bone of his bone. My face, in a much lesser degree of comeliness, was the face of my mother, but my mind and disposition were those of my father. I lacked his charm of manner and his scintillating wit; but I was his; nothing could dissever me from him. My very carriage, my intonation of speech, my weakness and my strength, the idealism of my nature—they were all his, and I could not find it in my heart to hate him. I could only suffer with him.[5]

Mary would do what was necessary, using the skills of survival she honed the year before to keep her family afloat. Mary quit her rooming house and packed up her trunk. She quit her job, sending all of her pay and money the doctor had sent to her mother, promising continual funds to the family through a new job promotion. It was a lie, but her mother needed to accept the financial support. Mary had a customer at the department store who worked as a prostitute at Custom House Place, the vice district of Chicago. Mary decided again to enter a bawdy house for her family's survival. Mary was not the frightened girl she had been before. She writes,

> The interview was brief and to the point. I was no frightened girl seeking refuge from the terrors of the streets. I was a woman driving the best possible bargain for the sale of my body and my soul. In reply to the questionings of Madame I said that I had been in a house before and spoke as if my experiences were much greater than the facts really warranted. I brought my dimples and my beautiful teeth into play, and Madame closed the bargain with me on my terms, which were not onerous. I knew the state of the market too well to make too many conditions.[6]

Custom House Place was not a house but a district of brothels in the First Ward, Nineteenth Precinct of Chicago. Depending on the year, the 30-plus brothels were found between Harrison and Polk Streets, parallel between Dearborn and Clark Streets.[7] It is impossible to know which brothel Mary entered at this time. Mary only uses the name Madame C and says she has broken English and allows unspeakable acts in her house, such as bacchanalian orgies in the basement rooms. Mary recollects that "she did not require the girls to do these unspeakable things if they did not want to, but she reproved me gently for the manner of my refusal, which made it seem that I felt myself better than the other girls."[8] Mary describes the house as full of "moral leprosy of which one hardly dares to think. I had never dreamed of coming into direct contact with such perversions." The man who rescues her from having to participate in the more detestable acts describes the house as a "notorious joint" and further tells Mary, "This house is one of the most notorious joints in the United States. I am not a rescue worker, but by Jove! It makes me hot under the collar every time I see a nice girl come into this place, although I am one of the regular customers. If you take my advice, you will get out of here at once."[9] The text also later shows that Madame C procured young girls for the likes of an elderly billionaire mentioned, who "had a perchance for innocent young girls." The text gives more clues describing the accent of Madame C. The madam cautions Mary, saying, "got ze beeg head wiz zem." Another clue was Mary's description of Madame C as "a French-Canadian who might have been foreordained

7. The Chicago Working Years

for the role she played, so admirably was she fitted to the part." Her disposition is described as, "She was hard and cold, and exacted her pound of flesh from every girl in the house" and as rich with insatiable greed. Another detail in the text is Madame C's use of immigrant girls. Mary describes these girls as "ignorant," unaware of the work or conditions they were signed up for. Mary does not say if they were tricked or coerced as the narrative of "white slavery" describes.

The clues combined offer a hint as to which house Mary may have entered, though this cannot be ascertained with total certainty. One such woman might have been Madame Carrie Watson, but descriptions of Watson seem at odds with *Madeleine: An Autobiography*. Watson's house was at 441 South Clark Street, which was not considered Custom House Place. She was from New York and did not have a European accent. Another aspect of Watson's character is that she was well loved and cared for her large family. Watson provided charity despite her working life, which was marred by tragedies and the sinful means of making her money.[10] After Watson's death, her will provided for her elderly parents' care and burial. She also left money to her deceased brother's children, listed as sons and daughters whom, for many years, she cared for. They resided on a farm in Kankakee under the best care and comfort and received an education. Watson also arranged for a young woman, 17, to be rescued (it is supposed from "the life") and cared for in a Chicago mission until the girl was returned to her father, who would arrive from California.[11] She was deemed by the newspaper a Good Samaritan even at the cost of her fortune.[12] It was said that women who worked for her did so of their own free will and could leave as they desired.

A more likely candidate was the infamous Madame Mary Hastings, born in Brussels, who had worked in her home country, France, and Canada as a prostitute and then as a notorious madam in Chicago. She was accused of utilizing "white slavery" in her importation of immigrant girls, and in this case, it was accurate. It was difficult to leave her house once a woman/girl entered. She sold the darkest of fantasies to men and had an arrest record of acquiring young girls in at least one instance in 1891 when she was arrested for having underage girls.[13] Karen Abbot wrote about Hastings in her book *Sin in the Second City, Madams, Ministers, Playboys, and the Battle for America's Soul* in such a way that it seemed to mirror what Mary wrote about her situation. Abbot noted, "During frequent trips to neighboring cities, she extolled the virtues of Chicago and its high-paying jobs, returning with gullible young girls aged thirteen to seventeen." Hastings took the girls' clothing and locked them in a room with six professional rapists. Once "broken in," the girls were sold to other madams for $50–$300 each, depending on age and appearance.[14] Later, when Hastings was forced to flee the United States, she went to Canada or Ohio, depending on the research, only to work under a new name.

Sick of the depraved conditions, Mary decided to try her luck at the newly built Dearborn house her friend had told her about when she first arrived. But to do this, she would have to devise a plan of escape. It would be impossible for Mary to quit and walk out. Even though she had paid off the debts incurred to the house when she first arrived and had managed to save money in the bank, Mary was afraid that madam might hold her trunk full of all her belongings. The plan Mary and her two friends devised was enacted. She recalls the plan as,

> This other man was to come down to the house and inquire for Madame; when he saw her, he would demand to know if she had a girl of my description in the house. He was not supposed to know that I was called Madeleine since that was not my right name, but he was to describe the clothes I had worn when I arrived; he would go on to say that I was his daughter and underage; he was to threaten all sorts of dire results if I were not forthcoming.[15]

It worked so well that her madam helped her pack. Thus began a short but happy time in Mary Regan's life. With the two men who helped in her escape, Mary spent two weeks at a hotel, enjoying shows such as that put on by Eddie Foy at the Crystal Palace, a performer and friend of Wyatt Earp, Doc Holiday, and Bat Masterson. She also spent time exploring the city. Mary describes this time as feeling a "deep sense of gratitude toward these two men, I had no trouble in finding words in which to express my joy for the unusual holiday which they were giving me; this was the first real joy my girlhood had ever known."[16] She explored the Art Institute and dreamed of someday becoming an artist. She shares in the text that she had a talent for drawing and still entertained dreams of a young woman who could see a life beyond the one she was trapped in.

Mary and the man who had played her father during the escape became lifelong friends. In him, she found someone to whom she could speak about literature and even studied the Bible with his interesting comparisons of the biblical Job to King Lear. These friends were the ones who helped her make the connection with the next house she would work for.

Mary was destined for the address of 2131 Dearborn Street, which, together with 2133, became notorious from 1900 to 1911 for its later connection as the Everleigh Club, run by Ada and Minna Everleigh. The home was a twin mansion described as an elegant brownstone known as a first-class establishment even before the Everleighs ran it.

Its world-class status began under the stern eye of one Madame Lizzie Allen, whose real name was Ellen Williams.

According to research, the Everleigh sisters purchased/leased the property in 1899 from Effie Hankins; by then, its glory had faded. Looking into primary and secondary documents of the time, the history of the building is as interesting as it is mysterious.

The front of 2131, 2133 Dearborn Street, Chicago, Illinois (*The Everleigh Club, Illustrated*, published by Minna Everleigh, 1911).

The mystery of the Dearborn property arises with the mention of Madame Carrie Watson not as proprietor but in a connection she and Lizzie Allen shared in the devilish persona of Christopher Columbus Crabb and his involvement in their properties and business dealings. Madames Carrie Watson and Lizzie Allen had business relationships with the well-known attorney Christopher Columbus Crabb, and in one source, Lizzie eventually married him.[17] However, no obituaries or newspaper reports covering her death and last will, nor her official Cook County death index report support a marriage. Instead, there is the general surprise after the death of Lizzie Allen in 1896 that Crabb in probate court is named executor, especially when he declares there are no heirs at law though her brother and sister reside in her Dearborn "home." The situation surrounding Lizzie Allen's death becomes even more mysterious in the weeks leading up to it. In July 1896, Lizzie Allen was reported kidnapped. Witnesses said that she was drugged and taken out of the city. It was suggested that she was taken against her will because of her wealth and accumulated properties estimated at $500,000. The police publicly stated she had gone away for health reasons,[18] but she had previously been involved in an investigation and court proceedings regarding the shakedown of police and purportedly Mayor Carter H. Harrison, III, for "protection fees" that were asked in the name of supporting his election.[19] The protection fees racket already suffered by brothel owners would become the way of business with the mafia.[20] One newspaper reports that her death was being investigated as she "died under peculiar circumstances."[21] Further, research shows that she did operate a house at Polk and Clark Streets in the levee district and then on Congress Street. The Dearborn Street address is recorded as Allen's from 1892 until her death in 1896 at 52.

Allen's death occurred at her house at 2454 Lake View Avenue. The Lake View and Dearborn properties would eventually fall into Crabb's hands. How Crabb obtained the property and all of Lizzie Allen's wealth is a story that reads like a fictional murder mystery.

Christopher Columbus Crabb, an attorney by profession, is often mentioned as a businessman and described by former mayor Harrison as an "imposing looking rooster" who had a mysterious connection to two of the most notorious Chicago madams.[22] In the book *Come to My Parlor*, it is written that when Carrie Watson died, Crabb joined up with Lizzie Allen, but Watson died in 1900 after Lizzie died in 1896, so some of the mystery remains.

Allen built the side-by-side mansions that would become the Everleigh Club for $125,000 and later catered to pleasure seekers of the World's Fair Exposition in 1893. Other sources say she entertained in her other properties, but with the enormity of the World's Fair, it is safe to assume that she would have wrenched every dollar from her properties and girls during the event.

Mary Regan would have entered Allen's house in the latter half of 1890 or early 1891. Documents suggest that Lizzie Allen's health was failing and that she retired in 1892 to her Dearborn address. The Dearborn residence was massive and would have accommodated Allen's brothel and a residential space. Mary notes Allen's presence as either living on the premises or having a constant presence, which is consistent with her living in one-half of her property. The research also noted that Allen was building a new house at Aldine Place for $100,000. Allen possessed vast wealth and power during a time when few women had either on their own. For most of her life, she was a savvy businesswoman with connections in the local government. Yet, with both, it highlights the need for the services of an attorney, such as Christopher Columbus Crabb, and as a woman, especially in her line of business, the ease with which a bad actor could emerge.

The research concerning Christopher Columbus Crabb uncovered investigation and court case documents from 1913. This attorney to wealthy prostitutes amassed significant wealth through inheritance. He would controversially acquire Lizzie Allen's massive fortune and properties just after her death but not without her family trying to fight back. Allegations were raised that this fortune was wrongfully taken from Allen's living siblings despite Crabb's legal victory in court. Crabb later married Helen Bean, the nurse who attended to Allen during her final days. Five years after their marriage, Helen Bean Crabb fell gravely ill and was attended by another nurse, Elizabeth Cummings. Following Helen's death, Crabb married Cummings, mirroring his earlier actions. Notably, both women—Lizzie Allen and Helen Bean Crabb—were nursed and passed away in Allen's Lake View home.

Then Elizabeth Cummings Crabb nurses Mrs. Mary Spiegel in the Cobb home at 2454 Lake View Avenue, where she suddenly grows ill and dies, but not before she changes her will, leaving Christopher Columbus Crabb $200,000. Mrs. Spiegel's brothers and niece demanded an investigation, noting that the signature on the will was not from Mrs. Spiegel and that the will had been changed days before her passing.[23] Lizzie Allen's family combined a suit with the Spiegel family to wrest the money he took and perhaps see him found guilty of murder. Yet just as before, even with witnesses and proof, Christopher Columbus Crabb won the case and walked away with the money. Even when the families tried to appeal, the judge overruled their attempt.[24] Although Mary Regan describes Lizzie Allen as a cold, stern woman, it highlights the dangers of prostitution, the seedy, dangerous characters, and the exploitation of women by men, especially of women who were pariahs in the eyes of society and the law. Even a woman as experienced as Lizzie Allen faced the reckoning of her life. Prostitutes had no protection except for their wits and cleverness.

Mary's descriptions of the Dearborn house rival that of its glory under the Everleigh sisters. Mary describes it not as the subpar descriptions of when Effie Hankins had the property but with the glorious details that almost match the elegance of the scarlet sisters. This suggests that much of the interior remained intact when the Everleighs gained the property. Mary describes the house in terms and room names that only existed after the Everleigh sisters took over. Mary writes, "The statues of Parian marble, the world-famous paintings, and bronzes, were no more beautiful nor perfect in their way than were the furniture, carpets, draperies, and other fittings. The famous Japanese room was the model for many similar rooms in the most exclusive homes in Chicago."[25] Mary describes the copper parlor where she first negotiates with Madame Lizzie Allen, the house entrance, the staircase, the ballroom, and the great Pompeian Room—hinting at the elegance of its first owner, Lizzie Allen.

Copper parlor at 2131 Dearborn Street, Chicago, Illinois (*The Everleigh Club, Illustrated*, published by Minna Everleigh, 1911).

7. The Chicago Working Years   85

View of ballroom at 2131 Dearborn Street, Chicago, Illinois (*The Everleigh Club, Illustrated*, published by Minna Everleigh, 1911).

Entrance to the hall at 2131 Dearborn Street, Chicago, Illinois (*The Everleigh Club, Illustrated*, published by Minna Everleigh, 1911).

The most interesting firsthand account of Mary Regan speaking of the Dearborn house was found in the *Los Angeles Record* 16 archives. Noted reporter Don Ryan interviewed Mary Regan about her time at 2131 Dearborn in 1924. He noted first in the article that "Madeleine Blair has been a boarder in the most famous institutions of the country, notably the establishment in Chicago, later known as the Everleigh Club." Further on in the interview, Ryan wrote, "She told me about going back last winter to see the old mansion at 2131 Dearborn Street, Chicago, the world-famous Everleigh Club."[26] Mary, at the time of the interview, still used the pseudonym Madeleine, said a Black owner possessed the property when she returned and rented the place out to other Black families. She recalled, "It had been a strange sensation, this revisiting a place that had once been famous for its splendor and its treasures of art." She said, "We stepped into the front parlor that had received leading American statesmen, businessmen, and professional men into the copper parlor." She noted that the owner and his family now live there. She said, "The embossed paper was still on the walls but hanging in shreds. From the ceiling, a poor, solid cupid still clung by one arm."[27] As she moved on into the now-faded interior of what used to be the Pompeian Room, a family lived in "where once were marbles that brought eager connoisseurs to this house." As she passed from room to room, one can imagine the feeling of time, both past and present.

The ballroom was full of families living together, and Mary noted in the interview that the "shredded tapestries still swung from the alcoves. Ragged fretwork depended dustily. While on the most expensive hardwood floor were heaps of coal and piles of frozen garbage. I thought of time and change. I thought of all the splendid men and women I had met in this house and all the beasts called men whom I also had known there. And I thought how different the popular conception of this past era is from what it really was." She said, "The life in one of these houses didn't do anything to a woman. It didn't make her anything she wasn't already by nature. If she were naturally hard, cruel, and avaricious, then she became a hard, cruel, avaricious gold-digger. If she were, by nature, kind, gentle, and tender, she probably grew more so as the years advanced. But under the skin, and despite popular opinion to the contrary, she was no wit different from her highly respectable sister. She was and always will be—just a woman."[28]

Mary Regan, by 1924, had already suffered through the scandalous Supreme Court case centered on her book *Madeleine: An Autobiography* in 1919. Her book had been banned and destroyed five years ago. Perhaps in that time, as the Roaring Twenties and the Jazz Age progressed, she felt she could come into the light. But no matter what prompted the

7. The Chicago Working Years

interview, one thing is for sure: she claims that she had worked in the house that would later become the Everleigh Club. The club was closed in 1911 when the Everleigh sisters' protection under John Coughlin and Michael Kenna was obstructed, and the new reformist mayor Carter H. Harrison, IV, son of the previously mentioned Mayor Harrison, made the club his first target in fighting vice in the city.

Mary, in her book, goes on to describe Lizzie Allen as "nearly sixty" and "sandy-haired, austere-looking woman, severely corseted and garbed in a plain, tightly fitting, high-collared dark-gray dress, who looked more like the severe matron of an orphan asylum than the mistress of the most exclusive 'house' in the United States."[29] The staff and rules were strict concerning cleanliness, style, and formality. The women would be formally dressed when they went down for the evening's work, unlike the robes at any of Mary's former places of employment. A hairdresser named Charlie was employed at the house, and at first, Mary refused his service. She found, however, that his services were at the behest of Allen, and a refusal was not acceptable. Charlie's services, however, went beyond the club as he also opened his house on Michigan Avenue for the girls to meet family if they did not want their secret employment to be revealed. Mary divulged that she worked in the Dearborn house for five years:

> During the subsequent years, as might have been expected, I developed into a female "Wandering Jew," who went to and fro on the earth, seeking a peace that was not in her own heart; but during the first five years, I always returned to the house on Dearborn Street; and invariably the first sight that greeted my eyes, when I came down-stairs dressed for the night, was Miss Allen enthroned upon that hard seat of the hall-tree.[30]

Mary's description is noteworthy, for it is a houseplant of striking color, sometimes called a "Purple Heart," that grows, trailing, climbing, and spreading in search of light. In many ways, this is exactly what Mary describes in her narrative. The plant also requires little attention or care, and Mary has carved out her survival alone with her wits and tenacity. Her description is also of a place that called her back through the years no matter how far she would wander.

Prone to adventures and exploring, one can only imagine what she observed while living in Chicago. Lizzie Allen was one of the most popular nighttime destinations for the rich and famous, businessmen, and the politically connected. The history of a changing world would have unfolded right before her. She does not write of it, but one can assume that she would have been among the crowd of 300,000 on May 1, 1893, when the World's Fair opened its magnificent city on the swampy shores of Lake Michigan. Perhaps, with her often walking in Jackson Park, she watched over the months as it was erected. Mary writes, "When I reached Michigan Avenue, I fell into the long free swing that has always made walking a joy to me, and I walked mile after mile through beautiful streets and tree-lined boulevards, across grassy park places and well-kept lawns, breathing in the fresh air that swept clean and strong from the lake and washed the stale odors of Dearborn Street from my nostrils."[31] She was adept at dressing down and could pass among polite society in her attempts to forget the traumas of the previous night. Perhaps she saw the spectacle of President Grover Cleveland calling forth the glorious lights that flickered to life in the "White City" as the World's Fair complex was named. No matter the circumstances, Mary was determined to survive somehow and even more determined that she would command her life and take possession of her choices.

Part of her survival depended on establishing connections with her scarlet sisters, who worked in the house. For Mary, this was not always easy. She often struggled with friendships and usually found it easier to connect with male friends. She recalls Olga Howard as one of her first friends in the household. Olga was from New Orleans and ended up in the Dearborn house because she had an "affair of the heart," which drove her north from her southern city. Mary describes Olga as an "ugly little thing" but notes she had "beautiful shoulders" and "beautiful teeth." Mary found her Southern drawl alluring and appreciated her intelligence and wit even more.[32] Mary describes Olga later in the text as five years older, and together, they explore the city after she convinces Olga to dress down to blend into society, a habit that Mary would practice all her working days.

As they grow closer, Mary learns of the true heartbreak of her new friend. Olga had been in love with a man in New Orleans who lavished her with gifts and showed her unfaltering devotion. In the text, it seems her life was one of a courtesan. Mary writes, "She thought she had won a secure place in his life and affections when she was startled out of her dream reading in the papers the announcement of his engagement."[33] Women came to life in a multitude of ways, and by telling Olga's story within her own, Mary seemed to refute the idea that all women were entrapped by way of cohesion and "white slavery."

Mary notes that they both were driven by secret ambitions and set aside money each week. Mary dreamed of becoming an artist, and Olga, though a fine singer, wanted to study dance. Olga convinced Mary to put off drawing lessons and take up dance with her on the West Side of Chicago. Olga was impressed with Mary's ability to design and sew dresses, a habit she used to save money even when negotiating with a dressmaker to sew them according to Allen's expectations.

7. The Chicago Working Years

The women also had poverty and large families in common and a love for children. However, Olga's family knew what she did for a living, and Mary still hid her secret life. Where Olga could easily send money to her family, Mary still sent funds to her family under the guise of the department store job she left behind long ago. Mary was not afraid of her family looking at her with shame; she was more worried about the grief it would cause them as a whole. She lived each day in fear that her secret would become known. Because of this, she could only send back small sums of money, lacking a means of explaining more significant amounts. Often, she and Olga gave money to the street children, the "street urchins" as they were called, a kind of surrogate for the charity Mary wished she could send to her mother.

Olga would teach Mary a lot about making money in the house, and they would occasionally work together to satisfy a client. Nothing in the texts suggests a queer relationship; however, such relationships were not uncommon. Although Mary would not commit to acts she noted as deviant in her former house, she does write at length about her and Olga satisfying a customer together over an evening and day within the book. The experience is recalled with disgust but also learning a new skill used by prostitutes to secure more money via a client's soft spot for alcohol and sex. Olga teaches Mary the art of reselling the same bottle of alcohol to an inebriated client who was too drunk to suspect otherwise, pocketing the money into their secret accounts.

Within the context of chapter X, Mary reveals that prostitutes of their caliber were savvy businesswomen, talented musicians, stylish dressers, and experts in engaging conversation. They were not just entertainers in the bedrooms but something more significant, feeding the egos and fulfilling the sexual and intellectual needs of the rich, famous, and politically linked of Chicago and the world. Mary writes that she was not favored among the "bloods," meaning the aristocratic class or older American monied. Still, she did find favor, she says, among the serious "higher class" assumed to be those men who were at the head of growing corporations and booming businesses of the fast-growing American economy. During this time, she would make connections and travel with her clients who wanted the company of a beautiful, intelligent woman. Mary would finally see the world she only knew from books.

8

Magdalene as Mother

MARY WRITES THAT FIVE MONTHS after her arrival back at Dearborn after an extended trip with a male customer to Quebec, she was told by her doctor that she was pregnant again. Mary was overwhelmed with fear at the possibility of pregnancy and childbirth once more. She begged for an abortion, but the doctor insisted she would not carry to term anyway and should await a miscarriage. He reported her pregnancy to Lizzie Allen, who sought Mary out in a fit of rage. Although Mary typically endured Allen's abuse quietly, this time she would not stay quiet. Mary tells the reader that her rage could not be contained:

> It was the impatience of a woman young and fresh for one old and withered: the scorn of the well-born, no matter how lowly their estate, for the ignorant and low-born upstart: the loathing of a woman who was reaching forth to grasp ideals for the woman who had no ideals and who, with great fortune at her command knew no other way of using it but to build a palace dedicated to sin and shame.[1]

Mary's unrestrained rebuttal against Allen is a verbal critique of the societal and moral tensions of the era. The text written years after the fact certainly held with Mary's feelings at the time, but it also reflects thoughts she grew into as a middle-aged writer. The 1890s experienced the tremors of a changing century, especially regarding the clash between generations, class hierarchies, and conflicting values. Mary was staring down this generational divide, where the aspirations and vitality of youth clashed with the outdated notions of the former generation. In Mary's mind, this stagnant, dangerous thinking kept women like her trapped in life and cut off from their families. It was laws and moral values that would prevent her from getting an abortion to save her life or contraception to prevent pregnancy from happening in the first place. This was Mary's moral judgment and attempt to make sense of her values against another who, despite her immense

8. Magdalene as Mother

wealth, uses it only to perpetuate vice and build a "palace dedicated to sin and shame." This explosive scene between Mary and Lizzie Allen parallels the tension between materialism and moral aspiration. It exposes Mary's developing and ongoing concerns regarding the societal conflict between those seeking a higher purpose and those squandering resources pursuing hedonism through privilege and moral decay, even if later in life when she encounters it, it will be under the guise of moral salvation.

Mary left with no desire to return. Thoughts of almost dying and her prolonged illness after giving birth to her dead child permeated her mind. In her chest, an ache for her mother grew. Mary did not desire an abortion because she was deviant or heartless, as early reviewers of the book suggested. She wanted the abortion because she had already gone through a difficult pregnancy and the loss of a daughter. She almost died then, and there were no guarantees that the outcome and dangers would be any different. The idea of a child growing for a time, only to die in her belly, was a horror she didn't think she could endure.

When her daughter was born years before, the body was taken, and the child she had felt growing and kicking disappeared. Mary did not get to see or hold the child or mourn properly. If she had been married and her situation socially acceptable, the mourning may have been public or at least shared with family. A burial would have followed, and a name would have been given. As a young girl, then only 17 and a prostitute, none of the social expectations were honored, and her bereavement, heavy as it may have been, was laid on her shoulders with no relief. The pain both in body and mind, though perhaps dormant out of necessity, must have been ripped open, the old fears and trauma rising to the surface. The recent refusal by the doctor meant, as far as she understood, she would carry the child until it died, either within her body or after birth. This was not an instance of Mary not wanting to be a mother. Instead, Mary was a woman feeling the very real fear of not knowing if she or a child would survive the ordeal of childbirth. She wrote, "I retained a most vivid recollection of my illness in Kansas City, and I wanted to see my mother before I had another experience of that kind."[2]

Mary must have also known from her scarlet sisters' knowledge and experiences that life would become more difficult if the child survived. For women—especially those who were mothers engaged in prostitution—the world was a harsh place. For many female sex workers, there weren't many choices: to keep the child would be as difficult as giving the child up. Mary was learning that the judgments of society fell harder on prostitutes who became pregnant. Prostitutes did not often keep their children, especially if working in a high-class house. Mary knew that if her family found out, she would be ostracized, married off, or worse. She also knew the real probability that she could die and felt an overwhelming need to risk being found out if only to feel her mother's warmth and love one more time before she underwent her ordeal.

If she survived, Mary was about to become one of the marked mothers who somehow had to circumvent their work and motherhood in often unimaginable circumstances, facing difficult choices for survival. Abortion and birth control, though available to some degree, were options usually out of reach for women across all social classes. Even when available, the procedures were often dangerous, and birth control methods were not always effective or practical.

Prostitution came with a multitude of health risks that many women were ill-prepared to face. Sexually transmitted infections, frequent pregnancies, and the physical toll of the work left many women in poor health. Accessing medical care was often impossible, especially for those judged by society as undeserving. Mary faced these issues with her first pregnancy, and the trauma and fear remained with her during the second.

Public health efforts focused more on blaming women than offering support. Mothers (low income and prostitutes) often struggled to get medical help for their children, as charities and hospitals sometimes refused to assist them. Disease and violence were constant threats, and mothers struggled to create safe spaces for their children. Often men, be they customers or husbands across all social classes who frequented houses of prostitution, brought disease to their married partners and the prostitute, creating a perpetual feedback loop of disease, which could also have adverse effects on pregnant women.

Women of the time were placed within the tight constraints of social expectations. They were expected to embody purity and sacrifice, ideals impossible for most mothers to meet and nearly impossible for the scarlet mothers. Being both a mother and a prostitute took immense courage. This courage was often learned through terrible circumstances by young women who were inexperienced and new to "the life," let alone motherhood. The hours required to work as a prostitute often meant leaving their children with older siblings, neighbors, or other caretakers. These arrangements were far from ideal, exposing children to neglect or danger. Some mothers made the painful decision to give their children up for adoption or place them in orphanages, hoping they'd have a better life or later, as in Mary's case, with a housemaid. Others fought hard to shield their children from the judgment of others and worked tirelessly to give them a chance at a brighter future, as Mary

8. Magdalene as Mother

would also attempt. However, this was often made difficult as prostitutes frequently faced arrest or problems with the law, which in court usually meant losing custody of their children, as courts deemed them unfit simply because of their profession.

Despite the hardships, women often found ways to support each other and their children. In red light districts, informal networks between the scarlet sisters provided emotional and practical help, such as shared childcare or pooling resources, offering lifelines for women juggling survival and motherhood.

Religious and charitable organizations offered help, but it often came with conditions such as expectations to leave prostitution and adhere to strict moral codes. This left many women feeling judged instead of supported. The hypocrisy of the time was that men who sought out prostitutes rarely faced judgment, while women bore the full weight of the condemned. This double standard, which Mary writes about at length, made life even more problematic for mothers trying to provide for their families through work that society deemed immoral.

The children of prostitutes faced immense difficulties and were often ostracized or excluded and had limited access to education and opportunities. They faced the lifelong shameful mark of illegitimacy and often ended up in the same situations as their mothers. Yet, for those children who survived, it was a testament of resilience to their mothers and the scarlet sisterhood who fought to give them a better life against overwhelming odds. Historically, the stories of these families have been sensationalized or ignored. Often noted for their deviation from societal norms, the mothers and children are viewed as sinners or victims, with little regard for their lived humanity.

All of the few options frightened Mary, who turned to her friends at a restaurant called Hogan's; these men were the very same ones who helped her escape Madame C's. She implored them to help her find a doctor to perform the abortion, but they refused, worried that the procedure would be too dangerous. Twice she has been denied choice by men who thought they knew better than her what she needed for her life and body, and as a woman, especially a young prostitute, there was nothing she could do.

Mary continued to push the issue over dinner. Her friends offered to help her monetarily, but she had money saved. For now, money wasn't the issue. She wanted a doctor's services to end the pregnancy. She writes, "We debated the matter all through dinner-time without coming to any understanding, and at length, one of them suggested that we send for Olga and get her advice in the matter." When Olga arrived, Mary announced she would go home to her family since she couldn't change anyone's mind. Her friends, including Olga, were surprised, as Mary had never shared anything about her family. They also implored her to rethink this decision, but in this, her mind was made up. She felt the outcome, no matter what it might be, would be traumatic if not fatal. Mary wanted to see her mother one last time. She would go home to Saint Joseph, Missouri.

In the morning, as she was leaving, a letter from Paul was delivered, and her plans changed to include going to Kansas City first before going to her mother in Missouri. Paul Martin, her man from Kansas City, had grown through letters into something more akin to a lover. With thoughts of a reunion with Paul and a deep need to see her mother, she left Chicago and the house on Dearborn. Paul was leaving Kansas City and going to Montana to look after business enterprises. He waited, however, for Mary's arrival. Mary had not seen him for a year. She writes, "For I had wired him that I was coming, he folded me in his arms, and I was all aglow with a rapture which made it hard for me to remember that I had ever known another resting place."[3] Their reunion is sweet, and their relationship is rekindled emotionally and physically.

With their bond renewed, Paul asks her to marry him, but she refuses, telling him she is pregnant. She realizes that although she loves him, her "work" is disagreeable to him and their personalities are so different, inviting a clash that would ruin a union. Mary refused to be molded into what a man wanted, as she had already done in her working life. Perhaps echoes of her parents' relationship haunted her, a marriage and two people that seemed so perfect in her early childhood but devolved into abuse and neglect all too soon. Perhaps she worried that although he seemed willing to forget what she did for a living if they married, this forgiveness would only last so long before it drove a wedge into their union. No matter the thoughts that arose, she steadfastly refused.

Paul insisted on going to the family home with her; this, too, she refused. He, in turn, translates her desire to remain independent as coldness. During this time, she had written and seen Paul occasionally, sometimes imagining a life with him as a married woman. She writes,

> With my whole being I wanted this man for my own, though I dimly foresaw the clash of wills which would make our lives anything but peaceful ones. During the time I had been a saleswoman in Chicago I had longed and hoped and dreamed of being this man's wife. Despite my harsh experiences before I knew him, I did not feel myself unfit to be the wife of such a man. He saw the scarlet brand as a vivid smear across my girlish brow, and he loathed the stain with all his soul, but his love for me was stronger than his loathing for the life I had led. To him the fact that I had known other men

embraced the whole question. It was all a hideous pollution in which there were no gradations; and I could not explain to him the difference between selling my body to a man of his own kind and selling myself to a man like Blanche Audley's "Beast," whose very presence was contamination.[4]

Paul is a constant throughout the book; if not always a lover, he remains a friend. He took her refusal hard, but not so hard that he cut off their communication or refused to help her many times throughout the coming years. He would send money whenever she asked and provide companionship, and Paul would later cross the Atlantic Ocean to aid her when Mary got into trouble in Europe. He would support her during the pregnancy and as she grows into single motherhood.

Mary did not marry him because she didn't love him. She felt in some ways that he was above her. She writes, "He could not understand that I could no more penetrate that wall than could he, nor that I would gladly have torn down the barrier that stood between us had it been in my power."[5] She understood at their parting that she loved him and loved him enough not to marry him.

For now, they said their goodbyes, Paul heading for Butte, Montana, and Mary to Saint Joseph to her family. For two weeks, Mary enjoyed the warm reception of her mother and family, who had not expected her arrival. Although pregnant, she was not showing and felt capable of continuing the lies of her life in Chicago. The visit was full of "great rejoicing" until her father arrived. Patrick was again aided out of trouble by a family member who gave him employment out east.[6] Older now and broken from alcoholism, he had Bright's disease (kidney failure), and Mary did not expect him to live long. As Mary notes, Patrick was a "man of the world," and he did not believe her story that she told her family. He went to Chicago, covertly inquired around, and discovered the truth about her way of life.

Earlier in her life, Mary Regan would have done anything to repair the damage, and in the past, she took the blame and beatings under his fiery temper, but she was not the child of before. He came to her in such a rage that she thought he would try to kill her. Although she did not go into detail about this altercation earlier in the book, she recalled the first time he beat her as a child using a switch, covering her entire body in bruises and cuts that took weeks to heal and wrecked her mental health.

But this time was different. Mary was no longer the beloved "Minnie" seeking her father's approval and love. She was no longer powerless before her father, a broken man who stood in judgment. She was still Mary Regan, but she was something more—independent, courageous, and world-wise to men like him. It was Madeleine Blair who faced off with Patrick Regan. She did not allow him to touch or judge her. She writes,

> I was no longer afraid of him. I turned on him, and all the pent-up bitterness of my childhood poured forth. I hardly knew him—he had changed so greatly—and my heart was torn at the sight of his physical decay and of his mental anguish at knowing that I was lost. But I did not spare him, though I did not raise my voice as I recounted his dereliction to his family. It was the first time in my life that I had acknowledged that anyone else was in any way responsible for my downfall.[7]

Mary recalls that she never saw her father again but that his face haunted her. Patrick never forgave her and never allowed her name to be spoken within the family again. She was erased and never mentioned in her father's, mother's, or siblings' family genealogical trees or obituaries. Even now, she is overwhelmingly omitted except in federal census records from her childhood. If one were to look, it might be assumed she died in childhood, and in some ways, Mary did. She writes, "They cast me out of their lives, and none but my mother remembered there had been another sister." This separation must have been traumatic. Mary had given up a new life and legitimate work so that she could support her mother and siblings while her father abandoned them time and again. Before leaving Saint Joseph for Saint Louis, Mary was a second mother to her siblings and incredibly close to her mother, but now the father, who had abandoned them, lost their home, and abused her, wielded the power of the patriarchy to erase her. For Mary, the only family remaining was the child she carried in her womb, and even this was shrouded in sorrow and very real fear.

In her book *Madeleine: An Autobiography*, Mary skips ahead to when her son is two years old. The surname of Fiske appears, and it is possible that she married, but more than likely, she simply used a new surname to protect her and her child's identity. Perhaps she wanted a measure of protection for her son, knowing it would be easier to navigate the world with a dead father rather than grow up as an illegitimate.

The two years previous are plunged into shadow. The year is not specified, but the assumption is that she is around 20–21 years old. In autobiography and memoir writing, the narrator is naturally unreliable due to the fickle nature of memory. Time reshapes recollection, filtering events through the shifting lens of personal perspective, emotion, and experience. Mary wrote her book many years later, from 1917 to 1918. What she forgets or omits may be as significant as what is remembered. Perhaps after her son was born, life continued in much the same way, with the exception of now having a child to care for. It remains unclear and no other documents were found to fill in the gaps of those years.

8. Magdalene as Mother

Although she skips over years and does not share the earliest days of motherhood, her tone in this chapter is that of a mother. Mary begins by expressing maternal jealousy for the nurse who kept her son. She visited him daily but had to leave for her work at night. Mary notes that she paid the nurse well and that both the nurse and the nurse's husband cared for her son as their own. Mary writes that she returned to Lizzie Allen's but that the cost of working there and supporting a child grew too high. Hers are the struggles of a working single mother with no real support.

During this time, Paul Martin visited her in Chicago. His work took him between Chicago and Butte, Montana, among other places. Her refusal to marry him did not quell their relationship. Mary notes that her attention drifted, and she entertained the infatuation of a "few" men who were "ardent" in their lovemaking. She described Paul as dependable and the only one she could share her son with, writing of her child's first steps, words, and smiles. Paul also sent money to help her when her debts grew and her savings dwindled.

One of the girls she worked with had spent the last summer in Winnipeg. Mary had previously described her trip to Quebec and expressed a love for Canada, where her father and mother immigrated from and where her beloved grandfather Cornelius Regan lived and died. Mary needed to make money; to do this, she had to leave her son in the care of her nurse. She decided to go in the summer and planned to stay for several months. Her plan to further her education was put on pause with the birth and attention of her son. A new desire to make enough money and open a legitimate business before her son understood what she did for a living was paramount in her mind.

Sometime around May or June, Mary took the train to meet Madame von Levin in Saint Paul, a woman described as stately and having ancestry to German nobility. Rather than travel with Levin's other prostitutes, Mary would travel alone and anonymously to the new house in Winnipeg. Only within the houses she worked in would she play the part of a prostitute. In public, Mary dressed down, melding incognito into society. Mostly, she traveled alone, preferring the role of respectability that came with not publicly associating with the women of her trade. If she went out for the day with a fellow worker, she insisted that they also dress down to better fit in with society. Since the houses were usually separate from the greater portion of the cities and towns they worked in, Mary could briefly enjoy intermingling with the proper citizenry. This practice was also followed in her travels throughout her life as a sex worker and may have been the only time she used her legal name.

Mary headed for Winnipeg's Thomas Street district, which lay apart to the west of the town on the prairie. Compared to the mansion on Dearborn, enclosed within the levee district of Chicago, Mary must have felt the closeness of the remaining western frontier with the Canadian Pacific Railway and Winnipeg's location as a crossroad into the West's advancing economic development. The Thomas Street district featured mostly female business owners of the houses. The businesses were highly regulated and enriched a small community of women who had agency within the constraints of their sector. Of course, the women faced the usual tides of law and moral enforcement. Still, Rhonda L. Hinther writes, "While ultimately limited by law enforcement trends and the whims of civic officials, these women learned to work within, manipulate, and oppose the system in order to achieve their own ends. In doing so, they created a colorful network and neighborhood and enjoyed various degrees of power therein."[8] Mary Regan felt that her experience in Winnipeg was life changing. She had time to pursue her artistry and drawing and, for the first time, admits to actually enjoying her work. Mary writes, "I had broken through the wall of my own reserve, that reserve which had been the cause of so much suffering, which had kept from me so much of the joy of life."[9] For the first time, she was able to rise above the pain caused by her father and the pain of losing her family and her first child. She writes, "My thwarted girlhood was behind me, and in my dawning womanhood, I felt that somewhere and somehow, I should demand from life the things that had been denied me."[10] Although prostitution has been looked at as a form of leisure for men, it could be said that prostitutes who operated at the top experienced a kind of leisure that women often did not experience. Whereas their nights would have been filled with work, their days offered time to pursue interests as they saw fit. Mary therefore describes her days there as personal and tremendously inspiring:

> I took a long walk before going to bed; for the dawn begins to break at two o'clock in midsummer, and every daybreak was a new revelation to me. I wanted to paint that first pink streak of dawn. I wanted to burst into poetry, and I did break into tuneless song as I tried to express to myself just what I felt was behind the rim of the prairies. Life became fuller and more beautiful than I had ever thought it could be.[11]

The district, she explains, was restricted from the rest of the town, described as the "American Colony," as most of the women were Americans. The money was exceptional, and the men who came spent with an exuberance not equaled in Chicago. The hours were early, and most business concluded by one in the morning unless the men paid for the pleasure of a whole night. This allowed Mary time to hike and ride out into the countryside, a pastime she would enjoy throughout her life. She also found herself a favorite among the men for the first time. Mary writes, "I rejoiced in my popularity" and describes her fascination with the prairie as a cause of spiritual and physical awakening. Mary also notes that the men were different in Winnipeg. They did not grow bored of the usual or demanded "perversions." She calls the men "fine, strong, and courtly gentlemen," almost in words carved out by Western romantics.[12]

Eventually, however, she had to leave and headed home in October, having made enough money to support her son. Mary did not stop missing her son the whole summer, and on the train, she wondered with anxiety if he would even remember her.

She arrived and found the nurse's house deserted. The neighbors told Mary that the nurse and her husband intended to keep her son. They claimed she had deserted her son and not once written of her whereabouts or plan to return. Mary felt the world stop—all of the money she made would mean nothing if her son was lost forever.

She had lost so much already that this thought drove her to action. Knowing the police would not help, she traveled to La Crosse, Wisconsin, where the nurse's family lived. Once Mary and the nurse's family found her son, the nurse's mother interceded with her daughter to give up the boy. Mary writes,

> When I reproached Nurse for her treachery and for the lies she had told about my desertion of Baby I found an unexpected ally in her mother, to whom she had told the same mendacious story. When I showed her the weekly letters which her daughter had written me, and photographs of Baby which she had sent, and the Dominion Express Company's receipts for large sums of money which I had sent from Winnipeg, she denounced her daughter and her daughter's husband in scathing terms. She herself was a mother, and she thought that the claim of a mother, who had done what she could, came before all others. She peremptorily ordered Nurse to pack up Baby's clothes and prepare him for the long drive to LaCrosse, otherwise she herself would go with me to the proper authorities. Nevertheless, the parting scene was a heartrending one, for Nurse clung to Baby and he clung to her. I would not tear him away by force, and I was at my wit's end what to do, when he became interested in the waiting horses which he could see through the window, and he allowed the driver to carry him out to the carriage. He would not let me touch him.[13]

Mary did not press charges. The journey home was difficult as her son did not recognize her and cried on the train. Mary describes how she felt: "My cup of sorrow was overflowing to know that my little son would make friends with everyone but his mother." Even so, just as she faced everything else, she knew she could get through it with hard work. She felt that being a mother was the most important work she would ever do.

When she arrived in Chicago, Mary found a small house to rent and hired a woman who had previously worked for her friend Olga at the Dearborn house to do the house chores so that she could devote all of her time to repairing the relationship with her son. The work resulted in a bond between them that she had so far, in a way, resisted. Perhaps going to Winnipeg and feeling freedom and then almost losing her son finally allowed her to fully embrace motherhood. Making a living independent of the standard bawdy house might have also opened her eyes to the possibilities of a life directed by her own agency, wherein motherhood could also be included.

This part of the Madeleine story gets ignored and is largely omitted from research and discussions about prostitution. This mirrors the sensationalism of the court case surrounding *Madeleine: An Autobiography*, the focus of which is centered on the body of the woman who is a prostitute and never on the other aspects that made her human.

This segment of women did have children and sometimes were married. Prostitution, while repugnant in most areas of society, was a means for women like Mary to provide for their families back home and the children resulting from work or even love. Mary was a complex woman with a love for nature and literature. She appreciated art and music, and just as she loved her family in Missouri who turned away from her, she loved her son who was learning to love her as his mother. She writes, "I devoted all my time to cultivating the friendship of my son. He was a strong, healthy child, remarkably bright, but with a quietness and poise not usually found in highly intelligent children. As soon as he had ceased to grieve for 'Auntie' (the nurse), he began to care for me, and we became very happy together."[14] Even though it took time, she worked to build the missing maternal bond.

Mary was happy in the small house, and although she could have had some of her clients come there, she decided to keep her mothering life separate from her working one. Only Paul was allowed into her tiny slice of happiness. She writes that her plans for a business were not quite ready, so she decided to "assignate" till spring. During this time, she already had styled herself as a widow and probably used the last name Fiske to better shield herself and her child from the truth of her work in her new home. Some records suggest that she married, but this only appears in her later marriage license to Septimus Whitney Sears, Jr., in 1916.[15] Mary always had a sense for self-preservation, including going through proper society incognito. This ability would serve her well in the next business venture, taking her from the house on Dearborn to the hidden places in well-to-do neighborhoods.

Assignation houses operated differently than bawdy houses. The

8. Magdalene as Mother   101

women were from various parts of society—some prostitutes, some married, students, artists, and some just working long enough to save money. The women "rented" rooms to meet with their clients or paramours. The houses differed from bawdy houses in that they were discreet homes where women were expected to dress and act without attracting attention. The reduction of attention was particularly important as the clientele were often from prominent positions in society, and the houses were located in respectable neighborhoods and furnished. A close description of what one of these houses might offer is from the New York Village Preservation Organization, which described one house as follows:

> 40 Amity Street (today West 3rd Street), Mrs. Ann Beach, also a widow, ran a house of assignation which, according to the 1870 "Gentleman's Companion," was "a first-class house of assignation. It is very nicely furnished, the house is always open, and Mrs. Beach gives her personal attention to visitors so that they may miss nothing which is required for their comfort and entertainment." Apparently, gentlemen were not the only members of the populace serviced. 372 4th Street received this review: "She (the proprietress) conducts a very quiet house, which is a fine resort for private young ladies to go to anticipate the pleasures of matrimony."[16]

Some information also showed that such houses allowed for discreet meetings of LGBTQ persons. Distinction as to the uses of such houses remains difficult as both laws and documents tended to lump all houses where sex work, sex, liaisons, and affairs took place together in an arbitrary binary way. What is certain is that those who participated in the various actions of sex work felt that what they did was different from what others did. For instance, a married woman having an affair certainly did not identify as a prostitute, and a woman who met a man once a week to make extra money to support her family might also deny acting as one. Yet during this era, all women who had sex outside of marriage, paid or not, would by definition be labeled as whore.

Mary lost out on one assignation house due to her honesty in working for years at the Dearborn house. The second house she applied to did allow her to use a room, but it was understood that if anyone identified her from Madame Allen's, Mary would be required to tell her client that she lied to the proprietress and quit the house without argument. In these houses, on the proper side of town, it would not do for an actual prostitute to operate. The men who frequented these houses wanted to believe they were with proper women, not a scarlet dove. The woman who ran the house wanted the women also to live there, but she allowed Mary from 1:00 p.m. to 7:00 p.m. to return home to her son.

It was here that she learned of two new "phases," as she calls it, of prostitution. She calls these phases occasional and clandestine. The names are precisely what they suggest. The women were not full-time sex workers. Mary goes into detail on the particular types of women who took rooms in the house while retaining their social standing in the real-world writing:

> There were several other women who came to the house and "sat for company," and others who were "on call." Most of these were the real articles of which we were the spurious representatives. These women came two or three times a week to meet friends, some of the married women keeping their engagements in the daytime because they could not leave their husbands at night. Some of the girls on call were students at the Conservatory of Music and at the Art Institute. One woman who came was a famous church organist, while still others had no other means of support. But all wore a distinctive garment which differentiated them from the public prostitutes whom they openly scorned. This convenient garment was the Mantle of Respectability.[17]

The women in this particular house role-played with the customer, either going along, requesting, or believing the role without question. Mary writes, "We were married women, widows, girls from good homes, working girls, business girls, professional women, or whatever else the men in question had ordered."[18] For Mary, she both scorned and loved playing the role, hoping that one day she would not "play at it" but reach the pinnacle of respectability. The situation worked for a time, and Mary was able to keep her small house until the double dealing that often resulted from unregulated sex work came for her. Through this interaction, she loses a considerable amount of money and her place in the house.

9

Living Picture of Sorrow

IN LOSING OUT ON WORK, Mary gained time with her child. She notes that her son was growing in "beauty of character and intelligence." She writes, "When I told him stories and watched the marvelous unfolding of his mind, or cuddled him to sleep in my arms, singing to him the songs my mother had sung to me, I thanked God from the bottom of my heart that the joy of motherhood had not been denied me. He was mine, this child who possessed such beauty of body and mind."[1] Mary spent countless hours playing with and sketching her son and even wondered about returning to a life of art. She was engaging in dreams that society had so far refused and felt at this point in her life that there was a chance at possibilities beyond the life she had lived so far.

It was during this time, while playing with her son, that her maid noticed she was putting on weight, and although Mary tried to brush it off, a doctor confirmed she was once again pregnant. She struggled with the thought of another baby without a husband and wondered why God allowed "the male parent to be such an unimportant factor in the scheme of life. A mere sower of seed who neither toiled nor reaped. Or why, since He had given me a limitless capacity for motherhood, had he denied me the usual emoluments of motherhood, a husband and a home?"[2] This news was not welcomed. She finally had a home, her health, and her son, and even though she did not have work, Mary, ever resourceful, was not worried. What did worry her was the returning fear of losing another child or her life, and this fear grew in her mind with her beloved son reliant on her and her alone.

Mary thought about abortion once more. On the one hand, abortion would risk her life, and on the other hand, having the baby would add to her burden as a single mother. She felt that both choices threatened her current happiness with her son. She went to the doctor, receiving confirmation, and with this new worry, she headed back home. On this doubly fateful day, her maid met her at the door with news that her son was sick.

The illness struck fast, and Mary sent for the first doctor. When this doctor could not offer answers, she called for other doctors who were no more helpful. Finally, she sent for the doctor who had delivered her son. He examined the child and told her the awful truth: Mary's son was dying.

Over the next six days, Mary watched her son struggle to breathe due to pneumonia. She was unable to do anything to prevent the greatest loss of her life. She tended to her son, never leaving his bedside. He cried out for her as his little body slowly succumbed to the illness. She writes,

> The frightful struggle for breath filled the room, but the brave little soul who had battled for his own life and supplemented our efforts for him in a manner almost uncanny in a child so young, looked into my face and asked me to hold him in my arms. As he struggled with failing breath the words he was striving to say found utterance, "Mother, I am your good boy." And then, as the beautiful eyes were fast glazing, "Mother.... I ... love ... you ... tongue ... can ... tell."[3]

Childhood mortality rates during this era were high, and mortality rates of children born to prostitutes were mostly unrecorded. Instead, the data reflected what then might be thought of as moral failings and sins of their mothers from abortion and infanticide. However, in one report from Dr. William Sanger, who worked for the New York City Almshouse at Blackwell's Island, single mothers who were working prostitutes lost their children at a 14 percent higher rate than general society.[4] Statistics and reports aside, no clear accounts were written in the first-person perspective documenting the loss experienced by women of this subsection of society except for that captured in *Madeleine: An Autobiography*.

No firsthand accounts come close to the raw anguish and sorrow Mary expresses in her book. Through all the newspapers and documents that followed the sensational courtroom drama that her book produced, there is no acknowledgment of her as a mother or of her loss.

Mary has no recollection of the week following her son's death. Her sorrow was overwhelming and incapacitated her to such a degree that she could not function. Olga made the funeral arrangements and sent a telegram to Paul Martin in Montana. The community of scarlet women from the Dearborn house sent condolences and offered financial aid but stayed away, respecting how their presence might cause a sensation within Mary's neighborhood since, at least there, she was not known as a prostitute. Although she was not physically alone, the loss separated her from those around her. Paul hurried to Chicago, but she responded angrily when he took Mary in his arms. She writes,

9. Living Picture of Sorrow

When he touched me, I drew back from him and struck him in the face with all my force. While I poured forth my protest against life, he stood motionless, with the red mark of the blow on his fair skin, but he gave no sign that he was hurt. "How dare you touch me? Don't you know that my baby is dead? Do you suppose I want a man offering me caresses when my child is not yet cold in the ground? Do you know that I am to have another fatherless child? That God has chosen me to be the mother of all the fatherless children that want to be born? Go away from me before I yield to the temptation to kill you; for you, too, are one of those who go thoughtlessly along the way, casting the seed of life wherever it may fall, not knowing and not caring that in some hapless woman's body, it may bear fruit."[5]

Mary, at 22 years old, was caught in the clutches of an almost unbearable trauma. All of her dreams for the future were gone. The culmination of past trauma—losing the child in Kansas City and now her son, her parents' abandonment, especially her father's cold hypocrisy, and yet another pregnancy most likely had her on the outer edge of sanity. Yet her words had a sharpness of truth that could not be denied. When Mary entered a sexual transaction with a man, she received payment, but for her and many other women, sometimes they got more than they bargained for. Pregnancy, venereal disease, and violence were all risks to be navigated alone. Many women had a similar background to Mary, with traumas such as abuse and abandonment. Mary, however, has written on the many different aspects of her life and humanity. On the one hand, the autobiography shows her in her role as a prostitute but on the other hand, as a loving mother. In much of the literature on Madeleine, the focus has been on her working side, and this mirrors the male gaze and use of the sex worker's body to the detriment of the very human side. Mary's sorrow, ability to love, friendships, and family are equally, if not more, important to study the whole person. Here, she is a mother. Here, she is a woman.

Women's bodies were seen by polite society as vessels to procreate within the carefully watched dynamics of marriage. Men could "sow wild oats," and their sexuality was considered a "need." Men could easily find forgiveness, but the women involved in the transaction were negatively impacted. Women did not have agency, especially where it pertained to their sexuality, and novels of the time reflected this. When a woman stepped out of the maiden or married mother role, dire consequences and social ostracization followed. Women like Mary were already outside the pale. Everything reflected this belief from literature, purity societies, medical providers, and the suffrage movement. There were very few options to help a woman like her, and of the ones available, punishment and isolation were usually the end result. It was one piece of the double standard with a higher burden applied to women.

Men were excused for sowing "wild oats," and scarlet women were expected to reap them alone silently.

Although her family was culturally Catholic, Mary could not find peace in the Church. Her spirituality, though usually strong, was in a compromised state. Mary did not have a church to turn to, nor could she turn to her mother and family. The only support she had was the community of women like herself. Paul stayed in town, but she refused to see him. Mary writes, "I hated him; I hated every man I had ever known, from my father down to the physicians who could not save my baby for me."[6] She plunged into a darkness that only women who have lost children would understand.

The issue of her current pregnancy deepened her depression. She took steps to terminate a month after her son died. She had already entertained thoughts of abortion, but now she would go through with it. She only tells the reader, "A month after my little boy's death, I made my decision. I would not bear another child, and I would not call on a physician to help me until it was too late for him to protest; then, I would call in my own. I made careful arrangements, and after the birth pangs had begun, I sent for him, for I knew that he would not refuse to aid me."[7] Abortion during this period and up until *Roe v. Wade* carried an extremely high mortality rate. More than a decade before, in the 1880s, all states had passed some form of laws restricting the procedure and stigmatizing the procedure with harsh penalties for women and doctors alike.

Mary had earlier sought help in getting an abortion before the birth of her son. She existed in a time when men sought to control women's bodies through outlawing contraception and the means to attain an abortion. During this time, the American Medical Association was the determiner of how a woman's sexuality and body would be governed. This was in response to more women entering the labor force and not moving from the control of father to husband. Here, the midwife's role in birth and other measures such as contraception and reproduction were diminished under the mostly male-dominated medical field of doctors. Norma Basch writes that during this era and the laws that came out of it,

> the law, the most effective instrument of social control in modern society, was in all of its manifestations males. It was created, shaped, disseminated, altered, and adjudicated by men. Men fashioned disabilities for women, subsequently devised ways of remedying them for women, and ultimately determined how far concessions to women should go. Few social institutions offer a clearer view of the way men debilitated the boundaries of women's lives than the law.[8]

Mary must have felt locked into a system that looked down on her profession but also expected her to give birth to children who, to society,

9. Living Picture of Sorrow

were unwanted, a spoke in a wheel that, for women like her, kept turning. Those who bought sex (casting the seed of life as Mary expressed it) were often the ones who ran from fatherhood and enacted the laws that governed female choice. Much of Mary's frustration, combined with grief, communicated this idea that was shared among many women, especially of the laboring class.

Mary must have known that the cost might be her life or freedom. Yet, with the overwhelming trauma and loss coupled with the fear of going through yet another delivery as a single mother, she makes the decision, leaving no room to change her mind. She could not economically or mentally be a mother at this time. Mary was told many times that she had no choice concerning her body, but in this instance, she took possession of choice and her body for her physical and mental health, as many women have done before and after her.

Mary does not say how she started the process. She only says that she does it alone and waits until nothing can stop the process before calling a doctor. She writes, "When peritonitis set in, he (the doctor) sent me to the hospital, and for the second time in a few weeks, I heard from his lips the words—there is no hope."[9] Mary almost died. The doctor (the very same who had tended to her son's birth and death) later told her she would have born twins if she had not interfered. Although she does not go into detail, it would seem that she, by inducing an abortion, suffered from a septic abortion, leading to an infection of the peritoneum (abdominal lining) as a result of retained fetal tissue. If a woman didn't die from the infection, they could experience renal failure, pelvic abscess, scarring, adhesions, or damage to reproductive organs such as uterine perforation.[10]

It is not known how she avoided prosecution for an abortion, especially if it was chemical, which was illegal. It can be assumed that her close relationship with the doctor and his desire to avoid prosecution also aided the discretion of all involved.

Mary describes a "dark veil of sorrow" that settled over her. She recovers physically, but mentally, she is broken. In one month, she has lost three children: her son and a set of twins. She has spent all of her money on doctors to save her son and lost her happy home and all that it had come to symbolize. There is nowhere to turn and no one to turn to.

Mary is not unique in this experience as women across all classes, regardless of status, who experienced the loss of a child through childbirth complications, miscarriage, or abortion endured deep emotional trauma. The rigid societal norms applied to women and the limited medical understanding of trauma compounded the emotional toll. The grief and mourning they felt were often suffered in silence, ignored, or dismissed. Open discussions about such losses were considered taboo, even with female family members, clergy, or friends. Women internalized the guilt and experienced self-blame, particularly in an era when their value was closely tied to motherhood and their ability to bear healthy children. When that value was removed, as it was in the case of prostitutes, the isolation must have been deafening.

The stigma surrounding pregnancy loss or abortion, which was, as noted, previously illegal in all states by this time, added layers of shame and isolation, leaving women to cope with their pain in silence. Women of all classes struggled with feelings of inadequacy and failure when pregnancy was lost or ended. There were no support systems or resources to navigate the map of emotional suffering. Women like Mary were left even more isolated to process their grief and, as prostitutes, were expected to go back to work, exposed to the men who contributed to their trauma—denying them the physical and emotional space to heal, perpetuating a cycle of silence and emotional repression.

With her home and money gone, she is forced to return to the full-time work she had hoped to be moving away from. Before her son's death, she had been saving to start a new, respectable life, one in which her son would never come to know that she had been a prostitute. Now barely recovered, physically or emotionally, Mary must go back to offering her body for money.

She refers to herself metaphorically as a living picture of sorrow in a house dedicated to joy. She is isolated within the framework of pain but still put out for the male gaze, many who knew what she had just lived through. Some clients who are friends come to see her, but she does not want company, despite desperately needing the money.

She feels the ache of her children and writes,

> My arms ached for the form of my beautiful son, and with strange perversity and inconsistency, I mourned for the twin children that I had deliberately destroyed. I yearned for the infant who had died at birth and who was laid to rest in Kansas City. Baby faces stared at me from the corners of my room. Baby hands upon my face awakened me from my troubled sleep.[11]

The happiest years of her life were spent with her son, but ultimately, her work and society robbed her of mothering other children. She would never bear another child.

Her writing expresses profound guilt, but Mary, under the circumstances, sacrificed everything. Perhaps she felt she could have done more and made some bargain with God to keep her son alive. She was one of many mothers who lost children during the year of the Russian flu epidemic. It is not known if this was the cause of her son's death, but it seems likely.

She found she could not pretend, and her mood filled the halls and made making money nearly impossible for her. Only her old clients and close friends braved her depression.

One night, her friend Olga, who had helped her through the ordeal, was singing a song requested by a client at the piano. The particular song was written by Henry Clay Work (1832–1884). Mary listened to the words until she said the lyrics were "beating themselves into my brain until I began to repeat them under my breath." Mary mentions the poem because it gave words to the feelings that were building within her. The lyrics of "Phantom Footsteps" read:

> Childish footsteps, just behind her,
> Softly patter on the green.
> Back she glances; tears may blind her,
> But no little one is seen.
> Blanched, as by an ill appalling,
> Home in terror hastens she,
> While a baby voice is calling,
> "Mother! Mother! wait for me."
>
> Phantom footsteps! hear them
> falling (falling, falling),
> falling (falling, falling)
> Now, wherever she may be!
> (hear footsteps falling!)
> While a baby voice is
> call- (calling, calling)
> call- (calling, calling,)
> "Mother! Mother! wait for me."
>
> Sobbing still but never lagging,
> Soon she enters the gate,
> And before her, on the flagging,
> Sees the symbols of her fate:
> Tiny shoeprints, plainly speaking.
> Of the salt and foamy sea.
> Hark! Was that the door hinge creaking?
> "Mother! Mother! wait for me."
>
> Half her night is spent in weeping,
> Ere she can forget her cares:
> Is there, not an infant creeping—
> Creeping slowly up the stairs?
> Venturing thither in her yearning,
> Only shadows can she see;
> But she hears the cry while turning,
> "Mother! Mother! wait for me."[12]

Mary was enraged that a man requested the song. She confronted Olga, asking, "What does any man know about phantom footsteps or phantom voices? What does any man know of anything but sexual gratification?"[13] Mary picked up the sheet music and tore it to pieces, running headlong to her room. Olga, who had been by her side since she first set foot in the Dearborn house, followed. At first, Olga begged forgiveness for the song, but then she changed tactics with her friend who was living life in a slow suicide. Olga ignored Mary's demands to leave her room and instead gave her stark advice and suggested Mary leave for a while and go to Montana, where Paul lived.

Mary remembered her treatment of Paul after her son died and doubted he would want to see her. Olga insisted, "Don't you worry about Paul not understanding. I had a long talk with him before he left, and I found him the most 'understanding' man I have ever met. He is waiting for you to tell him that you want him."[14] Through the years, Paul Martin has been a supporting force in Mary's life. He had started as a man who visited her rooms in Kansas City like any other "John" but had grown into someone more substantial. Mary considered this option, admitting that if he would forgive her, he might also be her salvation. Paul was the only man who shared her love for her son and understood her great loss. Mary desperately needed something to anchor her through the unbearable sadness. She chose to go to Montana and, for a moment at least, to try to live.

10

Mount Sinai

CHAPTER V OF *MADELEINE: AN Autobiography* is short but filled with vivid imagery and biblical allusion. This chapter, for so many reasons, renders the author in a state of vulnerability, contrasting the urban environment behind her and the natural one she enters. Chicago represents the darkened moments of her life, a haunted place of grief.

Mary describes the easing of her burden as her train passes through Minnesota. She personifies the wheat as "thrusting its head above the earth" in the imagery of rebirth. This journey and the symbolism used suggest possibilities for transformation. Mary also sustains herself in the journey by offering herself the possibility of self-forgiveness. She is not seeking societal forgiveness, nor is she seeking the forgiveness of God because she already understands that her God has not abandoned her.

She describes the prairie as cloth rolling out to the horizon.

On the train, she watched.

On the train, she was quiet.

The Badlands rose, and the prairie fell behind, reminding her of her barren desolation, so she closed the blinds. Her intense feelings colored what she saw projected on nature outside the window. The physical journey on the train paralleled her spiritual journey within the context of the lows of the Badlands and the awaiting highs of the mountains to come.

Mary, by this time, has faltered and risen many times. She has re-created the self in the most remarkable ways that are so often ignored in the study of prostitution. Mary represents the complex nature of sex workers and their multifaceted, often ignored identities. As a prostitute, Mary functions under the male gaze and the damnation of societal judgments. Prostitutes are often mothers but not viewed this way, and those who lose children, such as Mary, are not allowed a similar space to mourn any more than they are allowed to be functional mothers embraced by society.

She expressed thoughts surrounding spirituality, grasping teachings from her familial Catholic connections that still anchored her in some ways and even offered comfort. In this chapter, she contemplates her belief in a God who still loved her and guided her despite what the world believed of her character.

She tells of the starry sky as the train crept toward the mountains: "Somewhere in that vast starlit silence were the children that my heart cried aloud for, and as we ascended the mountain, I felt very near to them, but it was a kindly, loving nearness that brought consolation and peace." Mary says, "beliefs of her childhood were close" and that the mountains held a message.[1] Calling the mountains the "ramparts of God," she recalled Moses climbing Mount Sinai. Mary foreshadowed that the train was bearing her to a godless city, but not before God allowed her a quiet peace in the "silent places" where "he dwelt with his little ones."[2] Here in nature, away from the city, Mary could dwell for a moment with her God, love, and memories of her children as a woman beloved of God and as a mother who loved her children.

≋ 11 ≋

Greatest Mining Camp on Earth

It is late spring or early summer of 1895. Mary worked for a time at Dearborn before she could afford to go west. The West is new and raw, and Butte, Montana, is unlike anything she has ever seen. When she arrives, Butte has transformed from "the greatest mining camp on earth" to a boomtown engorged with money and vices that follow. According to the Mining History Association in 1896, "a five square mile section of the earth was producing 210,000,000 pounds of copper a year, over 26% of the world supply, 51% of the United States,' and employing some 8,000 men with a payroll equivalent to $44,000,000 a month in today's dollars."[1] Butte had employment for many single enterprising men and amassed riches, a flame to which many women, especially those in prostitution, gravitated to coming from cities such as Chicago, New York, and New Orleans. In the eastern cities, vice societies were fighting and winning a war against vice. In Butte, however, an anything-goes atmosphere filled the streets of the boomtown.

Mary calls the vices in Butte "naked, raw, and rampant." She describes a cacophony in the streets of ragtime piano, horse betting, and pool halls where men yell, "They're off at Hawthorne! Wildfire in the lead! Rubicon against the field! It's a hundred-to-one shot you can't win. You're crazy with the heat! They're off at Oakland! Come on, you Rubicon!"[2] Hawthorn Racetrack, newly opened in Chicago, was already capturing the attention of nationwide bets. Butte had a robust and rather mainstream gambling situation. Bookmakers and runners relied on the telegraph to communicate horse races from across the country. According to I. Nelson Rose, "Horse racing, for example, has been around forever. However, the invention of the telegraph and the parimutuel machine in the mid and late 19th century allowed poorer people to bet on contests. They did not have to be present at the track: 'pool rooms'—today, we would call them off-track betting parlors—sprang up in cities."[3] With the concentration of riches and wages in Butte, gambling was a favorite pastime for the wealthy and laborers. Mary's noting of the racehorse's Rubicon and Wildfire and the status of the previously mentioned winter wheat of Nebraska allows for closer dating.

With its 120 rooms, the Butte Hotel ran an expensive $3–$5 a night, indicating that Mary had some money at her disposal. The road in front of the Butte Hotel is filled with activity, which seems odd to Mary for a Sunday. Still, this activity is the norm for a booming mining town expanding into an almost overnight city. Mary notes this activity, but her mind is anxious, remembering how she last treated Paul in the madness of grief. Although she traveled across the country to see him and paced in her hotel room before asking for him from the staff, Mary finally learns that he is gone and will be for several weeks. Afraid of him rejecting her apology, she did not telegram ahead from Chicago.

Mary realized she had arrived alone to what she calls a "hole in the top of the world." Mary is entranced with the bustling activity outside the hotel. She describes the scene with amazement: "Men who wore the garb of labor hurried through the streets, carrying dinner pails in their hands, and Chinamen with laundry baskets on their heads mingled with the crowd of alert-looking businessmen, debonair gamblers, pasty-faced pimps, overdressed shop-girls, and painted, gaudily garbed harlots." Mary tells of the business being conducted, the stores and dance halls open, and variety shows at full steam. She was used to the city and its fast pace, but Butte was something different—wild and not yet tamed by civilization. Her observations are similar to the ones she made at 16 years old when she first arrived in Saint Louis. This time, however, she is older and more experienced in understanding the layers of commerce involved.

Although Paul was gone, a customer from a few weeks prior in Chicago was also at the hotel. He offered to show her the town. They visited two first-class houses, and she was surprised that something as nice as what she was used to at Dearborn could exist out in the West. She once again noted her wonder at the variety shows and dance halls.

Mary was experienced in the sex trade, but her experience was that of first-class houses and assignation houses. Nothing prepared her for what she would witness in Butte. She was horrified by the working conditions of the cribs on Mercury Street, also known as Venus Alley. The air, she notes, is permeated with the smell of sulfur from the mines, a sharp contrast to the peace she experienced on the train. Mary notices that women must parade here in Butte, unlike the Chicago and Kansas City houses where the men came to them. They line the road and pose in the doors of their cribs as men go by. Mary is repulsed by the conditions and describes what she observes:

Despite my shuddering horror, the sight fascinated even while it repelled me. It gripped me by the throat and forced me to examine it, even though I was sickened and faint at the horror of it. It filled me with many sad forebodings. I drew my skirts back from contact with the poor creatures who represented this seamy side of prostitution; I could not help it. I wanted to take them by the hand and tell them that I was one of them, but I could not touch them. I could barely touch my lips to the glasses of beer which they served.[4]

One of these women called her a "stuck-up parlor-house-tart." Mary says she didn't blame the woman. Mary was aware of the divisions within the subculture of her scarlet sisters. However, this is the first time she truly is close enough to observe the conditions of those who do not, for various reasons, share her privilege. The subculture of prostitutes was fractured within its own body from those who, like Mary, work in exclusive first-class houses to those who work in the streets, in smaller houses, and under the still frontier-like conditions of the West. The first-class houses were much like Mary described previously, with a focus on the class of clientele. The houses were well-appointed pleasure houses built to feed the imagination, where the women reflected the richness of their surroundings in how they dressed, entertained, and gave attention. On the opposite end were the cribs where Mara Laura Keire describes the environment as "routinized" where "men waited in line, paid from fifty cents to a dollar, got off, then went on their way." The attractiveness of the women usually matched the quality of their surroundings. "Prostitutes in down-market places often wore 'Mother Hubbards,' sack like dresses that went on and came off easily, while in midlevel houses women preferred kimonos, robes that enabled them to flash potential customers."[5] In the Dearborn house, Madame Lizzie Allen had expected her girls to be dressed in evening gowns; their clothes remained on until their services were fully engaged in the bedrooms. Mary couldn't fully conceptualize how a woman ended up in such dire circumstances.

It is during this tour of the lowest conditions to which a prostitute could fall that Mary encounters a former Dearborn housemate from Chicago named Norma. Norma calls to her from her crib, surprising Mary. Mary writes,

She caught her breath with a sobbing intake as she shook hands with me, and I was so embarrassed I did not know what to say to her; for girls of the higher class, who have fallen into reduced circumstances, feel their position as keenly as do women in other walks of life; the social gulf between the dregs of prostitution is as great as the gulf between the sheltered woman in her home and the streetwalker.[6]

Norma, once one of the most beautiful women in the Windy City and described by Mary as Allen's "star border," was now reduced to a shell, appearing 10 years older than her young age. Norma explains to Mary that she, like many women in the same condition, had taken up with a man who kept them, but then, as the men lost their funds through gambling and other vices, the prostitutes had to sell themselves in the deplorable crib conditions to keep their men. All of her money went to her man in the typical pimp-prostitute relationship. Norma warns Mary against taking up work in a house in Butte. She explains that the first-class house women are hopelessly in debt to the madams. The houses at first seem reasonable, charging low rent but charge double for everything else: cleaning, dresses, toiletries. Women are forced to stay due to their debt or lose everything they own if they leave. Mary is astounded, noting that the men are well dressed and seem in a position to pay well, but Norma tells her that the men pay high to gamble and drink but not for a woman's services. Any agency a prostitute might have had in the East does not exist in the West. Norma lost everything, and to survive, she turned to serving the unwashed "beasts" of the street.

Mary feels the first pangs of what would later in life become her mission. She realizes she is a part of a "sheltered class'" of prostitutes. She tells her Chicago companion,

> "I am sure I don't know," I answered, "but it all seemed so horrible and so hopeless to me to think of a girl like Norma living in this way. She is only twenty-six, and this is the beginning of the end for her. I can't express what I feel about it; my emotions and my thoughts are too chaotic, but this horrible town, and these awful streets of vice, with the women displayed like so much merchandise in the windows, while the endless procession of leering men of all races—whites, negroes, half-breed Indians, and Chinese—pass them in review, fills me with terror. Think of Norma having physical contact with that great, unwashed brute she was talking with when we came back to her. There are no depths of poverty nor stress of circumstances which could make me a thief, but I am not sure that I would not become a murderess if I were forced to consort with such creatures. I thought I knew all the horrors of prostitution, but I have learned tonight that I know very little about them. I have learned that there is a sheltered class and that I belong to it, yet I would have laughed yesterday had anyone spoken of 'sheltered prostitutes.'"[7]

Mary is shocked to understand that even as a working prostitute, she retains a certain measure of privilege that has kept her sheltered and safe to the degree that Norma and the women of the cribs do not have. Mary wants to help Norma and others like her, but there is very little she can do.

Mary's companion reminds her she can do nothing to help and asks her why she risks her soul by association, suggesting she should "forget her [Norma]." Mary remarks that she might not be able to do anything more than "stretch forth my hand; if not to draw her [Norma] back, at any rate, to let her know that somebody cares. It may be a premonition of what is coming to me that makes me want to be kind."[8] Her companion notes that she is experiencing the "premonitory birth-pang of the social consciousness."[9] Mary Regan does not understand at the time what her companion means, but she does understand the humanity of Norma and girls like her outside of the work—something history has not done for Mary, casting her only as Madeleine. Mary does not seem to be making a statement on sex work but rather the treatment of her fellow sisters and the hopelessness that often follows.

Later, she wanders the city alone—a tasteful, well-dressed woman, a novelty to Butte and not at all representing the prostitute class she is a part of. She buys drinks but doesn't touch them still resisting the temptation of alcohol in her life. No one aside from the two women before could guess her profession. Mary is content as an observer in this instance, not a participant. When she returns to the hotel, she tries to sketch what she sees and, even more important, what she feels, but she can't replicate the raw emotions that rattle through her brain. There is a sense of helplessness again, but she can do nothing to help others. Neither is she capable of rescuing herself from prostitution. Later, after the publication of her book *Madeleine: An Autobiography*, as the courts and even readers and researchers will surmise, her trauma began in childhood under the weight of abuse from her father and others, poverty, and lack of meaningful improvement. To her mind, the wound first started with the moral degradation of her father, which became infectious to those around him but particularly dangerous to Mary. The damages caused continually weighed on her mind and leeched their way into every aspect of her life, creating overwhelming shame for her. Although she is a prostitute, she styles herself in different ways for different situations and people. Mary seems to have a particular ability to adapt to her environment. Perhaps this was a means to preserve a small sense of self. In any case, Mary had a certain presentation reserved for Paul, and although he shared many of her most intimate moments, including those with her child, her past remained shrouded from him. Several pages later in the book, Mary describes this in more detail:

> On one thing, I was determined: Paul should never know of my wretched childhood. And because of this determination, eventually, I built for myself a wall which kept me apart from him through many years; for when once he had conceived the idea of educating me, he reverted to it again and again until he thought that nothing but sheer perversity on my part prevented my going to college. It was not strange that Paul failed to understand, for he had

no way of knowing that to my mind, poverty and ignorance were the cardinal sins and that these accompaniments of my unhappy childhood were to be concealed at the cost of my future happiness, if indeed that were the price of secrecy.[10]

Paul understood her work was to make money to support herself and her son. He also understood her need for independence and self-reliance in her early refusal to marry him. Although readers only have Mary's words to rely on, it seems Paul wanted to support and help her advance in the dreams he believed she wanted to attain. Even though they were close, he did not know that her education did not go beyond grammar school, or the extreme poverty and fall from society that her family experienced. It was not prostitution that caused her as much shame as her poverty and lack of education. When Paul insisted, it was a reminder of all she did not think she could ever attain and served as a reminder of the family trauma she could not heal. It was a wall that would forever divide the friends.

For now, Mary pushed these thoughts far back into her mind. She finally sent word to him, finding that he was in a remote part of the state, his business connected to placer mines. He quickly sent a telegram telling her there was nothing to forgive and to "come to me at once. Am anxiously awaiting you."[11] Mary hoped that Paul truly did forgive her as she packed for the journey.

For now, she would simply be a woman going to meet the man she loved.

12

Mountains and Valleys

Bannack's American history began with gold almost two decades before Mary arrived. John White and other men found gold in Grasshopper Creek that cut through the tremendous rolling hills that dipped into the valley below and climbed into the distant mountains in the early 1860s. The gold fever–infected horde of men arrived, filling the empty expanse with a population numbered in the thousands. By the time Mary arrived, the population had shrunk, and decades later, it would die, leaving the bones of buildings along its main street, forever a ghost town.

Mary tells the tale of Henry Plummer, the sheriff of Bannack and the surrounding territory, who was hung, accused of being the leader of a gang of road agents. He was respected for his "intellect in the community, polished, genial, and affable." His last words were, "Give me a long drop so that I may die quickly."[1] Mary wonders about him. Perhaps the dichotomy of character reminded her of her own. Plummer acted as "guardian to the town and leader of the road agents who preyed upon the gold-seekers." The town she arrives at, however, in 1897 was already a ghost town in decline. Earlier, Bannack had been a thriving mining town flush with gold fever. Founded in 1862 after the discovery of gold, Bannack was once Montana's first territorial capital before the boom shifted to Virginia City following the Alder Gulch gold strike in 1863. By the time Mary arrived in 1894, Bannack was already slipping from its peak in the 1860s and 1870s, and the population severely declined as miners and businesses moved elsewhere. It is unclear what business Paul had there, but some hard rock mining operations in the area remained connected to Paul's Butte-centered business operations.

Bannack had become a shadow of its former self, with many buildings abandoned or in disrepair, adding to the wildness Mary would come to love. Still, some of its mining culture and operations remained connected to Butte, which was thriving, as evidenced by Mary's writings, as a significant industrial mining city. Many miners who had once sought fortune in Bannack's placer gold fields had migrated to Butte, drawn by the promise of stable work in its vast copper mines. Historian K. Ross Toole noted, "As gold played out in the early camps like Bannack and Virginia City, miners moved to Butte, where copper mining offered long-term employment and industrial development."[2] Bannack, once self-reliant, now relied on Butte's economic network for supplies and equipment, as Butte had become Montana's commercial hub by the late 19th century. Although not direct, the transportation link between the two towns ran through Dillon, Montana, where the railroad provided access to goods and laborers traveling between the declining gold camp and the booming copper city.[3] Despite Bannack's population and economic power had dissipated, its mining past would serve as a reminder of Montana's shift from ephemeral gold rush towns to the enduring industrial power of Butte.

For Mary, the journey to Bannack must have felt like traveling back in time. She arrives when cattle stealing and highway robbery are still a threat. The area's wild, untamed environment excited her senses. Bannack is breathtaking with natural beauty, a balm from the abhorrent rawness of Butte. The land invigorates her in some of the ways of Winnipeg, but here, she will not work. She will be Paul's girl—clean, young, and without judgment. Gold is still moved under armed guard under the tall shadow of Road Agent Rock, and the "romance of the West" holds Mary in its grip.

Mary stays at the same hotel as Paul, though in a separate room. The hotel she describes is assumed to be the Hotel Meade, a red brick two-story building, one of the only well-appointed refuges for visitors to the remote area of rolling hills and mountains. Mary would have entered the hotel first observing the broad curve of the hotel's unique, beautiful staircase to the right and the rooms that were the seats of comfort and society in Bannack.

Because of how she presented herself, the community supposed she was a schoolteacher, offering Mary the respite she needed after Chicago's sadness and Butte's stress. Assuming this disguise, she and Paul could easily spend time together without anyone the wiser.

Mary's intellect and never-ending curiosity enchanted the townspeople. She explored the area of Hangman's Gulch, uncovering a burial ground on the back hill, each indicating the deaths of earlier inhabitants killed in a massacre by local tribes. Mary asked the town's longest inhabitants, but they did not remember the event or any stories concerning the lonely burial ground. One old story from the area speaks to a miner enslaving an Indigenous woman of the Bannock Nation. The

12. Mountains and Valleys 121

Mary and Paul stayed at the Old Hotel Meade while visiting and working in Bannack, Montana. John Vachon, photographer, 1942 (United States, Office of War Information, Overseas Picture Division, Washington Division, 1944. Film copy on SIS roll 11, frame 831. Farm Security Administration–Office of War Information Photograph Collection [Library of Congress]).

woman was able to get away after ongoing abuse and returned to her family, supposedly kicking off an ongoing dispute in the area in 1863. It is said 90 miners were killed, and perhaps these were the graves of those men. It was also told that the woman and her family, along with many of her tribe, were murdered. No matter the story, Mary was walking on land that had only recently been emptied of its historic first inhabitants.

The wide blue sky and rolling hills, held within the grasp of the mountains, inspired Mary. She calls this time and landscape "the most fascinating phase of Western life." She rode alone over many miles on horseback, exploring the countryside just as she had in Winnipeg, feeling a similar joy and healing.

She saw Paul at dinnertime. He arose early and went to work attending business with the remaining mines, leaving her the day for happy exploration on horseback. She talks about climbing into mine shafts and prospect holes and the exhilaration invoked by the surrounding nature. The evenings were spent with Paul, and the growing desire was building within Mary to have a future with him. Bannack and its unique isolation, surrounded by primarily undisturbed wilderness, separated Mary from the rest of the world. It was as if the town and broader area had been suspended in time, granting Mary a safe cocoon to imagine a life unburdened by what had come before. The romanticism of the place and relative calm she found there with Paul intensified Mary's sense that Bannack was a place where reinvention, if not resurrection, was possible. She wondered if the traumatized scarlet woman could finally disappear as a new pure self might be born again. The remoteness reinforced this fleeting illusion that this dream, though improbable, might be within reach—that here, in this quiet corner of the world, she could sever the ties to all that had once defined her. Mary writes,

> However, I was now so happy with him that I was ready to dismiss the future. I snatched every moment of happiness until I could have cried aloud for joy. But in my supreme moment, there came to me a haunting thought that would not be dismissed, try as I would to banish it. When I tried to formulate my thoughts and express to Paul the thing that troubled me, I could not make him understand because I myself did not understand the meaning of many things that are now clear to me.[4]

Yet, her thoughts from Butte intruded—the sense of suffering she acknowledged within the sisterhood of her scarlet sisters and the sense of the separation she maintained between herself and them. She felt a growing sense of responsibility and a false sense of superiority. By acknowledging this, she opened herself up to look at their collective suffering. The separation between us and them was falling, and she wanted to save her sisters and perhaps herself. The book was written years after she left the business, and in it, Mary notes in hindsight, born of experience, "Poor little fool that I was, I could not even heal myself." During this time, she receives word that one of the scarlet sisterhood has accomplished an almost unheard-of redemption. A feat that so far escaped Mary's grasp except in the illusion of Bannack. Mary read and ruminated on the letter in wonder, writing,

> About this time, I received a letter telling me the story of one of the girls that I had known in Chicago. She had been, apparently, so corrupt that no thought of her redemption had ever entered the minds of those who knew her. Two years before, she had startled us all by announcing that she was going to quit the business. We gave her a month as the longest possible time in which she could remain decent, but now at the end of two years, she was still making good. Of all the girls that I had ever known, she was the last one whom I should have expected to reform. But there was no doubt about it. When I read the story of her reintegration I began to realize something of the wonderful recuperative powers of the human soul. Then I began to see, as through a glass darkly, that every fallen woman who is restored to decency means more than an individual redeemed. It means the healing of a contagious ulcer on the social body.[5]

12. Mountains and Valleys

When she brought this up to Paul, he fell back on the old patriarchal adage of prostitution as a necessary evil. His views were not exclusive, but they were in the 1890s going out of fashion. Before the Industrial Revolution, sex workers were a somewhat accepted part of the social order. Wives were expected to remain faithful, birthing and rearing children. Men were excused as having appetites for sex beyond the expectation of marriage. This, to the view of many, prevented men from having adulterous affairs with married women. Men were also excused as having a need for constant sexual gratification. William Acton, a medical doctor specializing in gynecology in 1870, wrote a popular proposal called *Prostitution Considered in Its Moral, Social and Sanitary Aspects, in London and Other Large Cities and Garrison Towns*, which mirrored thoughts in the United States. He wrote, "Prostitution must be tolerated because their suppression is either impossible or attended with worse results than the mischiefs which they occasion."[6] R.K. Macalester, MD, wrote as late as 1895 in the *Journal of Cutaneous Diseases Including Syphilis*, "Would it be advisable for us, in our metropolis, to follow the example of the French, since so much good may be gained thereby? Would it not be better to recognize prostitution as a necessary evil, for it will exist despite all suppression by authorities, moral preaching from pulpits, and have it regulated by competent men?"[7] This idea of pseudoscientific need was the hot debate of the later 1800s, but the social justice and vice societies were gaining ground against the Victorian ideals of quiet toleration.

In the bigger cities out east, the vice societies were closing red light districts. More women were heading west and across borders to work in the sex trade. More within the social justice crusade were working to "rescue" women like Mary, but rescue meant different things to the social worker and the women to whom the rescue was intended.

Mary, during this time, surrounded by nature and in a small community that didn't know her trade, began to entertain thoughts in earnest that perhaps she, too, could fully reintegrate into society. Mary began to hope that Paul would propose. Maybe she thought marriage to a man she loved would save her. However, no matter how peaceful the dream of Bannack was for the two months Mary was there, it would not last. Paul did not revisit the subject, nor would he for the rest of their off-again, on-again years together.

When his business finished in Bannack and his proposal never came, it became clear that Mary must leave her dreams behind and face the realities of returning to her life. She considered returning to Chicago, but Paul convinced her to stay with him in Butte for another month. It's not clear how Mary felt about returning to Butte then.

Her relationship with Paul is altered when they return to the city.

To avoid a "scandal," Mary must stay in a separate hotel away from Paul and his social circle, and for the first time, Paul is not treating her as a lover but as a kept woman. It does not seem he is paying her (except perhaps in footing the hotel bill and living expenses), but it is equally clear that he does not want her working.

Butte, Montana, does not improve for Mary. She writes, "I did not see him every day, as I had in the mountains, for in the city he had his own circle into which he could not take me." There was no longer the wonderful outdoors, for the sulfurous atmosphere of Butte precluded the enjoyment of open-air exercise.[8] This is the first mention in *Madeleine: An Autobiography* that Paul is seeking to distance himself from her. In some ways, Mary's loneliness and isolation may have helped the return of the depression and shame she had been struggling with. By this time, she is only months into mourning the death of her child and months into recovering from the abortion. Whatever peace Bannack had given was now quickly erased in the toxic atmosphere of Butte.

To her, it is a devilish, depressing city. Without the ability to explore the outdoors and being left alone for long periods, she falls into a new vice, gambling, losing at times all of her money and the money Paul gives her. She describes the overwhelming feeling of being completely broke and knows sex work would have fixed her problem. However, since coming to Montana, Mary has been a kept woman; she has not worked except in relation to Paul.

The break begins in this isolation. She writes that "time hung heavily" in her hands, so when she met an old acquaintance from Chicago, she decided to go to dinner with him. She reasoned that Paul "had neglected" her for his society friends, and although she was Paul's girl when required, she was free to do as she pleased when he was not around, which was becoming more frequent.

Over dinner, the male caller told her about a nightly card game that women were barred from. However, he invited her to the game, stating, "Everything goes in Butte if you know the ropes." She writes that she went along, thinking she could quickly "shake him" if he got involved in the game. Mary still did not drink, and money was something she had a responsible relationship with. She didn't gamble but instead saved her money for her future goals. Mary had no intention of staying, let alone playing. After a while, she began to make her exit, but she was called into the game by one of the men also watching. The man offered to coach her, and she decided to try her hand.

Mary ended up walking from the game at four in the morning with $220 either from the men being kind or "fool's luck." Either way, she was hooked on what she perceived as easy money. When she arrived at the hotel, Paul waited in her room full of jealousy and rage. He asked if there was "anything you want to tell me" supposing she had stepped out with another man. Although he seemed relieved that she had not slept with the man, he was not happy that she was out gambling, calling it worse than whiskey.

Mary writes that he kissed her and left and that "since 'everything went' in Butte, he could visit my room whenever he liked, or stay as long as he liked, and I was sorry that he had not chosen to stay." In some ways, her developing addiction to gambling was not only a cry for help but also a quiet rebellion to being controlled. Time and again, she loses all the money Paul gives her in a day.

Paul bails her out, but by this time, their relationship is coming apart under the strain of secrets and social and cultural division. Before, he could visit her house in Chicago where she was comfortable with her child, and in Bannack, they could pretend she was someone else, a schoolteacher, an innocent. In her line of work, she sold lies, pretending to be anyone but herself, and perhaps for the first time, she truly saw that it was no different with Paul in many ways.

Soon after, Mary leaves Paul and goes back east, probably to Dearborn in Chicago, and from there, she writes that she travels the world for three or four years. She lists Europe, Mexico, the Orient, and Canada and, in her line of work, saw that the conditions of her sisterhood were similar no matter the country. Mary describes what she experienced and observed:

> I saw them all, the "lost sisterhood" of the nations. I met them in Europe and in, the Orient, in Canada and in Mexico. And I met more American women than those of any other nation, for they were in every city and every land that I visited. I met the public prostitute, the clandestine prostitute, and the occasional prostitute. I met the trusting girl who had been betrayed and the unfaithful wife. I met the college woman and the illiterate child of the slums. I met the deserted wife and the wife of the profligate; the girl from the sheltered home and the girl who had been allowed to run wild; the girl who had sold her honor for bread and the girl who had sold it for luxury and fine clothes. I met the girl who should have been a nun and those others who were "predestined by ancient conditions" for the life of a harlot. But the one girl I never met in all these years and in all the cities and the countries that I visited was the pure girl who had been trapped and violated and sold into slavery and held a prisoner unable to effect her escape—the so-called "white slave." Because I had more intelligence than the average harlot, I was enabled to go into many places that they could not enter and to make money in many ways not open to them.[9]

In this part of the book, Mary clearly distinguishes between her reality, the reality of other sisters, and the popular social justice concept of "white slavery." Mary did not believe in the 1890s or when she published the last edition in 1924 that "the pure girl" is ever held in "white slavery." She always maintained that the prostitute's life is a choice and that to leave is a choice. This is a belief she holds to the end of her life. She did not view prostitutes as powerless, perhaps because, from the beginning, Mary needed to believe she had the agency to change her life. Her developing personal agency was not just theoretical but helped to shape how she lived and worked within the confines of her profession.

Mary always worked hard not to owe the house she worked in, making her clothing, not drinking, and saving up every penny she could. Yet she always functioned at the higher end of sex work. Butte, Montana, opened her eyes to how destitute and dangerous the conditions could get for women of her profession. Her travel abroad illuminates that the problem of prostitution is not an American one but a global issue as well.

She writes that after Butte and her solitary world travels, she lives with Paul for a year.

> At length, I went to live with him, and after this, I gambled no more. For one year, I had much happiness, mingled with much sorrow and bitterness; for we belonged to different spheres of life, and we had but the one point of contact, our love for each other. And that was not great enough to cover the multitude of disparities between us.[10]

Eventually, Mary moved to Helena, Montana, with Paul, where they shared a house for a time. Although they still do not marry, she describes this time as both bliss and bitterness in the slow death of their relationship. Another blow Mary suffered during this time was the death of her father Patrick Regan in November 1898. Mary was neither invited to nor attended his funeral, nor was she mentioned in any newspaper obituary notices. The father she was so conflicted about remembered in equal love and sorrow was gone, and with him, the rest of her family. So erased was she from the family line that she was only found in old census records as a young child.

⇒ 13 ⇐

Northwest Canada

AROUND 1900, ONE OF HER closest friends, Nona Blake, invited Mary to work in Canada. Her friend opened a bawdy house in northwest Canada two years before, and although it was small and housed only three women, the returns made Nona rich. By this time, Mary and Paul's relationship was under tremendous strain. She does not tell the reader why but writes that after a "prolonged and bitter quarrel," she decided to go to Nona for six weeks, not knowing then it was the start of a new adventure that would last six years. Mary, now 28, commits to making the trip, leaving Helena, Montana, for Great Falls, which would be the first leg of a difficult trip. Money, always a great motivator for Mary, combined with her desire for adventure, once again inspires her to make a huge change in her life and location by taking her to the wilds in Canada. She writes,

> It was the lure of the "just beyond" which caused my vagrant feet to turn in a northerly direction. To my mind, the Canadian Northwest represented a land of great adventure, an unexplored country in which there was something hidden from me; when once I had heard the call of it, my restless heart could know no peace until I had gone "to search behind the ranges."[1]

Mary traveled the rail line nicknamed the "Turkey Trail," a route that spiked through the vast open prairie, and arrived in Macleod, a town that developed just beyond the boundaries of Fort Macleod. The fort, established in 1874, was the first North West Mounted Police (NWMP) post in southern Alberta, created to bring order to the region. The NWMP was tasked with enforcing laws. The Mounties had the difficult job of curbing the illegal whiskey trade that plagued the area and maintaining peace between hunters, traders, settlers, and Indigenous peoples. The arrival of the railroad and the construction of the fort had transformed the area into a growing hub of activity, attracting settlers, traders, and lawmen, an activity that would stick in Mary's mind. Macleod's development reflected the rapid changes brought on by westward expansion, as the town grew around the fort to serve as a center for commerce, governance, and settlement in the frontier.

Mary was met with a harsh, cold wind when she got off the train. The wind blew incessantly with violence that made Mary unsettled. It would be six months before she adopted the northern skin to ignore the never-ending winds of the Canadian prairies. From there, the rails took her to Calgary. The city was experiencing an economic boom, which meant workers with money to spend. What Mary found at Nona Blake's place was hardly the romantic adventure she had pictured. She describes the house as "ramshackle" and provides further details of the environment:

> The wallpaper was torn and discolored, and the plaster had fallen from the ceiling in many places. The carpets, from which the pattern had long since been torn away, were ragged in spots, with only a few upstanding tufts of nap to bear witness that in a better day, they had been Wiltons. Apparently, the mattresses were stuffed with brickbats, and the springs on the beds sagged down until they swayed like hammocks; again, there was not a comfortable chair in the house. On account of the difficulty of getting laundry done, the dining table was covered with a white oil cloth, on which was placed a miscellaneous assortment of cracked china and tableware splotched with occasional flecks of silver, proving that it had once been plated.[2]

Mary was used to first-rate houses, and although the house in Winnipeg so many years before had been primitive compared to Dearborn, Nona's house was squalid. To Mary, it must have reminded her of the cribs in Butte and perhaps made her wonder if she had fallen even further into the depravity of prostitution. Her choices were not the same as in her youth, and now at 28, she was older, no longer considered the "handsome" younger woman of the house.

She wondered how her friend Nona could live in such an environment, noting that the place could have been made livable for $1,000. Nona, who operated in "first class" houses in the United States, understood the dynamics of prostitution in Canada. Nona explains that she would rather be able to take her $1,000 in cash and leave if necessary, as no house in Canada has a guarantee that they will remain open. To work in Canada also meant that one might have to leave at a moment's notice.

The women in the house were older and were given to vices that Mary was the victim of or had recovered from and avoided. She notes that the money was plentiful, but the area's cost of living was high. The business was either busy with rough men or filled with long days of nothing to do and no customers. This caused the women to drink heavily and get into fights. For Mary, it was intolerable, and after 10 days, she had had enough. Nona tried to get Mary to stay, but nothing, not even their close friendship, would change her mind.

She decided to go to Banff. Nona tried to warn her away, citing a dislike among the folk and governmental bodies for women of their ilk. Nona's strongest warning was to avoid the mounted police, but this did not dissuade Mary in her plans. She had always prided herself in being able to meld into society. Mary, though 28, claims to still look younger than her age and describes her blending in ability as follows:

> At times I tried to live up to this appearance of respectability; at other times, I tried to live it down. I never quite succeeded in either effort. But some inner sanctity which remained undefiled by my mode of life kept from my face the brand of infamy. My own conscience will keep my speech and manner free from contamination, and because of these things, I knew that I could go wherever I liked and not be subjected to questioning.[3]

Her appearance was also on her mind when she thought of the future. Her looks, though younger, were, as she says, entering the "old-timers class," and she knew her working days as a prostitute were numbered. She would need to figure out something different to survive. So it was to Banff she decided to go for rest and to plan her next moves.

Banff is located in the Alberta Rocky Mountains. The raw beauty that Mary appreciated was centered within Banff National Park, established in 1885. Mary probably took the Canadian Pacific Railway there and, like most visitors, stayed at Banff Springs Hotel. The picturesque five-story hotel is surrounded by the majestic Bow and Spray Rivers. The view from the hotel would have been breathtaking, as Mary's eyes swept across the valley to the rising heights of Mount Rundle.

Mary found peace and relaxation there, writing, "I went up to Banff and crept a little nearer to God for a little while." She describes the mountains as a "temple" where she didn't go to pray but to "feel the touch of the infinite." She also decided to write to Paul, requiring a better understanding of their relationship. Although she didn't doubt his love, she didn't feel he understood her and asked why he could not take her as she was. Mary goes into detail on her understanding of their relationship:

> In the nature of things, I should lose Paul someday. Notwithstanding our love, our lives had been led apart except for a few brief weeks of nearness, which had only made our apartness seem wider. We had lived in the same house with a world of misunderstanding between us. And we had lived on different continents when the understanding between us was so great that we seemed to be holding hands, for both of us had the disposition and the power to forget all unpleasantness once it was over. During the past ten years, I had traveled thousands of miles to be with him, and he had crossed

the continent and the Atlantic once when I greatly needed him; but in the end, the wall always rose between us. Paul had other ties and other interests into which I could never enter, and on my part, no man could ever fill my life, no matter how much I might care for him. It was part of Paul's paternal nature which made him want to guide and direct the woman he loved. It was my nature to find a trail for myself, no matter what the cost might be. If I went out into the mountains, and two trails lay before me, one of which was cleared and blazed and the other narrow, dim, overgrown with underbrush and almost impassable and leading no one knew where I invariably took the unmarked trail. Paul was conventional to the core and would follow no path which had not been marked out and trodden by the members of his own class. We could never hope to be any nearer than we were at present. Someday, Paul would marry, and I must then depend upon myself. I was getting into the old-timer's class, notwithstanding my youthful appearance. If I ever intended to have any money of my own, I must grasp my chance in this land of opportunity.[4]

Mary didn't wait for Paul to respond before planning for what she believed was her only secured future.

She doesn't say what kind of capital she began with, but she lays out a goal of having a working capital of $20,000. With a business and additional savings, she could feel fully independent. She left Banff and headed to Edmonton to search for a location in what she called "this land of opportunity." Mary eventually decided on a town that she pseudonymizes as "Malta."

Mary gives clues as to the actual location of her bawdy house. First, some businessmen objected to the town's "closed" boundary. This means the town was closed to vice—gambling, drinking, and prostitution. The "hundreds" of single men who worked there would leave to find entertainment, spending their wages in other towns and not in "Malta" where they earned them, suggesting it was a "closed" mining town. Businessmen were, in essence, losing revenue.[5] She goes on to explain that Malta closed vice due to "dissolute squaws and half-breed women ... and an alarming increase in venereal disease."[6] She attributes the problems to the Indigenous prostitutes, a shared belief of the time. If Mary believed the white women working in the deplorable conditions of the cribs in Butte, Montana, were at their lowest, then those who were Indigenous figured even lower. The views of the time were evident through the unassuming use of the label "squaw." Traditionally, Indigenous women held power in their respective nations, and the diminishing of their role through the tools of colonization was a means of suppression of First Nations' power and agency.

Mary did not seem to understand that the plight of the women in the cribs of Butte was similar to those of Indigenous women. In many ways, what the Indigenous women and prostitutes faced was worse in the erasure of kinship and culture and the absence of economic means to support their families. Whereas white skin allowed for some agency, prostitutes who were Indigenous, Black, or Asian faced hardships that would have been almost impossible for Mary to understand from her position of whiteness.

Canada was no different than the United States in its tactics to suppress and eliminate the culture of a people, even at the threat of extinction. L.K. Bertram suggests the problems arose because of racism and power:

> Why were Indigenous workers so aggressively targeted by officials who quietly tolerated (and potentially patronized) white-run brothels in the 1880s? Scholars often convincingly attribute these anti-prostitution campaigns to ideas about race and the much larger political or ideological threat that the image of Indigenous women in this underground economy posed to white, monogamous Christian colonial ideals. But in the 1880s, as the specter of real-time armed Indigenous resistance loomed large, it is also clear that some officials feared it could also strengthen Indigenous resistance.[7]

This race-based segregation included Black people, Chinese, and those of mixed blood who were not considered Anglo/white. This influenced how red light districts were operated and who was allowed to open an establishment. Mary was white, had money, and understood the game. She was not garish or flamboyant in her manner or dress and could convince the men in power that she would run a quiet establishment that would follow the set rules.

Mary carefully consulted the commandant of the Mounted Police, who it can be assumed was none other than Captain Burton Deane of the NWMP, an Anglican, God-fearing man but known to treat prostitutes with a measure of respect as businesswomen. The chief of the municipal police allowed bawdy houses to open but only if the establishments ran orderly. Thus far, it is impossible to determine the location. In her exceptional book *We Don't Talk About Those Women*, Belinda Crowson thought perhaps it was Lethbridge, Alberta, and offers convincing details. However, Lethbridge was never fully "closed," though an effort beginning in 1894 led by a Presbyterian minister named Charles McKillop ensued. McKillop and another Methodist pastor "called a public meeting to discuss the 'flagrant violations of law relating to liquor selling, gambling, and public morals."[8] McKillop demanded that the town council "rid itself of these evils, particularly the soiled doves."[9] Captain Deane, who consequently also lived in Lethbridge for 14 years, "preferred a policy of supervision over the compact, segregated red-light district, out in the open where he could exercise a measure of control."[10]

His opinion states that "if [the pastors] would turn their attention to the juvenile depravity and promiscuous fornication that going on under their own eyes and in their congregations, they would be kept so busy that they would have no time to think of the professional ladies, who at all events are orderly, clean and on the whole not bad looking."[11] Later, Deane wrote in his memoire, "The Red Light District used to cause a disturbance now and then, but, as a rule, one capable man could easily handle that and any other spasmodic trouble."[12] Although the issue would arise many times over the years, including the years Mary lived and worked in Canada, prostitution within Lethbridge was a steady business beyond Mary's time in the country.

Valuable insight, however, on the area during Mary's time in Alberta is highlighted through the memoir of Captain Burton Deane. He was sent to whip the Mounted Police into shape for the Northwest Territories. With his wife and five children, he came to a land that was still untamed and wild. He describes the prairie as "carpeted with wild roses."[13] He writes that the "first line of study that it was incumbent upon me to take up was obviously criminal law."[14] Having been a military man previously, he was "familiar with Military Law."[15] The situation he worked in was, in his words, "complicated, for only certain statutes were in force in the Northwest Territories: having ascertained from Colonel Richardson, the senior stipendiary magistrate, which those were, I set to work to epitomize them into the form of a manual which a constable could carry about with him, so as to inform himself as occasion might require."[16] The territory was not lawless when Deane came in 1884 but was comparable to the western United States in the 1870s, with many of the same issues brought on by colonization. How they differed in Deane's words was in a "dominion statute prohibiting the importation, sale and even possession of intoxicants by any person within the Northwest Territories except by permission of the Lieutenant Governor and it was the duty of the Mounted Police to enforce this Act."[17] Deane writes to the then governor that he "considered it to be an infringement on the liberty of the subject, and calculated to bring into disrepute a body of officers [NWMP] without whose co-operation the existing prohibition law could not be enforced."[18] Deane had the power to give liquor permits, and he did. In many ways, this was how he approached the prostitution and bawdy house issue as well, ultimately working to Mary's advantage.

Other towns that could be Malta were early Calgary, which is doubtful, and other outlying villages that ran along the rail line. Initially, Mary notes Malta was closed (no prostitution within the limits); all other previous houses were shut down due to the effects of venereal disease and the deviant behaviors of the prostitutes and their callers. The town she chose appealed to her because her house would be the only house; therefore, there would be no competition for callers or their money. However, the location had to have either industry and/or be large enough to have the customers she lists later in the chapter. The area must also be a crossroad of ranching and mining with an available rail connection. Another clue offered in *Madeleine: An Autobiography* in the Book/Part III Chapter I section is that the workers would leave the town to spend their money elsewhere on drink and sexual activities since they could not do it there, suggesting that perhaps the men went to Lethbridge or some other larger town for amusement. Mary also mentions that she had to travel to Lethbridge to meet Paul at the train station, which indicated she traveled from "Malta" to meet him.[19]

The patrons combined suggest a larger town that could employ all the positions she mentions. Mary also writes that the town bars close at 10:00 p.m. Monday through Friday and 6:00 p.m. on Saturdays. She notes that the "sporting houses" (houses of prostitution) were open as long as they liked, so she figured the most significant business would be over the weekend.

Mary takes further action by obtaining a loan on her jewels to buy an eight-room house for her establishment. However, she needs $1,000 more before she can take possession. As she has done in the past, she contacts Paul, who, unable to deny her anything except marriage, sends her the funds.

Paul is concerned about the business she is entering into, and after multiple telegrams are exchanged, he decides he needs to convince her to change her mind in person. Paul struggled with Mary's line of work but resolutely was against the proprietors of such houses. Mary writes that Paul "looked upon the keeper of a house of ill fame as a modern Moloch who could be appeased only by the souls of the women victims who fell into her insatiable maw."[20] When she met him in Lethbridge, he pleaded with her to return with him. Her mind was made up, and she knew then that their social status was the great rift that would forever keep them apart. She notes, "I had seen it too often when some woman of the underworld loved a man in a different station in life. Sometimes it was many years coming, but the final rupture was inevitable." The truth of her life was that she could not find true happiness with Paul, that she was a prostitute of the underworld. If she complied, she would always be just Paul's woman, not wife with the shackles of the underworld firmly affixed. She writes,

> I endeavored to make the matter clear to him, but, like all other men, he believed that he would never change. He had cared for me for ten years ;

> he had gone to Europe to find me and bring me home when I was sick and friendless ; he had paid my gambling debts times without number; and he had never refused me anything within reason that money could buy. What was it that I wanted?

She needed to carve out a life with at least some agency. He tried to convince her to come back with him to Montana, but she stood firm. Finally, he proposed marriage, saying the words she had longed to hear. Her answer was, "It's too late."

Mary must have felt the excitement of adventure and the sadness one feels as one part of life comes to a close. She doesn't pause her acquisition of the house and begins preparations to open in the fall. She hires a Chinese immigrant named Fawn Kee, who would deal with the routine maintenance of the house, keep up with supplies, and see to the cleaning and cooking. Mary writes that she furnished the house well for comfort, but Fawn had to outfit and set up the kitchen as she didn't have much to do with kitchens or cooking since she was a child. She and Fawn would become close friends over the years, and the tutoring lessons in English would also strengthen their friendship she would give him when their work was finished for the day.

As far as girls to hire for her house, the pickings were slim. She notes, "Every town and hamlet was a port of missing women, or the wrecks of women, time battered derelicts who had drifted up from the states seeking an undiscovered harbor. But these derelicts, far from being water-logged, were usually sodden with whisky."[21] In her observations, alcohol usually claimed women when they came to the territory. Mary, still resistant to alcohol, noted that all of the women who came seeking work were under its influence, and this was not what she wanted for her house. Instead, she sent for three women in the United States she knew to be "not overly given to alcohol."

Finally, with her house in order, she opened in November 1900. The day, which began with good weather, quickly turned a chill as the wind kicked up. Mary felt like her opening evening would be ruined, but she could not have known how popular her business would become in the area. She writes,

> As soon as it was dark the men began to arrive in buggies and in hacks, in hotel buses, on horseback, and a foot-men of all sorts and conditions, gentlemen, hoodlums, and all the gradations between. There were railroad men and bank officials , cowpunchers and professional men, wheat-growers and business men, Mounted Police in mufti, bartenders, clerks, and most of the male choir members of the English church. Inside of an hour after my house was opened I had discovered that I could make no social distinctions. If I did not want the house torn from its foundations, I would have to admit any white man who came to the door.[22]

She tried to turn men away as they filled every room, noting that each group kept to themselves, but all were hostile to the Mounted Police with whom she had agreements. There were too many men for the three women. By midnight, many had departed, and one disgruntled customer had put a lamp through the window, letting in snow. The weather turned from snow to a full blizzard by morning, and Fawn Kee, who had nowhere to sleep due to the sheer numbers of customers, had left to rest elsewhere.

≈ 14 ≈

Somewhere Beyond Redemption

MARY FINDS SUCCESS AND PROFITS enough to add a ballroom to the house in her first year. She had begun to think of money as more preferable to love and honed her skills as a successful businesswoman. She was well liked by her working women, though she was considered a strict disciplinarian and the favorite among her customers. She kept the "warring factions" of police pleased with her, which also helped her business. Even the public, which "believed that prostitution was a necessary evil," conceded that it was best to have a stern "straightforward" woman running a house of ill repute than a vulgar, openly public one. Mary says she never paid "graft" to the Mounted Police, but she does tell the reader that they took tribute in other ways.[1] Some attempted not only to extort money but also her body. She complied with money payments to keep her business open, but her body was at this point of her life under her direction.

In her second year of business (1901), Mary hired Mildred as a housekeeper. However, Mildred would function as much more. Mary had known her for many years, although she chose not to mention their association. Mildred would run the house and act in Mary's stead when she was away. It would be one of these times that Mildred would be arrested for procuring women from the United States. Mary, who was with Paul at the time near Chicago, writes,

> A few days after I left two girls in Spokane had written me for railway tickets to bring them to Malta. Mildred had sent the transportation and the girls arrived a few days later. A few days after their arrival they had asked to borrow clothes so that they could make a presentable appearance; they explained that they were going down-town to meet an acquaintance from Spokane.
>
> Mildred had dressed one of them in her own clothes, and had drawn on my wardrobe to clothe the other; thus attired they had gone to the Mounted

Police and represented themselves as innocent girls who had been inveigled into Canada for immoral purposes.

A man confederate appeared at the proper juncture and declared himself a near relative who had followed them into Canada, to save them from a life of shame. Evidently they had reckoned on making the complaint and then demanding a big sum of money or their silence. It was a case of "shake-down" pure and simple, and I was the intended victim, since they did not know of my absence when they sent for the railway tickets. But as I was not in Malta, the conspirators made a scapegoat out of poor Mildred.[2]

She returned and found that this was a complicated case of extortion. Yet, the whole affair was a financial burden, as Mary had to hire an attorney for Mildred and return to the States until after the trial to avoid complications such as arrest and conviction. Mildred was acquitted but was convicted and fined not as an employee of Mary but as a "principle" for selling alcohol. Mildred, who was loyal, took on the conviction, thereby keeping Mary and her house out of further legal trouble.

This was the beginning of discontent. With the ending of the prosperous winter season, the women of her house grew bored and unhappy. Mary's house had grown bigger by this time to accommodate customers; therefore, more women were working for her. It grew harder for her to keep the women in line, and they began to go into town, attracting attention by their attire and behavior. More and more the law visited. Both the municipal police and the Mounted Police chiefs came to her with threats to manage her girls or close up the house for good. She resorted to only letting two women out at once and only if they were modestly attired. Mary tells the reader her rules for the house were tightened:

> Both the city police and the Mounted Police held me to strict accountability for the actions of my girls, not only in the house, but in the streets as well. If the girls went down-town shopping and attracted attention in the streets, either by their actions or their attire, I was sure to receive a visit from the chief or be called up on the carpet by the commandant of the Mounted Police. I protested that it was unfair to hold me responsible for whatever some irresponsible girl might do when she was out of my sight. But my protest was unavailing. It was my business to manage the girls, and I must do so or shut up shop. I could not put the lid on their going out whenever they claimed to have business, but I forbade more than two going out on the same day. This order was attributed to tyranny on my part, and in self-defense, I was forced to urge the chief to give his orders in person to the girls.[3]

The women bemoaned her rules on alcohol and lovers, both of which Mary felt led to the darkest of corners for a prostitute. To fill their off time, Mary tried to teach them how to sew without much success and when that failed, to read and write, which was also a failure. She writes, "At that period of my life I thought that my own class of women were the only empty-handed, idle minded women in the world, but I can see them now on every hand, women who have never learned to use either hands or minds and whose sole object in life is to murder time."

Perhaps the dream of owning her business was becoming a burden or maybe life's traumas were catching up to her. She was becoming cold and calculating, not unlike her former Dearborn keeper, Madame Lizzie. Her business cares harassed her day and night, stealing her sleep and her health. Mary calls this time her darkest and a "delusion of a dreadful dream." She develops insomnia and turns to whiskey to fall asleep and quiet her anxious mind, fracturing the last self-preserving rule she had kept all her life. She began to drink secretly, and the disease that had gripped her father now took hold of her.

Mary speaks to the soothing effects of whiskey at first helping her sleep and smoothing her prickly disposition. She began to make excuses to herself for her need:

> Liquor had at first a most soothing effect upon me, and on this plea I excused myself for taking it. I needed something to soothe my tortured nerves, for under the stress of my many business cares I had begun to grow irritable; it was only by the greatest effort that I now preserved my equanimity and my smile in the presence of the customers, the girls, and the servants.[4]

Some of her troubles were attributed to a new house built near hers. The madam of the place allowed her girls to run "wild all over the town." Two months after this woman opened her house, both houses were raided, and everyone on the premises, including Mary, was arrested.

A similar story arises in an article from the *Edmonton Bulletin* on June 4, 1904. The report said five houses were rounded up, and fees that ranged from $20 to $50 were charged. Mary tells of the new house that was opened beside her own but does not allude to the reader if there are more. The arrests certainly cost her money, and depending on how many girls Mary had working, she would have paid out a lot of money for herself and her workers for their collective release.

Another story arose out of Medicine Hat in 1904 with striking similarities. In Medicine Hat in 1904, the NWMP had a presence and a busy railroad depot. Medicine Hat at the time was growing in population, with miners and workers working various jobs that would be needed to support a growing town and connecting railroad. The town was under the watchful eye of Captain Deane and the NWMP. In 1904, there was no cure or a way to diagnose syphilis, but Medicine Hat had a developing problem. Researcher S.W. Horrall writes, "The deputy Attorney

14. Somewhere Beyond Redemption

General in Regina received an anonymous letter which claimed that over 100 new cases of syphilis had been treated by a doctor in Medicine Hat." Deane remarked that "he didn't believe there was any truth to the accusations. The only case he had heard of was that one of the hotel clerks was infected by an entirely unprofessional source."

The NWPM was mostly in charge of the activities of vice as far as allowing prostitution, gambling, and alcohol under certain rules and permits, so Deane handed the investigation to his NWPM officer in Medicine Hat. According to Horrall, this man was Inspector C. Starnes who originally suspected the Reverend Nicholl of the Church of England who had been trying to shut down a bawdy house outside of town. Horrall notes that the house was mostly left alone as it operated "quietly two and a half miles from town and that no one else seemed to support the minister." Starnes first investigated the three in-town doctors, one of whom, Dr. C.F. Smith, reported treating six cases in 10 years with many more cases of gonorrhea. Horrall writes, "Dr. Smith stated he was called to the house run by Stella Hattley quite frequently as she was very particular about the health of her inmates." Dr. J.G. Calder alternatively stated that "he had treated 50 cases in the last six months, more than he had seen in the previous 16 years. He claimed to have traced the majority of cases back to the prostitutes. According to Calder, the inmates [prostitutes] did not use proper antiseptic precautions. He accused the madams of allowing their women to get drunk and to neglect themselves." Eventually, the two houses were raided, and "two keepers, 10 inmates as well as two Chinese cooks and 12 customers we fined." It should be noted that Mary was very keen on keeping her women healthy and paid one doctor well for the care of her house. She also did not let her women go into town except on appointed days in groups of two and in plain attire.

Meanwhile, the women in the house next to hers did not keep such rules, and it was because of their behavior that both houses were raided. Horrall writes that although the syphilis epidemic was "deliberately exaggerated," it was done in an attempt to close the houses. Also, "Deane instructed Starnes to obtain medical certificates for each girl, informing him that if any was diseased, she was to be told she could not stay in business. The two madams, Stella Hattley and Marjorie Dale, were summoned to the police detachment" and told to obtain such certificates.[5] In addition, the madams were made to agree that their inmates would no longer be seen in town except for one day a week to purchase necessities. What Mary writes in her book cuts so close to the Edmonton and Medicine Hat stories, suggesting that the location of Malta might be one of the two.

Mary had ongoing trouble with the town's police and not as much with the Mounted Police. She felt at least one of the men wanted her gone, but she claims she had information that the town police would not want the NWMP to have their hand in her destruction.

It was not the police or officials that finally brought Mary to her knees, nor was it her gambling or wandering. The culmination of years of traumas and abuse was catching up with her. Her childhood loss of her family and loss of her children—all the ghosts were pressing their weight into her being. It was a weight she could no longer push against or travel far enough away from to get relief. After a particularly difficult night, she writes, "I went out into the ballroom, which a slow crowd had been holding down for several hours, and I told Mildred that I intended to put a little ginger into them by treating them to a bottle of wine. Mildred looked her astonishment, but I repeated my order; then, seeing that one bottle would not go around, I ordered two."[6] It didn't stop there. She writes that that first spree lasted for weeks. She claimed it "soothed her disposition." Mildred begged her to travel and get away. Mary first went to Spokane, lost a fortune, and then drank more until Paul had to be called to rescue her after not seeing him for two years. He did not reproach her, finding her pitiful and sick. Mary describes this first long binge and its results:

> I was in bed for a week as a result of my dissipation, and then Paul was compelled to return to Montana. But before leaving, he prevailed upon me to go out to the coast for a while until I could get a hold on myself. I went to Seattle, where I remained for a week, and then took a steamer to San Francisco. I did not make any acquaintances in either place, but I was not lonely, for I had always possessed the faculty of entertaining myself. After three weeks in San Francisco, I went to New Orleans, stopping for a few days in El Paso.[7]

During this time of solo travel, she felt the weight lifted for a moment—the stress created by her business, the viselike pressure of the town police or NWMP, and the traumas of her life were pushed back in her mind. She was able to stop drinking and wrote to Paul, often telling him of her travels. While on the road, she was a woman of means, traveling for pleasure. In some ways, she was living the life she so craved, but like so many things in her life, it would not last. Canada, her business called her back.

Mary lasted two months before she started drinking again. The alcohol did not have its soothing effect but made her into the kind of bawdy house madam that she always abhorred. Mary says she "drank and drank; I went to bed drunk, and I got up drunk, and every time I thought of the many scurvy tricks that life had played me, I took another drink. I insulted every customer who gave me the opportunity to do so,

14. Somewhere Beyond Redemption

and my business decreased until I was not making expenses. But I went on drinking and antagonizing both my customers and the authorities."[8] What Mary was experiencing was not uncommon. It might be understood as a kind of self-sabotage, a call for help, death, a change, or an end of pain.

Paul once again came to the rescue, and Mary was able to stay sober when she was with him, but she also felt he did not love her anymore. Mary heard he was finally engaged to another woman. She notes, "We went through a scene that was filled with anguish for both of us—I, crushed and broken, with no other hand to cling to, and he, filled with sorrow because he believed that no human power could save me from the pit that I had dug for myself. He said, sorrowfully, again and again, 'Madeleine, you are beyond redemption, you are beyond redemption.'"[9] Mary's consumption of alcohol was telling in that it was never social but always done alone. She describes her drinking as not in anger but in sorrow. Some might relegate this to an internal feeling of guilt, but it was the crushing weight of trauma, the loss of children, the constant battle of survival in a world not made for women that drove her to seek numbness. I would argue it was not so much born of a feeling of sin but the sins committed on her body and mind in servitude to the appetites of men from her father, the lawmen, to the customer.

She went back to the house and stayed to herself now, fearing that she was "the most hated woman in the Northwest Territory." Mary soon after experienced a curious interaction with a Presbyterian preacher who mistook her plain attire as a housekeeping wife. He had come to preach against the Madame "Madeleine Blair." Mary, now 34 and desperate for some sort of salvation, played along. He found her copy of *Voices of Doubt and Trust* and read aloud the poem:

> All the world over, I wonder
> In lands that I never have trod,
> Are the people eternally seeking
> For sins and the steps of God?
> Westward across the ocean
> And northward ayont the snow
> Do they still stand gazing as ever?
> And what do the wisest know?[10]

Mary was moved by the words, and from here, they dived into deep conversation. Mary did not lose sight of the irony that in another manner, this man had shaped her as all the others before into the vision he required. She writes that they "spoke on equal terms, he with no idea that I was the notorious woman that he had come to excoriate and I, oblivious of the fact that I was a harlot and a drunkard, who, in the very nature of things, was not supposed to know nor think of those things which pertain to the Spirit."[11] She wondered how she dared this deception with a man of God, but her answer was that she was "trying to analyze her soul." Mary notes that her struggle was "war with society, and every man's hand was against her."[12] At this moment, she was a whore hiding in the guise of a "good" woman. Later, she would be a "good" woman trying to hide the past trappings of living the life of a prostitute.

The hiddenness was not her choice but forced on her. It did not matter which guise she took in the moment because society would hate her, and men would punish her no matter the decision she made. Later, she looked at her reflection, searching her face for "signs of vice and dissipation which should have been there." She says, "My eyes looked very weary, and in repose, my face was so inexpressively sad that it was a subject of much comment, but it did not bear the scarlet brand."[13] This realization of Mary's that she did not have the mark of prostitution was telling in the ways in which she would think on this subject in the future.

Mary wanted salvation, but she was economically tied to her business. Issues with the law were almost to a boiling point, and she could not break the cycle of alcoholism. It was not lost on her that she was taking the road of her father and destroying everything and everyone around her. Paul had finally washed his hands of her, unable to watch Mary's mental and physical health deteriorate. She was lost but could see no way out.

She was attuned to the self enough to know that the mark she bore was that of trauma unseen that went unaccounted for in the fervor of the religious and social justice movements. When reformers and moral crusaders spoke of rescue and reclamation, it almost always involved retiring from society, quiet work, or entering respectable marriages. New voices were rising, such as Jane Addams, Louise Creighton, Maud Miner, and Judge Ben Lindsey, who viewed prostitutes as victims. The connecting vices, such as alcoholism and substance abuse, were symptoms of the trauma suffered by the victim. These new voices called for reformation in the treatment of prostitutes and the examination of issues that contributed to prostitution, such as the economic circumstances of the "white slave trade" (which Mary denied existed) and double standards. A belief arose that prostitution could be controlled with simple remedies and with a rationale that the "behavior of both individuals and society can be controlled and regulated."

Progressives thought they could apply laws and compassion with their firm belief that no woman entered prostitution of their own volition. Progressives, however, in their rational campaign, failed to note

14. Somewhere Beyond Redemption

that prostitution was not simply "white slavery." It ensnared women of all races. The issue was far more complex and beyond the notions of virtue or rationality. In some ways, the progressives may have been correct, alluding to a 1909 Federal Immigration Commission that reported, "The novice prostitute had learned, through suffering, to become resourceful," adding that the "innocent victim had become so nervously weakened, so morally degraded, that she cannot look to any better life, and apparently even loses desire for any change."[14]

Mary was not the kidnapped woman but a woman of circumstance trying to grasp at opportunity and agency in a world that made it nearly impossible for women. The dream of living a socially acceptable life always seemed to escape her. There were times when Mary tried to leave and times when the agency and independence she experienced in the life served her. In the past, each time she was pulled back into life, it was always to serve others—her mother, siblings, and son. In all of this, she did so with love.

Now she needed to love herself, and it is with this need that at 34, she found herself in a Catholic church. She is ready to make a choice and radically change the trajectory of her life. She desired to take a pledge of sobriety, but it is much more than that. Mary meets the priest and confesses:

> I told him that I was not a girl, but a woman of thirty-four, that I had not been sober half a dozen times in the past year, and that for two years I had been drinking heavily.
> He then asked me where I lived, and I gave the name of my house, which was known as the Windsor Club. He nodded his head gravely and told me that he had heard of this notorious place and of the iniquitous person who kept it, but he could not credit that I was that kind of a person.
> I looked him squarely in the face and told him that the keeper of that house was not so black as she was painted; that I was the iniquitous woman to whom he had referred.
> If I had announced that I was the Prince of Darkness he could not have looked more astounded. But he asked, kindly: "Why did you come to me, my child? Are you a Catholic?"
> I told him that I was not, but that I had come to the place where I could no longer help myself; that unless a higher Power could rescue me from alcohol, I was lost indeed. I had heard of him and of his kindliness to those who sought his aid, and so I had ventured to believe that he would not refuse it, though I was not a Catholic.
> "You did right to come, my child," he said, gently. "It makes no difference that you are not of our faith."
> Then, for half an hour, he talked to me as a mother might have talked to a sick child, soothing, healing, strength-giving words, that bore no resemblance to preaching. Then, before giving me the pledge, he exacted a

promise the fulfilment of which would leave me almost a pauper, but I gave it unhesitatingly.

After I had made the promise he handed me a crucifix and, bidding me kneel down and repeat the words after him, he gave me the same pledge that I had signed as a little girl when I had joined the Band of Hope, except that he added, "To abstain from the use of liquor for one year from this date, and to avoid the occasion of temptation."

Then he knelt down beside me and asked me to say the Lord's Prayer with him. It was all so simple that I wondered that I had not thought it out for myself long before.

When we arose from our knees I asked him why he had said one year.

"My child," he said, "there are times when our Lord, seeing that we can no longer go on alone, takes us in His arms and carries us for a part of the way as a mother carries the child who has grown too weary to walk. But He will not always carry us. After a while He puts us down, then we must rely on our own strength and walk alone, for God would not have us weaklings. Trust Him and do not fear. You will be able to walk alone at the expiration of the year."

As he bade me good night he admonished me, "Remember what you are to do, and that you are to do it to-morrow."

"Yes, Fa—" I hesitated over the word. "Yes, Father, I shall do it to-morrow."[15] What she was "to do" was walk away. For Mary, it was either leave the life and all that went with it, even the financial stability, and work out her salvation or die.

The next day, she packed her muted street clothing, books, and pictures. She wanted to sign the house over to Mildred, but her friend would not take it. Mary sold her jewels to cover her debts. Mary's friends thought she had finally cracked or was going to search out Paul, but neither was true. She would go to "work out her salvation, alone as she always had done. Mary would catch the train the next day, never to return to the house or the life."

15

Resurrection

Between 1911 and 1917, major bawdy houses and red light districts, such as the Chicago levee and the New Orleans Storyville, shut down due to the increased pressure and push of social justice, Christian, and purity crusades. The crusaders wanted to clean up the underground but did not consider the human cost to those who lived and worked there. What would the women do, ripped from their livelihood and the only sisterhood they knew?

In 1917, right at the precipice of Mary's writing her book, a prostitute, Reggie Gamble, entered a church with other prostitutes in a last-ditch effort to save their profession. Hundreds of women waited on the steps of the Central Methodist Church for the Reverend Paul Smith and crowded in behind Gamble as she took the pulpit. Gamble begins,

> "We, women, find it impossible to exist on the wages of six to seven dollars a week—" The air is full of applause and women's voices in agreement. "Most of the girls here present came from the poor." Gamble looks to the reverend, who is the edge of the sword and would cut off their livelihood.
>
> "Your sphere is among the well-to-do. These girls are better off in houses of prostitution that they would be as individuals because at least they get what little protection can be afforded to them by the house. The curse of us women is disease. In my years of experience in this life, I have learned why it is that so many children are born blind, and so many homes are made wretched. Nearly every one of these women is a mother or has someone depending on her. They are driven into this life by economic conditions. People on the outside seem oblivious to this fact. One of the girls told me that her brother, a Methodist minister, when she applied for help to him, only told her to trust in God. You can't trust in God when shoes are ten dollars a pair and wages are six dollars a week. You said that you didn't want women like us to come near your church. You want this section of the city to be free from their presence. That is quite different from the attitude of the Son of Mary toward the Magdalene. Jesus did not scorn the Magdalene as you have done."[1]

Whether Mary worked in a San Francisco house during her travels is unknown. It is not known if she had connections in the city to help her as she began a new life or if it was because she could remain anonymous that she chose San Francisco. Earlier, when she struggled to get sober, she had traveled there, New Orleans, and the Southwest, so she would have had some familiarity. On this day, if she was not in the crowd, she certainly read about Gamble featured in an extra edition of the *Bulletin* in "The Voice from the Underworld Series," titled "Underworld Women Plead with the Rev. Smith at Church." This speech was given two years before Mary started her work on the book, and in the 1924 edition, she mentions reading and following such topics in the *Bulletin*. The realistic reporting and stories in the *Bulletin* moved Mary. In the self- and society-imposed isolation that she had entered, it must have been a moment of being "seen" even if it was through the voices of her scarlet sisterhood. She wrote,

> I did pray that somewhere a woman would arise who would shed some new ray of light on the subject of the scarlet woman. Someone who would divest her of all the hideous or the romantic trappings with which society had invested her and, not mitigating one iota of her follies or misdeeds, present her to the world as simply a human being. "She may be human, alive, with the same feelings that all other women in the world have. Life may mean exactly the same thing to her; she may have youth with all its vague and beautiful longings."[2]

Mary did not yet see herself as a voice in the darkness; she still struggled with her past and how it could be used for a higher purpose.

In her new life, she did not always go unrecognized or unknown, and she was harassed occasionally, costing her jobs and places to live. Mary refused to be fully shuttered away from the world, as was the custom of the majority of purity reclaimists. She tells of one instance where a woman of "means and position" hounded her from one boarding house to another and places of employment. When Mary confronted her begging for peace, the woman "declared that she knew all about my former life and that I had no right and no place among decent people; that my place was in the red-light district, and that she would fulfill her duty to society by seeing that I returned to it."[3] Mary knew that when a woman who had been a prostitute married well, she could expect "few difficulties placed in her path by society," but the single woman such as herself at the time must "[go] forth alone to fight for her soul who finds every hand against her, and every door of opportunity closed in her face. She is cut off from the world she knew, and the larger world, outside the door of the brothel, seeks to drive her back as if she were a wild beast who had strayed from her cage." This is why very few women left the life even if

15. Resurrection

they wanted to. For those like Mary, a life leaving the sisterhood was lonely and full of peril.

Mary was a natural explorer of her environment and the self. She knew she wanted to help women like herself, but she lacked direction. So it is not surprising that at the Empress Theater in San Francisco, a lonely week after Christmas 1912, she found the first awakening of inspiration. Fresh out of prison for a burglary conviction, Donald Lowrie spoke to the Empress audience about redemption in his "My Life in Prison" presentation.[4] Mary was impressed but recalls, "When I left the Empress, there was a little pang of envy gnawing at my heart." She saw that Lowrie was using his experience to help men, but she could not fathom a way to help women who were caught in the prison of prostitution she had left five years prior. She would go on to respect Donald Lowrie's message for the rest of her life, following his work and buying his book. It could be that watching him slowly gave her the courage to write her book, *Madeleine: An Autobiography*.

Mary notes that within those five years, she struggled to "gain a foothold in decent society." Finding work was equally challenging. Her reintegration was lonely and difficult. Mary understands that there is a double standard for repentant men compared to women. Whereas men can testify about their sins and salvation, women are relegated to silence, shadow, and humility. Men can speak to their experience and reenter the world, gaining employment and carrying on as if they had not fallen. Women like Mary must work diligently to reinvent themselves and hide the sinful parts, always living under the real fear of discovery. Donald Lowrie was able to help others and live off his experience, gaining employment through the *Bulletin* as an editor. Mary hardly knew where to start.

Her conviction was at war with a deep desire for solitude. Others had made demands on her and her body during most of her life, and revealing her story would be no different for the attention it would garner. Mary tried at first to join the social justice causes around her. She writes in her 1924 epilogue, "It seemed to me that there must be, somewhere in the world, a woman who could do this work, but I told myself it could not be I."[5] She hopes for a younger writer of the sisterhood to step forward. She tried to convince herself that she had no obligation, "that having reclaimed herself," she "had done all that society could reasonably expect of her," including her silence. She noted that in Lowrie's book, he wrote about purpose, and his words began to have an effect:

> No man or woman suffering a ruptured life in a prison cell is a less important unit in the evolution of humanity than the money king, the man with the hoe, or the minister of the gospel. No man has yet lived, and no human

being now lives who has not or does not serve some purpose in the great scheme of things.⁶

Mary never went to prison, and there are no records of short jail stays, but the life before and her life of reclamation after felt like a sort of prison. The bars of steel she faced were of exposure and judgment that framed her into silence with feelings of being a pretender in society. Until she started writing her book, Mary tried to keep her past well hidden.

Mary worked to become a helpful part of society but understood why more of her sisterhood did not. The risk of revealing oneself was too dangerous in a society that valued purity. The sex work that she did clearly defined what society thought in opposition to her inner knowledge and self-reclamation. She writes of one woman at the head of the San Francisco social purity campaign whose "activities are as wide as her ignorance is deep." The woman made a comfortable living and gained fame in her campaign to save the prostitute. Mary recounts, "She reproached me for my selfishness and my indifference to present-day social conditions and insisted that I was a dreamer, who by keeping aloof from the world was enabled to preserve my youth and retain my illusions, but who knew nothing of real life." If only the social justice reformers knew of her wealth of knowledge on the issue of prostitution. The women around her made assumptions based on the careful outer shell she crafted to keep her previous life in the shadows. The woman wanted to school her in ways of the depraved and advised Mary to "wake up." The fear that followed Mary was that one day, when faced with the words of ignorance from the privileged women surrounding her, she would lose her temper, revealing that her knowledge was formed within the dirty womb of the underworld they claimed to know so much about. In an analogy of the 1919 edition, she wrote,

> I may liken my state of mind to that of a physician who has spent years in the dissecting room, in the hospitals, and beside the couch of pain, who loves his fellow men, and who would gladly devote his life to their service, but who, for a sufficient reason, is forced to conceal his knowledge and remain silent, while those who never saw a dissecting-room, and whose hospital experience is confined to a case of measles, endeavor to teach him the science of medicine.⁷

It was difficult for Mary to keep silent, especially to the continued cry of the "white slave trade," which she argued was a false narrative. She calls out the hypocrisy of the supposed Christian society in its accusations of herself and the sisterhood in one breath and their feeble claims they will help in the next. She points out the long history of prostitution:

The scarlet woman has been looked upon as one who, in sheer wantonness, had chosen her evil mode of life. "Very well," said society, "she has made her bed, now let her lie in it." That countless thousands of its fairest and best came to lie in it also matters not at all. It was left for the enlightened twentieth century to create the Great American Myth. "White slavery is abroad in our land! Our daughters are being trapped and violated and held prisoners and sold for fabulous sums (a flattering unction, this), and no woman is safe."[8]

Mary often points out in her book that she did make a choice. At the same time, it was true that many women suffered abuse and victimization and fell into vices that matched their customers', just as Mary did. Sometimes she despised her lifestyle; sometimes her customers were her closest friends. Mary understood the financial power of prostitution and its agency, which was impossible for most women of the era. Mary traveled the world and gained enormous wealth with times of blissful leisure. While working, she was othered, but she was also able to pass in polite society. Yet she understood this was not the norm for all of her sisterhood.

Why would women leave their lives if all they would know was separation, shame, and silence? The reality of salvation was often too much for a human to bear. Mary writes in her afterword, "But sinner or sufferer, victim or fool, or an amalgamation of these elements, the position of the woman who would come back to a life of usefulness has not changed a particle. The present-day Judah, who shares her guilt, still says with the Judah of old, 'Bring her forth and let her be burned.'" And the multitude still cries, "Let her be stoned." Frequently, the woman whose own sins are the blackest casts the first stone.[9]

Mary also believed there was a financial motive for the spread of the myth of "white slavery" and that it started in the "pulpit" and "was promulgated," producing revenue for reformers, churches, and governments.[10] It was easier to spread fear about "white slavers" than to teach a girl about her body and sexuality or allow for knowledgeable independence and agency. It was easier for the anti-vice societies to speak of sin and damnation rather than note hunger and homelessness, which made sex work necessary, if not appealing, for food and shelter security. For all of its problems, the sisterhood offered more than the local church. So why would women leave their lives if all they would come to know was a different kind of misery in the silence of supposed salvation? Mary knew that women like her would need something different. The crusade system was polluted with hypocrisy and only really offered further destruction and shame placed on the bodies and souls of the women.

Mary read books such as *A Mind That Found Itself* by Clifford W. Beers, another man like Lowrie who transformed a social catastrophe into helpful humanitarian work. In her 1919 afterword, Mary also says that she worked for 10 years after leaving the profession to further her education and do "everything in her power" to help women who "needed a friend." She wanted to deter girls who might follow her path and offer help to those still caught in the sex trade.

In 1914, she wrote and published a poem titled, "Into the Mountain." She seems to have styled herself as a writer as Mary Agnes Fiske. The poem, which appeared in the official Los Angeles and Monterey Diocese Catholic paper *The Tidings*, offers a glimpse into her reformed path and growing spiritual relationship. She writes,

> From the sacred Sinai,
> Unto Moses spake his God.
> Gave the law unto His people
> Marked the path which Moses trod.
>
> To preach the greatest of all sermons
> Jesus went into the mountain.
> Spoke the words which made men brothers,
> Taught that all could speek the fountain.
>
> Though fair and smiling lies the valley;
> In the mountains we seek God.
> Climbing upward to snow peaks—
> Leave behind the soft green sod.
>
> Farbelow in all their splendor
> Lie the kingdoms of the world.
> Round about us gray cliffs threaten,
> Which the ages there have hurled.
>
> Oh, the loving deeds, and handclasps
> From the pilgrims on the way—
> Through their feet are torn and bleeding,
> Climbing up to meet the Day.
>
> Often we faint from pain and hunger,
> As we pass beneath the rod.
> Until alone upon the mountain,
> Face to face we meet our God.[11]

Mary revisits the same themes and symbolism as in her Mount Sinai chapter, finding inspiration and strength from God and the natural environment around her. The fleeting feeling of forgiveness and salvation that she had tried to grasp in 1894, when she had taken the train from Chicago to Butte, Montana, after her son's death, seems finally tangible to Mary in 1914. Later at the end of her life, she is given full

15. Resurrection

rights of a Catholic burial, so it is possible that she converted or reestablished her salvation during the early years of her reclamation.

In 1916, two things occurred that once again changed her life. It is not known which came first. On November 13, 1916, she married Septimus Whitney Sears, Jr., whom she called Silas.

Septimus Whitney Sears' remarkable heritage is worth noting. His grandmother was a prominent suffragette and one of the greatest diarists of the previous century and the current era. Her name was Emmeline B. Wells, and it is due to her diary that records of Mary's husband Septimus were revealed. Mrs. Wells, during the great migration of the Latter-day Saints, married Newel K. Whitney in Nauvoo, Illinois, as one of his eight plural wives with Brigham Young as the officiator. Newel K. Whitney was a founding member of the church. Emmeline would go on to Salt Lake City and eventually become a committee member of the National Women's Suffrage Association, the National and International Councils of Women, and the National Women's Press Association. Within the 47 or so diaries, many records of daily life are recorded, including that of her grandson, whom she called Sep.

Her writing revealed that Septimus was born on January 26, 1874, to her grandson Septimus Wagstaff Sears and Isabel Modalena Whitney. He was baptized as a member of the Mormon church on September 14, 1882. In 1895, he was the assistant bookkeeper in a mining office in Butte, Montana, during the same time Mary would have been there. He lived in San Francisco as early as 1896, and in the same year, he married Esther Julian, reportedly having one child. Esther lived from 1878 to 1910, so it is interesting that he next married Gertrude Trindle on November 30, 1902, suggesting a plural marriage. Gertrude died in 1913.[12]

He married Mary Agnes Regan Fiske in 1916. Fiske was either a short marriage, which seems unlikely, or the name she styled herself when she and her son had a home in Chicago or sometime after. There are no records on how Mary met Septimus, who went by the name Silas. It could have been through the beginning of her work with women's issues, the homeless, and women like her still stuck in the life. Two archival records confirm his identity and the marriage to Mary, recorded in his grandmother's diary and on a marriage certificate from the California State Board of Health.[13]

The marriage certificate shows Mary's signature using her middle name as first and her maiden name as middle—Agnes Regan Fiske. It shows that she moved from San Francisco to Los Angeles. Silas resides in San Francisco but later moves to LA. She lists herself as a writer and he as a contractor. They both give their ages as 43.[14] The marriage was reportedly very happy, though brief, as Silas died on September 8, 1922, in an automobile accident and is later buried in Salt Lake City. It seems that Mary did not convert to Mormonism but retained her Christian spirituality beliefs till death. This may be one reason why she is not noted in any obituary, and in Salt Lake City, the announcement reported his death by an accident with a streetcar and that he was recently engaged to an unnamed woman instead of married to Mary since 1914.[15] Later, at Mary's burial, only one of Septimus' family members attended the funeral—most likely his sister Laura Lucille Sears who lived in Los Angeles. It should be assumed that the family most likely knew something of Mary's past life and, like the Regans, sought to bury any connection to her and her scarlet past.[16]

It should be noted that Septimus Whitney Sears, Jr., lived and worked in many of the same places as Paul, including work as an architect and as a bookkeeper to a mining office in Butte,[17] Montana, and eventually living in San Fransico.[18] Besides location and work, there are no other indications that they were one and the same, but the parallelism is noteworthy.

The second event was that Mary began writing her story. She worked on the book for two years. In the 1924 edition, she thanks a man and his wife who helped her with the book's direction. Based on the

Judge Lindsey and wife Henrietta, a husband-and-wife duo in social reform. They were supporters and mentors to Mary Agnes Regan Sears (Bain News Service, George Grantham Bain Collection, Library of Congress).

15. Resurrection

quantitative data collected, it is believed that this was Judge Ben Lindsey, who wrote the introduction, and his wife Henriette. Their stylometric fingerprints matched Mary's in striking proximity. This, of course, is a theory but the nearest explanation using the techniques of textual bibliography, genealogical study, and stylometric technology.

Mary Agnes Regan Sears went on, eventually married, and dramatically changed her life. Even though she changed, turning away from a life of prostitution, she did not abandon her sisters. She managed to renew her promise to Miss Laura Lovejoy so many years ago in Kansas City: " Whenever I hear anyone denounce the women who lead this life, I shall think of the kindliness I have received from those I have met in it, and I shall defend them."[19]

≈ 16 ≈

The Well-Defended Barrier

MARY LIVED IN SAN FRANCISCO in 1911, and even though she was an avid reader, it is not fully understood where she gained inspiration for the writing and format of her book. Some clues come from her writing and interviews. Like much of the city, she read the San Francisco *Bulletin* closely. During this time, the *Bulletin* started to approach topics in their reporting that other newspapers wouldn't touch. The topics, especially those about reclamation, captured Mary's attention and allowed her, if not publicly, to grasp hope from the stories of others. Literature always had a calming and inspirational effect on her life, pulling her from the darkness when she was facing the very edge. The *Bulletin* began having a similar influence, impacting how she would eventually communicate her own story.

The paper ran a series of purported firsthand accounts between 1911 and 1914 that drew Mary's interest. The first was the earlier mentioned Donald Lowrie, whom she had seen speak—the recently reacclimated convict, fresh out of the San Quentin prison, wrote an installment about his life and reclamation. Mary wrote, "His was an absorbingly interesting story with a poignantly human appeal, and I had followed every installment of it eagerly. I marveled at the man's courage in attempting the apparently insuperable task of convincing a callous prejudice and incomprehending public that the convict was a human being, and that his problems were simply human problems."[1] Donald Lowrie was paroled on August 1, 1911, and shortly after, his articles began serial publication in the *Bulletin* in 1911; almost immediately, he was viewed as transcending his past. This act of transcending one's past was something that Mary desired. Instead of hiding as she was forced to do, Lowrie could live in the light and even make a living off the sins of his past.

Lowrie was offered a job at the San Francisco *Bulletin* before his release. Fremont Older, the managing editor of the *Bulletin*, wrote,

16. The Well-Defended Barrier

I told him that, in my opinion, the best way for him to face the world was to do it openly and without reserve, and I suggested that he write a series of articles under his own signature stating frankly his prison experience and in no wise hold anything back or to endeavor to extenuate his infractions of the law.[2]

Men who crossed society's boundaries were not forced into silence and shadow. Their testimony, especially if shared with the world, was considered a valuable service to humanity. Mary noted that Harold Bigbie, who wrote the 1909 *Twice Born Men*, carried a view of women that was damning, a view reflected in much of society. After reading the book, she notes a double standard applied to women's writing: "The only *women* to whom this author attributes the semblance of a soul are the poor spineless creatures in the rescue home, working out their repentance in *silence* and *shadow* and *humility*." This is not to say that Mary did not appreciate the salvation of men like Lowrie, who had walked through hell; she was happy for those who pulled themselves up from the depths. Rather, she noted the walkway was narrow, and women were not allowed to travel it. She continued in her epilogue, "None of his men derelicts—not even the most vilely depraved among them, is required to work out his repentance 'in silence and shadow and humility.'"[3] For Mary, there were no examples of women writing similarly. This changed in 1913 when the San Francisco *Bulletin* decided to allow a woman to have the same treatment and exposure as Lowrie in a serialized story of her own, titled "A Voice from the Underground."

Like Mary, the pseudonymized author Alice Smith has remained a mystery and garnered little attention beyond the years the *Bulletin* published her narrative. However, the story of Alice Smith and the letters to the editor that followed provided a remarkable example of inspiration that served Mary well. Before her book *Madeleine*, there was very little in the way of firsthand accounts of working or retired prostitutes. Research notes that Mary knew of the "Voices from the Underground" series; some even attributed it to her, but she denied it. It is possible she drew inspiration from the brave writing of the author and the following letters from women who recount similar experiences. It is likely that the series, as well as other writers she noted, helped guide her in how to tell her story. Writers are often inspired by the writing of others, making agreements with the words and judging if the themes and ideas are communicated correctly.

In Mary's case, it was the blossoming of an idea that she could find a way to tell her story and therefore help society to understand and, even more important, rescue the few girls and women who might choose differently. Mary was an artist and knew how to sketch what she saw and understood, highlighting details and shadowing others in the background, contributing to the narrative. The artist in her transformed into the writer. However, it was through the study of others that she drew inspiration and noted what boundaries could be crossed and still allow for society's readers, the very readers Mary wanted to reach. These works and letters that directly resulted from them offered her a framework, teaching her that intimate, unfiltered accounts could challenge societal boundaries and capture readers' attention. For Mary, reading other women's unvarnished, honest voices validated her urge to share her story. It does not seem that she had a misplaced sense of empowerment, but Mary did feel a keen sense of the injustice and unfairness in the treatment of women such as herself. She had spent most of her life in the shadows, and she wanted women like her to have peace and a time of true reclamation—a chance to step out into the light.

When the story of Alice Smith came out, many women wrote in wondering if, through letters, their stories could be told as well. The *Bulletin* published many of them, allowing women to take up full pages of the paper. It was revolutionary.

Women bravely shared their stories, though they rarely shared their names. They included warnings, horrors, hardship, sadness, and stories that contradicted the "white slavery" narrative. They questioned the double standard set against women as Mary had done. One headline in the *Bulletin* read, "Horrors of Prison May Be Described but Not the Horrors of the Brothel." The headline directly referenced the Lowrie serial story and compared it to the newly printed Alice Smith memoir. The letter writer, who did not give a name, wrote, "You have stirred the people by telling of the prison horrors, but no one but the girl herself knows of the horrors within the walls of a prostitute's room."[4] This unnamed woman spoke of a "prominent, successful" married man in San Francisco as an example of the male predator. The writer describes how she was sexually assaulted, illuminating that girls in her position, even when it is reported to the police, watch as their attackers go free. The shame of the assault opened the door to prostitution, and her testimony suggests that she was not from a destitute family, as the virtue societies and experts believed. She writes, "We in this life receive so little kindness. The men are cruel to our bodies—the women cause us to suffer mentally. If the so-called 'good people' could only understand."[5] Another woman, who signed her name as Mable, also had much to say about social purity reformers:

> Why do all these would-be good people wonder because a poor, unfortunate girl, friendless, out of a job, and broke, goes into a house of prostitution? Perhaps you will ask why they don't apply to a charitable institution for

aid. Most girls, before they come down to the redlight district, have applied to these charity dealers. Some have received an offer to work for their board, but most of them got a dry crust, some spiritual advice, and a cold shoulder; a few had prayers thrown in for good measure.[6]

Many women in the letters suggested that it was the charities and social societies and other women of society who were the most uncaring and cruel, first in their hour of need before going to the underworld and damning when a woman attempted reclamation after.

One woman who signed as Cecil Linden of the underworld wrote to the *Bulletin*, "I know hundreds of girls who have tried to reform, but they can't. No; once a prostitute, always one." Cecil continues, "I could tell you a story that would make every mother in the United States shed tears, but what's the use? You can't help us because, in your heart, you don't want us."[7] Overwhelmingly, what Cecil said was true. Although Progressive era feminist groups, physicians, religious organizations, women's clubs, and social societies sought to "help" prostitutes, they often struggled to see the women beyond the work they did to survive. Society commonly believed that only a certain "type" of person fell into prostitution or coerced via the "white slave" trade. Jane Addams, who was one of the three reviewers of *Madeleine: An Autobiography* and held more progressive views from her work with prostitutes, noted the economic issues surrounding low wages that contributed to prostitution. Addams, in her book *A New Conscience and an Ancient Evil*,[8] noted unprotected young women who left home to work were in particular peril regarding sex without the moral support of their family. Sex and the workings of the human body, particularly the female body, were not topics that society talked about, and young girls were often left to figure it out for themselves. Their first lessons came from the men they married or, as in the case of Mary and evidenced by many of the women who wrote to the *Bulletin*, men who preyed on their innocence and vulnerability, throwing them out after their bodies were used.

The dominant theory across the varying anti-prostitution movements was the continued cultural myth of "white slavery," a pervasive idea that purity was stolen and the prostitutes themselves were "dirty" victims. Their rescuers were on a mission to save them—that is, pull them from the underworld—but for the most part, beyond the saving, they were left alone and unmoored in a world that did not want them before prostitution and wanted them even less after. Emma Goldman, an activist during this time, declared,

> Society creates the victims that it afterwards vainly attempts to get rid of. The meanest, most depraved and decrepit man still considers himself too good to take as his wife whose grace he was quite willing to buy, even

though he might herby save her from a life of horror. Nor can she turn to her own sister for help. In her stupidity the latter deems herself too pure and chaste, not realizing that her own position is in many respects even more deplorable than her sister's of the street.[9]

The purity crusades attempted to force religious ideals of morality into a social apparatus not set up to meet the needs of women who, when "rescued," faced social conditions and circumstances that did not support the societal version of morality or living. There could be no job or support, such as when Donald Lowrie was offered right out of prison. There were no meaningful jobs or marriages for the rescued but "damaged" women. Thus was the importance of the public testimonies offered by women of the underground who wrote to the San Francisco *Bulletin*.

Many of the women who wrote spoke of the hypocrisy of their would-be rescuers. One prostitute named Bessie wrote in the *Bulletin*, "The clergyman from Palo Alto states that reformed sporting women have been treated kindly by the church. Why did he not add that they were treated in a pitying, patronizing way: in other words, it was a case of 'Poor sinner, we will pray for you.' You may come to our church, but WE WILL NOT CALL."[10] Mary understood this heavy burden of isolation, learning early in her life the overwhelming familial rejection and societal banishment that came from working as a prostitute.

In her book, Mary also discussed the isolation of leaving her life and the constant fear of discovery. She had been discovered and chased off by an upstanding female member who threatened to reveal her secret. Mary also understood what leaving meant, having done so a time or two, once long ago in Chicago and later when she left for good and settled in California.

For most women, reassimilation to society typically meant being hidden away and silenced in a mission home. Others who had the means chose to dwell in the shadows under a new persona and name as Mary had done. Another letter to the *Bulletin* headlined, "Watch Your Chance She Tells Women." The writer's words were penned as one who had escaped the life and now focused directly on her fellow sisters in prostitution, including the steps needed to start life anew:

> The world is wide. Make any kind of start in some place else, no matter how humble. Do not accept the protection of any man under any circumstances short of marriage. Don't look to church people for help or encouragement—you will be given a stone. Be willing to suffer. Keep a closed mouth. Every household has some sort of a skeleton in the closet. In the end you will win. It is well worth while, and you will have become useful to others and incidentally to yourself.[11]

The writer, who signed "For obvious reasons I must remain UNKNOWN," pointedly called men "moral cowards" who were all too willing for the prostitute to take on the fury of society and the burden of sexual sins rather than defend, help, or protect them. This writer also asked that her sisters "not take the condemnation of the world as a final and because of it, believe you are done for here and hereafter; do not pay it the compliment of respecting opinion, weighed with prejudice."[12] Mary, who worked with her fellow sisters to help them leave the life noted that her work was better done alone than with outside help. She particularly felt that men were ill-equipped to help women in prostitution. She wrote, "I came into contact with intelligent women, I discovered that they were *trying* to understand their less fortunate sisters, but they were sadly handicapped because of the fact that they were compelled to get their knowledge second hand from the class of men who knew very little about the matter (and that little was false). The intelligent men who could have told them a great deal were silent."[13] Her suggestion that men who had intelligence refers to men with experience due to their habit of visiting brothels not as saviors but as customers. Mary understood how men contributed to the problem, including the profits extracted by government bodies, judges, police, physicians, and landlords, all of which often benefited from the prostitute's labor. The problem of prostitution was never about sin or purity; it was a complex problem created by the conditions of the society that sought to damn such women. The entirety of the problem would not be solved as a whole, but Mary believed it could be solved one woman at a time.

17

American Magdalene

MARY'S LIFE AFTER MADELEINE REMAINED obscured until recent findings. Her life after prostitution was no less colorful, full of her wandering, writing, and invigorated by her passion to help not just her scarlet sisterhood but also women and children oppressed by systems that made them a second thought. Her passion, it seems, became a mission and was not lost after the scandal of her book in 1919.

On February 14, 1927, two years after the second edition, the *Los Angeles Times* published a remarkable interview that in 1919 would have been front-page news. This interview, however, barely made a ripple printed on the back pages of the paper. The headline stated, "Banned Book's Author Known." Other bylines followed, stating that "Mrs. Agnes Sears" wrote "Madeleine," followed by, "Writer of Work on Social Evil Found in Hospital." How did the unnamed reporter find her, and why were they looking?

It's unknown why the reporter sought her out, convalescing at the hospital. Perhaps the reporter was acting on a tip or other information. Mary was often very outspoken on social issues and had made friends and many enemies in the process. It could be that once again, purity and social societies, especially those run by religious men, were trying to silence her by illuminating her past life and writing. It might also be true that because of her former sex work, she knew of the sins of those in power who would have good reason to reveal her identity and force her back into the shadows. Mary was known as a writer then but not for *Madeleine: An Autobiography*.

The interview that followed was sensational and possibly dangerous for Mary Agnes Regan Sears, for not only did they name and interview her while still convalescing from an operation, but they also gave her home address. Research shows that she made a living as a writer and as a writer of children's books, and this would have threatened her financial and professional situation. It has been only seven years since the book caused an uproar across the country, and many of the same laws would still be on the books; many of them, such as Comstock laws, are still in effect today.

The reporter recounts the New York Supreme Court case and the arrest of Harper & Brothers and Clinton T. Brainard. Much is made about the court case and the social praise and damnation the book received. Mary, up until that moment, remained in the shadows incognito, using her middle name, Agnes, and her Sears surname to stay separated from Madeleine Blair, fully embracing a life of redemption. The article states, "Despite legal attacks, authorship remained a mystery until *The Times* last night found Mrs. Sears."[1] Mary is described as middle aged and scholarly. It is reported that she decided to come forward, revealing herself to the world as the author of *Madeline: An Autobiography*. Under the circumstances, one has to wonder if she was coerced into the revelation or did this of her own free will.

She does not hold back, using the moment to shed light on the plight of women like her. She tells the reporter, "I feel that 'Madeleine' has been of some value to the American literary world." Mary continues, "Because it is a true and first-hand story and has stood the fire of courts and has been vindicated, which may ease the ban of censorship."[2]

Mary tells the reporter, "Madeline was written as a warning concerning existing social evils. I tried my utmost to point out a way to relieve a sociological situation that extended its tentacles into American ideals with astonishing and disheartening results. My book has the misfortune to be made an issue in a political warfare raging in New York at the time of its publication. Its publication was not so much an issue, but the political situation surrounding personalities in its fight for existence made grist for certain factions in New York's political mill, and Madeleine suffered as a result."

The reporter asks, "Why have you remained anonymous for so long?"

She replied, "Because I felt that my book would be of greater value and go farther toward serving its purpose under that condition." The article goes on to state that "one of the foremost contentions in 'Madeleine' is that the so-called white-slave traffic is a myth and popular fancy, while the authoress takes issue with some of the methods employed by authorities and welfare workers in dealing with prostitution concerning women of the underworld."[3] Even in 1927, Mary retained her beliefs that choice was at the heart of the profession because women lack so few relevant choices in life.

During this interview, Mary says she makes a comfortable living writing short stories and has been a widow since 1922. The paper also says that although *Madeleine*'s author managed to keep the secret, she is well known as a writer and lecturer in Southern California. Mary claims to have written several books since but declined to name them as her publisher demanded in her contracts that she must never be known as the author of *Madeleine*. The newspaper and Mary agree that two or three of her books were widely circulated in 1927. There are many entries about her as a writer of children's books, poems, and editorials.

Mary mentions the vindication that she hoped would ease the ban of censorship. Despite the 1920 overturning of the conviction of Clinton T. Brainard, Harper & Brothers, and comparisons of *Madeleine* to *Tess of the d'Urbervilles* and *Jude the Obscure*, *Madeleine* remained a banned book.[4] The ruling proved that Brainard was the inconvenient member of an ongoing extraordinary grand jury that threatened the power of New York mayor John Hylan. However, in the summer of 1920, opinion had shifted. The *Brooklyn Daily Eagle* reported "the suspicion that no prosecution would have been undertaken" if Brainard had not sat on the grand jury that threatened the top governmental powers in New York.[5]

At the end of summer in 1924, attorneys Cassell and Stafford of Los Angeles applied for a mandatory injunction in the District of Columbia to permit circulation through the mail. The attorneys represented Hollywood Press, who brought the suit as they published a second edition of *Madeleine: An Autobiography*. Sensational details emerged from this injunction, such as a $50,000 gift to the NYSSV after the arrest of Clinton T. Brainard, president of Harper & Brothers. Some papers of the time declared Mayor Hylan behind the court case and the money "gift."[6] Although the case was overturned, someone (perhaps Charles S. Sumner) went to Washington to successfully see that the book remained banned if sent by post. Mary says in the interview that she got her chance to confront Sumner, secretary of the society. She described the interaction between her and Sumner in detail:

"Is there anything obscene in my book?" She demanded.
"No," admitted the moral mentor (Sumner).
"Then why do you suppress it?"
"Well," Sumner told her, "It won't do to teach that a woman can go wrong and then come back."
But that is exactly what Mary decided to do with the rest of her life.
"What about Christ and the woman taken in adultery? What about Mary Magdalene?" demanded the indignant author.
Mr. Sumner didn't know 'what about them.'
When questioned further about the case, Mary's fine brown eyes flashed as she recounted the incident.
"That's what I'm up against," she said warmly and continued, "they shall not pass! Neither in life nor literature. Even the working women, who owe

a debt of gratitude to the Magdalenes of the last decade, are unwilling to admit the reformed outcast to society. Yet the old-time woman of this class was the advance guard to the army of modern women workers. The first battalion mowed down, but making possible the industrial emancipation of women who followed her."[7]

Prostitution has always been a commercial enterprise embarked on by women to supply first the needs of a human for survival and second as a means to improve conditions. When Mary set out to do sex work, it was initially for basic needs—food and shelter. When she began work in Chicago, her needs were met, but now she had to earn for her family because her father failed in his duty. Later, it was to provide for her son and also build savings to open a legitimate business in the future. Sex work was also one of the most plentiful means of labor in the cities and out west during the 19th century. From Mary's viewpoint, the work was no different than an unhappy marriage if understood under the concept of trade and labor. She writes,

> A lie that is half a truth is ever the blackest of lies. This lie that they love the life, that they always go back, is the blackest invention of the Father of Lies. Few women, indeed, love the life, but many love the ease and luxury, the power over men, the idleness and freedom from responsibility, which they enjoy. If they pay for these with their souls, they differ in only one respect from the women who sell themselves into unloved and often loathsome marriage they do not cheat in the delivery of the merchandise for which they are paid.[8]

Whether it was prostitution or an unhappy marriage, Mary felt women were caught in a male-dominated construct of using their bodies in a transaction for survival in a world that did not support women as individuals with rights or agency over their lives or bodies. Mary did not see a difference. The female body had always been at the mercy of men, religion, and society.

The prostitute has always been compared to the biblical Mary Magdalene. Even in his introduction, Judge Ben Lindsey uses this comparison to show that Mary's book and testimony of a life had value. The Magdalene saw what no one else saw and believed when no one else believed. Yet her story was diminished in the connection to the prostitute who humbled herself before Jesus. Former prostitute or not, she was the first to see Jesus after he rose from the grave, but this is not what usually comes to mind when you hear or see her name. Usually, to see her name is to be reminded of the prostitute, not the disciple. Madeleine is no different when encountered in research. But like Mary Magdalene, Mary Agnes Regan Sears dedicated herself to helping her sisters in need. When *Madeleine: An Autobiography* was published for the second time, she became a friend to the fallen women, spending much of her time and money assisting missions on the streets of Los Angeles.

Mary R. Sears was known to the down and out, the prostitute, and the hungry, offering assistance in her later days along Main and Los Angeles Streets, sometimes named "Skid Row," in Los Angeles.[9] She worked with Christ Faith Mission, Mary Covell of the Midnight Mission, the Big Sisters, the House of Friendship, and interestingly, the Sisters of the Good Shepherd in San Francisco. She also stood up in exclusive women's clubs when meetings looked into issues of prostitution. In one such meeting where Dr. R.C. Barton, executive secretary of the Morals Efficiency Commission (a type of governmental vice society much like Sumner's in New York), spoke, trying to rouse the women into reformative action against the immoral acts of sex workers, Agnes was said to have asked "mildly potent questions from the floor." Described as a neat gray-haired woman of 50, Dr. Barton responded, "You, my dear lady, cannot possibly know the conditions of which I speak."[10] But Mary did know. She knew better than most of the doctors, social workers, women, and preachers who filled the room. After this incident, Mary wrote,

> I always had to bite my tongue to keep from hurling the truth in his face—that I might be able to tell him a great deal about them, including the fact that he and his cohorts could discharge more poisonous salacity into the atmosphere inside of an hour, I had ever heard in a month within the walls of a "sporting house."[11]

Mary had other dealings with Barton and noted, "Time and again I have heard this man blatantly assert that, 'the only thing to do with these women is to drag them into police court, throw them into jail instead of giving them a fine, and then give *us* a chance to reclaim them.'" Mary points to men, especially those that she classified as the roué, the worst barrier for women to get help; she lists them as the psychic roué, actual roué, reformed roué, and the staunchest of these defenders of the barrier between the "good woman" and the "bad woman" was the burned-out, reformed roué who "not infrequently owed his material prosperity to a woman on the other side of the barrier."[12] Noting that the roué made money off those needing reclamation and also participated in the sin they pretended in society to abhor, it was her opinion that men ultimately created the problem with their needs, fed it with greed, controlled it with their power, and cursed it when caught. She believed that if men were taken out of the equation, women would stand a chance at finding a solution. She did not expect to effect radical change with her book or street mission, but she did hope that with her unique ability to cross the barrier, she might "be able to lay a foundation for those who came after her to build upon."[13]

Social hygiene became a bigger social cause with laws passed against "white slavery." Bawdy houses, hair and nail parlors, and laundries were raided, and anywhere where women were primarily the labor force was suspected. James Bronson Reynolds, who was a one-time assistant district attorney in New York City, was counsel for the National Association for Social Hygiene and made speech after speech declaring that prostitutes were educationally and mentally deficient. In one speech, he said, "The Massachusetts Commission had found 51 percent of defectives among cases investigated."[14] He was followed by Dr. R.C. Barton, who spoke on the work of enforcing red light abatement, which included closing women-owned businesses that were suspected of prostitution.

The front pages of the 1924 edition of *Madeline*, published by Hollywood Press, have the inscription, "Printed from Harper & Brothers Original Plates." Somehow, Mary got the plates back for her book. This directly rebuffs the earlier belief and research that they were destroyed. Her fortune was gathered from her years of work, and the sales of the 1924 edition were spent on aiding girls and women who were caught in the life she left behind. She walked Skid Row in Los Angeles, offering aid to those in need. She worked with various missions. Friends revealed that the last years of her life were spent emulating Mary Magdalene and offering a hand to those women who wanted rehabilitation.[15] Mary was involved in mission work that helped women secure jobs and places to sleep through the Christ Faith Mission, focusing on jobless and destitute women.[16] Mary always faced frustration in her street mission work. She describes this in her epilogue of 1924:

> Whenever I encountered a case that I could handle unaided, I usually met with a considerable measure of success; but whenever I had to work in conjunction with others (with a few notable exceptions), I found my best efforts frustrated by the invincible ignorance, blind stupidity, or the criminal indifference of those who were ostensible, aiding me in my work. Whenever I tried to suggest to these persons that they failed to produce results with the scarlet woman because their ideas about her were all wrong and their information erroneous, they would inevitably inform me that they had statistics to prove their contentions and that I had only my own supported opinion.[17]

Mary also fought for "idle women," a contrary description for women who lost their jobs or were destitute. This included women who could not find work after leaving prostitution. In one instance, Mary was named Mrs. Agnes Sears in the newspaper and was a representative of the Christ Faith Mission. The mission took care of women with a capacity of 70 beds. However, the need was so great that they managed 130 beds, and when they needed more, they housed women at the Natick Hotel. The mission did this without the help of the Community Chest or city funds. What made the Christ Faith Mission different was that they took older women between the ages of 30–60, and whereas they were overflowing, similar missions had many empty beds because they took only young women.[18] Mary discovered through her work that it was not just the reformed prostitute but also teachers, stenographers, and bookkeepers who were women from the labor class. Once they reached their 30s, they were no longer considered useful and often fell into poverty and homelessness. Sexism and ageism further complicated life for women, especially in labor, in which youth and beauty were part of the requirements.

Her writing and wandering during the 1920s did not stop after she wrote *Madeleine*; the money she made from her books was always used to help women and children. She moved around California during the 1920s and 1930s. For a time in 1920, she moved from San Diego to Auburn,[19] perhaps thinking of settling down with Silas to quiet married life, but this changed after his death. Later, in 1928, she either visited or resided at a writers' retreat in San Diego or lived there for a short time and is listed in the 1966 *Books and Authors of San Diego: A Checklist*.[20]

A portion of an allegorical essay published in the 1928 *Troubadour* was said to be an editorial in the *San Diego Herald*, which is contrary to the paper's running time of 1851–1860. In the *Troubadour*, Mary is cited as an editor of the paper, but this wasn't true. The short-lived paper's editor was John Judon Ames, and the timing was before her birth.[21] Might this persona as an editor of a defunct paper be another use of pseudonyms to publish and have her voice heard? The piece "Where Does a Butterfly Sleep at Night?" matches the stylometric markers as Mary's writing and exemplifies the continued growth of her writing craft and the intense thoughts and concerns for women and girls living in a world that catered to men and left little else for women. Mary writes,

> Day after day, I sat in a crowded courtroom looking at unlovely people and listening to tales about the evil that men do until I had begun to wonder if there was anything of beauty or goodness left in the world. I had listened to the equivocation of witnesses, the whisperings of spectators, and the wrangling of attorneys until the sound of catbird's voice would have been music in my ears. I had not realized that there were so many uninspiring words in the world. Words! Words! Words! Never a winged, flaming, scintillating word, but dull, prosaic, leaden words that fell upon the ear like sounds of dried clods of clay falling upon a coffin lid.
>
> On Saturday morning after that discordant week, I awoke with a poignant

longing for the sight of cool green mountain meadows, for the sound of breakers along a lonely sea coast, with a great desire to flee from the sights and sounds of the city and the endless stories of man's inhumanity to man. As I sat down to my desk, the telephone rang, and a voice reminded me of the forgotten engagements.

There was an all too brief drive through the cool greenness of Balboa Park; then I found myself entering a room where a group of alert looking boys and girls were gathered. Standing before them was a tall, scholarly-looking man talking, and in front of the man, there was a table filled with birds and butterflies and sea shells, and green twigs. When he finished speaking, they bombarded him with questions: How long does a butterfly live? "How high up in the air can a butterfly go?" "Where does a butterfly sleep at night?"[22]

The piece above seems to contrast the evils of the courtroom and men to the outer natural world, and a reader cannot help but wonder if she intentionally allegorized women as the butterfly.

Not one to suffer without trying to change her luck, she continued her hard work and was appointed to the Federal Housing Commission, set to earn a wage of $125 a month. It was reported that she was hard at work on a book concerning Mormon emigrations, of which she would have had an interest and some knowledge since her grandmother-in-law was Emmeline B. Wells through her husband Septimus Whitney Sears, Jr. It was also reported that Mary had secured another contract on a finished book with an eastern publisher.[23] Unfortunately, her mighty heart would not sustain, and she died of a heart attack in her rooming house before seeing the harvest of her recent work.

Mary died without a penny to her name and was to be given a pauper's cremation, but those who loved her fought for something else. Friends and a Catholic priest, Father George M. Scott, claimed her body, and L.F. Utter & Co. donated full funeral services.[24] Depending on the newspaper, a few friends or hundreds attended her funeral. Another paper reported that she was mourned by thousands of friends and the many unfortunate girls she had helped.[25] Alma Whitaker, whom Mary cited as a brilliant writer, described the crowd at Mary's funeral as odd and motley humans. She was given full Catholic rites of burial and was buried at Saint Vibiana's, suggesting she converted or returned to the faith of her grandfather.

It seems poetic that Mary Agnes Regan Sears, historically known as Madeleine Blair, was received into the Cathedral of Saint Vibiana. Saint Vibiana herself is a mystery. The saint embodies the unknown and forgotten whose history is obscured in shadow. She is only known as a martyr. Los Angeles deacon Eric Stoltz, who dubbed Vibiana "the Patron of Nobodies," offered this take on what she could mean to the faithful:

Who was she? She is an enigma. She is nobody and everybody. Her feast is celebrated only by us here in Los Angeles. Because we don't know the details of her life, in one way, it is difficult to ascribe to her particular virtues we can imitate. Yet in another way, this makes it easier for us to identify with her. All we know about her is that she was a martyr. And that is enough. She stands for all of us, the insignificant ones who will never be written about in history books.[26]

This viewpoint could have stood as Mary Agnes Regan Sear's obituary. Mary has stood as the example of the prostitute in countless research papers, books, and websites. When American prostitution is brought up in serious conversation, her image as we conceive it comes to mind. When we think of prostitutes, we think of sin, dirt, and disease but rarely their humanity. Mary was described as beautiful even in her old age, with dark brown eyes and an easy smile. She was described as witty, intelligent, wise, and full of heart. She was so much more than we have ever known: a remarkable woman, mother, sister, daughter, friend, businesswoman, writer, missionary, friend to the prostitute, and a sister in the scarlet sisters. She faced every year of her life with inconceivable courage and grace.

Mary was more than Madeleine. She was our American Magdalene.

Appendix: Transcribed Epilogue from *Madeleine: An Autobiography*, the Discovered 1924 Edition

Below, I have included the epilogue from the unknown edition for readers. This is not widely available, but it offers context to Mary Agnes Regan Sears' thoughts after she won her court case against John Sumner, which allowed for legal printing in the United States. The income from the 1924 edition was used to support women, girls, and others in Los Angeles, particularly those on Skid Row. This is a faithful transcript, including grammar, spelling, and syntax.

Epilogue—The Well-Defended Barrier
Madeleine: An Autobiography, 1924

I WAS AMONG THE AUDIENCE AT the Empress Theater in San Francisco when Donald Lowrie made his first appearance on the stage. I had never before seen a man whom I knew to be a convict, and I had some naive idea of the *convict* type. Before Mr. Lowrie came to the stage. I had conjured up a burly individual with a sinister cast of countenance and a slouching gait. When I found myself confronted by a clean-cut, tall young fellow, who looked more like a professional man than a paroled convict, a two time loser—I fell back on the usual platitudes of the person whose preconceptions of a class have been rudely shattered: "Of course, this one must be *quite* different from the rest."

Donald Lowrie had only been paroled from San Quentin Prison a short time before this. He was then engaged in lecturing on "prison reform" and writing his own story, "MY LIFE IN PRISON," for the San Francisco *Bulletin*.

His was an absorbingly interesting story with a poignantly human appeal, and I had followed every installment of it eagerly. I marveled at the man's courage in attempting the apparently insuperable task of convincing a callous prejudice and uncomprehending public that the convict was a human being, and that his problems were simply human problems. That the cruel, barbarous and inhuman modes of punishment then in practice in prisons of California not only did not lessen crime, but helped to foster it. And last, but not least, that the intelligent man who had been a convict, living the life of a convict, among convicts, knew more about the criminal both in his outlook on life, and his failure to society—and societies greater failure to him—than the most earnest outsider could possibly know. No one who read Donald Lawrie's story with an unbiased mind could doubt that he spoke with authority.

On the occasion of his talk at the Empress, he was plainly suffering from stage fright, and even the calls of encouragement that came from those newspaper men who were in the audience, did not serve to set him at ease. Yet notwithstanding his halting speech and his diffident manner, I was deeply impressed by his sincerity.

When I left the Empress, there was a little pang of envy gnawing at my heart: Here was this man, with the prison pallor not yet gone from his face, who was utilizing his dearly-bought knowledge to help the men he had left behind him in prison; and here was I, a woman who five years before had left behind her prison of a different kind; who knew the hearts and needs of the human creatures in that prison as no outsider could ever know them; who knew a great deal about their failure to society, and society's failure to them—and yet I dared not speak.

My experience during five years of struggle to gain a foothold in decent society; to earn a living, and to lend a hand to other women who were making the same upward struggle, had left me with no illusions as to society's attitude toward the woman who once been definitely outside the pale that separates the prostitute from the rest of the human race.

Society has not only established a double standard of morals, but (as a direct and logical result of this same double standard), it has a double standard of regeneration and rehabilitation as well.

This second double standard is strikingly exemplified in Harold Begbie's remarkable book TWICE BORN MEN. William James calls this book "a clinic in regeneration." As a clinic in *masculine* regeneration, it is, indeed, an interesting and valuable human document. But the only *women* to whom this author attributes the semblance of a soul are the poor spineless creatures in the rescue home, "working out their repentance in *silence* and *shadow* and *humility*."

None of his men derelicts—not even the most vilely depraved among them, is required to work out his repentance "in silence and shadow and humility." Each man of them, after his come conversion, goes about his business of earning a living: of lending a helping hand to his brethren who are still held in the bondage of sin and drink, and have working out his own salvation in the work day world.

This is exactly what Donald Lowry was doing. Through the generosity of Fremont Older, Managing Editor of the *Bulletin*, he had a position on the *Bulletin*, which served the double purpose of arousing interest in his work and affording him a living. And in his prison reform work, he had the aid and support of representative business and professional men, and of prominent and influential women. While I envied this man his opportunity, I did not seek to emulate him. I would never have had the temerity to speak in public, and at that time, the idea that I could write had not occurred to me.

But I did pray that somewhere a woman would arise who would shed some new ray of light on the subject of the scarlet woman. Someone who would divest her of all her hideous, or the romantic trappings with which society had invested her; and, not mitigating one iota of her follies or her misdeeds, present her to the world simply as a human being. "*She* may be human, alive with the same feelings that all the other women in the world have. Life may mean exactly the same thing to her; she may have youth with all its vague and beautiful longings."

It seemed to me there must be somewhere in the world, a woman who could do this work, but I told myself it could not be I. I had neither been called nor chosen for such an apparently insuperable task. It would have to be a younger woman, one better able to are the stress and strain of cutting a trail through the unchartered morass; and it must be one whose economic position was more secure than mine. I tried to convince myself that I had no obligation in the matter; that having reclaimed myself I had done all that society could reasonably expect of me. I had indeed done far more; for through the world for though the world appeared to be filled with iron-tongued reformers engaged in what they were pleased to term "reclaim-work," most of them proclaimed with loud and arrogant assurance that there could be no reclamation! Although I knew this was false, and that I myself was a living proof of the falsity of it, I did not want to engage in any such unequal warfare. I was tired and no longer young, and in my heart was a deep and abiding longing for solitude and for peace.

It was not a great while after I had seen Donald Lowry at the Empress that I left San Francisco to take a position in another city. I still followed his career with interest, and I rejoiced to hear that he was meeting with success in his chosen work. He had stirred something deep within me though would not again become quiescent and yet his second book MY LIFE OUT OF PRISON, was published some years later and I had still taken no steps towards making public my own experience.

There was one sentence in that second book of Donald Lowrie's that kept haunting me day and night: "No man or woman suffering a ruptured life in a prison cell is a less important unit in the evolution of humanity than the money king, the man with the hoe, or the minister of the gospel. No man has yet lived and no human being now lives who has not or does not serve some purpose in the great scheme of things."

That is what I would have written about "the other kind of woman" had I known that I was able to write. I had day by day, come to realize that I had become a *useful* member of society, and if I, why not many other women I had known? Why this appalling waste of a potentially useful human material? Except that I possessed a little more of the quality of grim endurance and blind persistence than the average person, I had no reason for supposing that I was in any wise different from many other women I had known in other days.

It was sometime early in the year 1914 that I came across a copy of that miraculous book A MIND THAT FOUND ITSELF by Clifford W. Beers, and then I came to know another man who had transmuted his social disaster into social victory, and who on the very foundation of that disaster, was building up great a great humanitarian work.

While it is true that insanity is a disease and not a crime and that Mr. Beers had committed no crime in becoming insane, he could hardly hope to entirely escape the stigma which society in its blindness, has placed upon an insanity. Many of the phrases used in connection with this disease belonged to the terminology of crime and not of disease. "Charged with insanity tried for insanity!" "These terms are in the very nature of arraignment and not of diagnosis." And if these opprobrious phrases are falling into disuse, and if the public is changing its attitude toward the insane, by the shadow of a degree, it is due to the great humanitarian work of the Committee for Mental Hygiene, which Mr. Beers was instrumental in founding. And that this man should have taken his own unhappy experience as a foundation for this splendid work was nothing short of marvelous.

But even with this inspiring example of these two men—each in his own field proving that great good could be accomplished by the handicapped individual, and that the man need not remain socially disqualified because he had once been so—I did not rush to pen and ink to record my own recovery. I did not feel qualified to write without someone to direct my work, and I realized that the person who would undertake to direct it must have an understanding heart and have motives and ideals that would be similar to my own. Even after I found this prospective counselor and guide, it required two years for me to muster up the courage to approach him on the subject that lay so near my heart it will be seen that the writing of MADELEINE was not lightly undertaken.

During the *ten years* that have elapsed between the time I gave up my old life and the time I began writing this book, I had (aside from the serious business of earning a living) but two interests in life; but these two interests were tremendous ones: I wanted to improve my education, for the sheer joy I've always derived from the mint from mental effort; and I wanted to do whatever lay in the power in my power for other women who might need a friend. But I wanted especially to hold out a deterring hand to other women who are on the downward path; and to lend a helping hand to women who are struggling to emerge from the underworld.

Whenever I encountered a case that I could handle unaided, I usually met with a considerable measure of success, but whenever I had to work in conjunction with others (with a few notable exceptions), I found my best efforts frustrated by the inconceivable ignorance, the blind stupidity, or the criminal indifference of those who were, ostensibly, aiding me in my work. Whenever I tried to suggest to these persons that they failed to produce results with the scarlet woman because their ideas about her were all wrong and their information erroneous, they would invariably inform me that they had statistics approved their contentions, and then I had only my own supported opinion.

It has always been my misfortune to be rather guileless looking and individual, and apparently somewhat helpless. For this reason I've always had to submit to much patronage on the part of those who would instruct me in the ways of the world. There was, in the city to which I came to make my permanent home, one good brother, very prominent in commercialized reform, who always tried to crush me kindly: "But my dear little lady you do not in the least know what you are talking about a woman with your innocent mind is easily taken in by such women. I've been investigating these women for 20 years and you cannot tell me anything about them."

I always had to bite my tongue to keep from hurling the truth in his face—that I might be able to tell him a great deal about them, including the fact that he and his cohorts could discharge more poisonous salacity into the into the atmosphere inside of an hour, than I'd ever heard in a month within the walls of a "sporting house."

Time and again, I have heard this man blatantly assert that "the only thing to do with these women is to drag them into police court, throw them into jail instead of giving them a fine, and then give us a chance to reclaim them."

More and more, as I came into contact with intelligent women, I discovered that they were *trying* to understand their less fortunate sisters, but they were sadly handicapped because of the fact that they were compelled to get their knowledge second hand from the class of men who knew very little about the matter (and that little was false). The intelligent men who could have told them a great deal, were silent.

The most astonishing thing that I learned during this time was that the staunchest defender of the barrier between women of the upper world and women who had been out of the underworld, was not, as I had been led to suppose, the pure minded woman: it actually was the roué, the psychic roué, and the reformed roué and that the staunches of these defenders of the barrier was the burned—out, reformed roué—and not infrequently one who owned his material prosperity to a woman on the wrong side of the barrier. For as that brilliant writer Alma Whittaker has truthfully said: "This Lord of creation has cheated them both, and only that impassable barrier has saved his face."

After I fully realized this truth about the staunchest defender. I began to hope that I might allude his vigilance and crossed the barrier with a message for the decent, intelligent women on the other side. Men had been muddling about ever since the beginning of recorded history, trying to find a solution for the problem of prostitution, and all they had ever been able to accomplish was to make a bad matter worse. I believed that the so-called "good woman" and the so-called "bad woman" were to get together and discuss the matter, with naught extenuated and naught set down to malice; without patronage and without a price being set upon pruriency and hypocrisy, we might be able to do something about it.

I did not expect to bring about any radical reform to the accompaniment of brass bands and marching banners; but I did hope that I might make a small breach in the barrier, and, once on the other side, I might be able to lay a foundation for those who came after me to build upon.

That I did make an opening in the barrier it has been attested to by the generous response that MADELEINE has met with from women. And that it would arouse the staunch defenders to rally to the breach, was one of the things that entered into my calculations when I wrote the book.

In giving my book to the world I have followed the light of my own intellect and my own conscience. I believe this book to be a valuable human document as well as a valuable contribution to sociological literature, and I'm not alone in this belief. One woman, whose father was a famous preacher, has written me: "Your book is a greater sermon than any my famous father ever preached and it holds out a great hope for fallen humanity. I shall always have a different viewpoint towards the girl who has 'gone wrong.'"

The Judge of a Juvenile Court in Ohio has written: "I am asking nothing for women on the ground of chivalry, but it is high time that something was done on the ground of simple justice. I should like to have around me a few welfare workers who have the qualifications so richly given to you." A YWCA secretary, dear friend who stood staunchly at my side whenever I would have faltered, has written, "You are in mental ability and moral worth, the finest woman I've ever known." You have been tried on the fire, and you are—And a great writer has written to me: "It is a big book, and I believe an enduring one.... It is a book that Jesus would have loved, and that all the Pharisees will want to strangle you for."

But if I had no other reward, the generous support given me by the man and his wife, under whose direction I wrote my book, would be sufficient. And in the following paragraph, which came in a letter from my preceptor after my work was done, I'm more than repaid: "You needed little but little guidance from the very first; all I did was to act as a sounding board for your own thoughts. My share of the work has been purely a labor of love; you cannot possibly have enjoyed our work together more than I have, and spiritually, I am in your debt."

Chapter Notes

Introduction

1. Emma Goldman, *Anarchism and Other Essays* (n.p.: Sahara Publisher Books, 1910), 184.
2. Paul S. Boyer, *Purity in Print: The Vice-Society Movement in America* (New York: Scribner's, 1968), 50.
3. Anon., *Madeleine: An Autobiography* (New York: Harper & Brothers, 1919).
4. New York Society for the Suppression of Vice (NYSSV), founded in 1873 to enforce laws for the "suppression of trade in and circulation of obscene literature, and illustrations, advertisements, and articles of indecent and immoral use, as it is or may be forbidden by the laws of the State of New York or of the United States." The organization was spearheaded by Anthony Comstock, who served as the secretary of the NYSSV as well as an agent and inspector for both the society and the United States Postal Service. The early annual reports of the society make clear that information or appliances for birth control, contraceptives, or abortion were considered obscene, even pornographic. All of this obscene material, including pamphlets, newspaper advertisements, pills, and powders used by abortionists, was to be confiscated and destroyed by the society. See New York Historical Society and Museum, March, 27.
5. Anon., *Madeleine*. Citations refer to the 1986 Persea edition.
6. "Brainard, Found Guilty of Selling Vile Book, May Get Jail Sentence," *Washington Times*, January 24, 1920, 1–2.
7. "Brainard, Found Guilty," 1–2.
8. Anon., *Madeleine* (1919), xxx.
9. Anon., *Madeleine* (1919), xxx.
10. Anon., *Madeleine* (1919), xxx.
11. "Brainard, Found Guilty," 1–2.
12. F.M. O'B, "The Book of Madeleine Who Is Not Magdalene," *New York Herald*, November 2, 1919, 58.
13. *Battle Creek Enquirer*, November 20, 1919, 3.
14. "Filthy Fiction," *The Tennessean*, January 27, 1920, 6.
15. Anon., *Madeleine* (1919), xxix.
16. "Brainard, Found Guilty," 1–2.
17. New York Supreme Court appeal records of appeals, argued by John Larkin on behalf of Harper & Brothers, 1920, 982–1107.
18. New York Supreme Court appeal records of appeals, argued by John Larkin on behalf of Harper & Brothers, 982–1107.
19. Julia Watson and Sidonie Smith, *Before They Could Vote: American Women's Autobiographical Writing, 1819–1919* (Madison: University of Wisconsin Press, 2006), 442–447.
20. Belinda Crowson, "We Don't Talk About Those Women—Lethbridge's Red Light District 1880's to 1940," Lethbridge Historical Society (1970, repr. 2010), 46–48.

Chapter 1

1. Emma Goldman, *Anarchism and Other Essays* (N.p.: Sahara Publisher Books, 1910), 175.
2. *Sunday News* (Wilkes-Barre, PA), Sunday, January 13, 1895.
3. Anthony Comstock, *Frauds Exposed: Or, How the People Are Deceived*

and Robbed, and Youth Corrupted (New York: J.H. Brown, 1880), 418.

4. Comstock, *Frauds Exposed*, 5.

5. Robertus Love, "Side Lights on a Relentless Veteran in the War Against the Indecent and Obscene," *Grand Island Independent*, October 27, 1906, 4.

6. Frank Bixby Gilbert, *Criminal Law and Practice of the State of New York, United States: vol. 1–2* (Albany: Matthew Bender, 1918), Article 106.315b.

7. Jay A. Gertzman, "John Saxton Sumner of the New York Society for the Suppression of Vice: A Chief Smut-Eradicator," *Journal of American Culture* 17, no. 2 (1994): 41, doi:10.1111/j.1542-734x.1994.00041.

8. S.J. Kleinberg, "Children's and Mothers' Wage Labor in Three Eastern U.S. Cities, 1880–1920," *Social Science History* 29, no. 1 (2005): 45–76.

9. U.S. Census Bureau 1923: 478; Perlmann 1988; Hunter 2001.

10. Kleinberg, "Children's and Mothers' Wage Labor," 45–76.

11. Loralee MacPike, "The New Woman, Childbearing, and the Reconstruction of Gender, 1880–1900," *NWSA Journal* 1, no. 3 (1989): 368–397.

Chapter 2

1. *New York Tribune*, Friday, October 24, 1919, 10.

2. New York, Supreme Court, Appellate Division, 1st Division, vol. 4255, 981.

3. Dawn B. Sova, *Literature Suppressed on Sexual Grounds* (New York: Facts on File, 2006), 153–154.

4. New York, Supreme Court, Appellate Division, 1st Division, 982–1107.

5. Office of the State Historian, U.S. Diplomacy and Yellow Journalism 1895–1898, http:// history.state.gov.

6. Office of the State Historian.

7. Sova, *Literature Suppressed on Sexual Grounds*, 153–154.

8. Paul S. Boyer, *Purity in Print: Book Censorship in America from the Gilded Age to the Computer Age* (Madison: University of Wisconsin Press, 2002), 50.

9. Henry Pringle, "Comstock the Less," *American Mercury* (1922): 58.

10. New York, Supreme Court, Appellate Division, 1st Division, 982–1107.

11. New York, Supreme Court, Appellate Division, 997.

12. New York, Supreme Court, Appellate Division, 982–1107.

13. New York, Supreme Court, Appellate Division, 1033.

14. New York, Supreme Court, Appellate Division, 1043.

15. New York, Supreme Court, Appellate Division, 982–1107.

16. New York, Supreme Court, Appellate Division, 1st Division, 982–1107.

Chapter 3

1. David W. Levy, "Review of *The Quest for Moral Reform*, by David J. Pivar," *Reviews in American History* 2, no. 1 (1974): 94–98, https://doi.org/10.2307/2701355.

2. Levy, "Review," 94–98.

3. Levy, "Review," 94–98.

4. Levy, "Review," 94–98.

5. Claudia Goldin, "The Work and Wages of Single Women, 1870–1920," *Journal of Economic History* 40, no. 1 (1980): 81–88, http://www.jstor.org/stable/2120426.

6. Goldin, "The Work and Wages," 81–88.

7. Anon., *Madeleine: An Autobiography* (New York: Harper & Brothers, 1919), 17.

8. Anon., *Madeleine* (1919), 19.

9. Emma Liggins, "Prostitution and Social Purity in the 1880s and 1890s," *Critical Survey* 15, no. 3 (2003): 39–55, http://www.jstor.org/stable/41557223.

10. Liggins, "Prostitution and Social Purity," 41–42.

11. K. Burns and L. Novick, "Roots of Prohibition," PBS, 2011, http://www.pbs.org/kenburns/prohibition/roots-of-prohibition/.

Chapter 4

1. Ben Barr Lindsey and Harvey Jerrold O'Higgins, *The Beast* (New York: Doubleday, 1910), 10.

2. *Washington Post*, January 25, 1927.

3. Lindsey and O'Higgins, *The Beast*, 15.

4. M. Susan Yetter, Inventory of

Benjamin Lindsey, collection no. 389, Colorado Historical Society, 1986.
5. Yetter, Inventory of Benjamin Lindsey.
6. Lindsey and O'Higgins, *The Beast*, 15–16
7. Lindsey and O'Higgins, *The Beast*, 15–16.
8. Lindsey and O'Higgins, *The Beast*, 16.
9. Lindsey and O'Higgins, *The Beast*, vi.
10. Lindsey and O'Higgins, *The Beast*, 152.
11. Marjorie Hornbein, "The Story of Judge Ben Lindsey," *Southern California Quarterly* 55, no. 4 (1973): 469–82, https://doi.org/10.2307/41170502.
12. Lindsey and O'Higgins, *The Beast*, 231.
13. *The Survey*, vol. LV (New York: Survey Associates, October 1925–March 1926), 473.
14. Philip B. Gilliam, "The Story of Ben B. Lindsey," *Brand Book* XXV (1969): 27.
15. *San Francisco Examiner*, March 27, 1943, 3.
16. Ben B. Lindsey, introduction to *Madeleine: An Autobiography* (New York: Harper & Brothers, 1919), xxx.
17. Lindsey, introduction to *Madeleine*, xx.
18. Lindsey, introduction to *Madeleine*, xxxii.

Chapter 5

1. *Catholic Record* XX, no. 1010 (February 26, 1898), https://www.canadiana.ca/view/oocihm.8_06663_1011/8.
2. "Cornelius Regan," *Catholic Record* 1, no. 31 (May 2, 1879), 3, www.canadiana.ca/view/oocihm.8_06663_31/5.
3. Anon., *Madeleine: An Autobiography* (New York: Harper & Brothers, 1919), 5.
4. *Catholic Record*, February 26, 1898.
5. *Catholic Record*, February 26, 1898.
6. Anon., *Madeleine* (1919), 3.
7. United States Census, 1880, National Archives and Records Administration, image 253 of 645, Film Number/Image Group Number: 005161244.
8. *Unionville Republican* (Unionville, MO), Thursday, November 13, 1879, 3.
9. *Unionville Republican*, Thursday, November 13, 1879, 3.
10. Anon., *Madeleine* (1919), 4.
11. Anon., *Madeleine* (1919), 6.
12. Anon., *Madeleine* (1919), 6.
13. *Canadian Encyclopedia*, www.thecanadianencyclopedia.ca/en/article/american-civil-war.
14. National Park Service, "6th Regiment, Missouri Infantry (Union)," Civil War Soldiers and Sailors Database.
15. National Museum of Civil War Medicine, www.civilwarmed.org/ptsd/.
16. Jonathan Lewy, "The Army Disease: Drug Addiction and the Civil War," *War in History* 21, no. 1 (2014): 102–119.
17. Anon., *Madeleine* (1919), 3.
18. *Missouri Republican* (Saint Louis, MO), Tuesday, October 14, 1873.
19. *Unionville Republican* (Unionville, MO), Thursday, March 3, 1881, 1.
20. Anon., *Madeleine* (1919), 9.
21. Anon., *Madeleine* (1919), 10.
22. Anon., *Madeleine* (1919), 11.
23. Anon., *Madeleine* (1919), 11.
24. *Saint Joseph Gazette*, February 7, 1889, 4.
25. A house of assignation is a term used in the 1880s and early 1900s to describe rooms in a house rented by the hour or hours for sexual activity.
26. 1880 United States Federal Census, Missouri, Saint Joseph, microfilm 056.
27. Anon., *Madeleine* (1919), 13.
28. Anon., *Madeleine* (1919), 15.
29. Ben B. Lindsey, *The Companionate Marriage* (New York: Arno Press/New York Times, 1972), 364.
30. Anon., *Madeleine* (1919), 13.

Chapter 6

1. Carroll Smith-Rosenberg, "The Hysterical Woman: Sex Roles and Role Conflict in 19th-Century America," *Social Research* 39, no. 4 (1972): 656.
2. Anon., *Madeleine: An Autobiography* (New York: Harper & Brothers, 1919), 18.
3. Anon., *Madeleine* (1919), 25.
4. Anon., *Madeleine* (1919), 32.
5. Anon., *Madeleine* (1919), 30.
6. James Smith, *Ireland's Magdalene Laundries* (Notre Dame: University of Notre Dame Press, 2007), 29.

7. Elizabeth V. Cardinal, untitled email written to unknown recipient, July 18, 2006, http://archiver.rootsweb.ansestry.com/th/read/GOOD.-SHEPHERD-HOMES/2006-07/1153260852.

8. Anon., *Madeleine* (1919), 55.

9. *Kansas City Star*, September 23, 1886, 1.

10. Thomas M. Spencer, *The Other Missouri History: Populists, Prostitutes, and Regular Folk* (Columbia: University of Missouri Press, 2004), 228.

11. Anon., *Madeleine* (1919), 58.
12. Anon., *Madeleine* (1919), 62.
13. Anon., *Madeleine* (1919), 61.
14. Anon., *Madeleine* (1919), 64–65.
15. Anon., *Madeleine* (1919), 66.
16. Anon., *Madeleine* (1919), 70.
17. Anon., *Madeleine* (1919), 71.
18. Anon., *Madeleine* (1919), 73–74.

19. B. Donovan, "The Sexual Basis of Racial Formation: Anti–vice Activism and the Creation of the Twentieth-Century 'Color Line,'" *Ethnic and Racial Studies* 26, no. 4 (2003): 707–727.

20. William A. Davis, "'Irréconciliables,' 'Reclaimables,' and 'First Falls': Lady Mary Jeune and the Fallen Woman in *Tess of the d'Urbervilles*," *Hardy Review* 10, no. 1 (2008): 69–82, http://www.jstor.org/stable/45300330.

21. Davis, "'Irréconciliables,' 'Reclaimables,' and 'First Falls,'" 77–78.

22. Lord Byron, *The Ethical Works*, vol. I (New York: Little, Brown, 1854), 153.

23. Anon., *Madeleine* (1919), 81.
24. Anon., *Madeleine* (1919), 85.
25. Anon., *Madeleine* (1919), 88.
26. Anon., *Madeleine* (1919), 88.

27. *Fessenden Diamond Jubilee, 1893–1968*, 108.

28. *Fessenden Diamond Jubilee, 1893–1968*, 87.

Chapter 7

1. Anon., *Madeleine: An Autobiography* ((New York: Harper & Brothers, 1919), 97.

2. Obit, January 4, 1905, Bismarck, Burleigh, North Dakota, United States, ancestrylibrary.com.

3. Anon., *Madeleine* (1919), 99.

4. *History of Buchanan County, Missouri, containing a history of the county, its cities, towns, etc.*, 1881, 210–222.

5. Anon., *Madeleine* (1919), 99–100.

6. Anon., *Madeleine* (1919), 101.

7. W. T. (William Thomas) Stead, 1849–1912—Stead, William T., *If Christ Came to Chicago! A Plea for the Union of All Who Love in the Service of All Who Suffer* (London: Review of Reviews, 1894). Information was retrieved using the 19th Precinct and 1st Ward at Chicago by Stead W. T, in his book *If Christ Came to Chicago! A Plea for the Union of All Who Love in the Service of All Who Suffer*, records 46 saloons, 37 "houses of ill-fame," and 11 pawnbrokers in 1894.

8. Anon., *Madeleine* (1919), 105.
9. Anon., *Madeleine* (1919), 104.

10. *Inter Ocean* (Chicago), Thursday, October 25, 1900, 3.

11. *Inter Ocean* (Chicago), Sunday, November 25, 1900.

12. *Inter Ocean*, Thursday, October 25, 1900, 3.

13. *Inter Ocean* (Chicago), Friday, September 2, 1892, 3.

14. Karen Abbot, *Sin in the Second City: Madams, Ministers, Playboys, and the Battle for America's Soul* (New York: Random House, 2008), 12.

15. Anon., *Madeleine* (1919), 117.
16. Anon., *Madeleine* (1919), 118–119.

17. *Chicago Tribune* (Chicago), Monday, January 7, 1935, 14.

18. *Chicago Tribune* (Chicago), Wednesday, July 29, 1896, 12.

19. *Inter Ocean* (Chicago), Monday, June 25, 1894, 4.

20. *Inter Ocean*, Monday, June 25, 1894, 4.

21. *Chicago Chronicle*, Wednesday, September 9, 1896, 5.

22. Charles Washburn, *Come into My Parlor* (New York: Knickerbocker Press, 1934), 114.

23. *Day Book* (Chicago), Saturday, April 5, 1913, 7.

24. *Chicago Tribune*, Sunday, December 20, 1914, 19.

25. Anon., *Madeleine* (1919), 120–121.

26. *Los Angeles Record*, Friday, August 29, 1924, 1. This interview is part of a larger interview referenced in this book.

27. *Los Angeles Record*, Friday, August 29, 1924, 1.

28. *Los Angeles Record*, Friday, August 29, 1924, 1.
29. Anon., *Madeleine* (1919), 122.
30. Anon., *Madeleine* (1919), 127–128.
31. Anon., *Madeleine* (1919), 145.
32. Anon., *Madeleine* (1919), 131.
33. Anon., *Madeleine* (1919), 152.

Chapter 8

1. Anon., *Madeleine: An Autobiography* (New York: Harper & Brothers, 1919), 160.
2. Anon., *Madeleine* (1919), 161.
3. Anon., *Madeleine* (1919), 163.
4. Anon., *Madeleine* (1919), 166.
5. Anon., *Madeleine* (1919), 167.
6. In this case, it is said a relative helped her mother and stepped in to get Patrick out of jail and gives him employment. With the difference of years, it can be assumed this is another event of a run-in with the law and rescue, this time by a relative. The previous had been a friend of her father who was an attorney. The relative is listed as being from the East, which most likely means Canada.
7. Anon., *Madeleine* (1919), 168–169.
8. Rhonda L. Hinther, "Manitoba History," *Manitoba Historical Society* 41 (Spring/Summer 2001), http://www.mhs.mb.ca/docs/mb_history/41/oldestprofession.shtml
9. Anon., *Madeleine* (1919), 178–179.
10. Anon., *Madeleine* (1919), 178.
11. Anon., *Madeleine* (1919), 179.
12. Anon., *Madeleine* (1919), 179.
13. Anon., *Madeleine* (1919), 184–185.
14. Anon., *Madeleine* (1919), 186.
15. "California, County Marriages, 1850–1953," *FamilySearch*, entry for Septimus Whitney Sears and Agnes Regan Fiske, November 13, 1916.
16. Sarah B. Apmann, "Was My House a Brothel?," *Village Preservation Organization*, 2016, 3, 17, www.villagepreservation.org/2016/03/17/was-my-house-a-brothel/.
17. Anon., *Madeleine* (1919), 189.
18. Anon., *Madeleine* (1919), 189.

Chapter 9

1. Anon., *Madeleine: An Autobiography* (New York: Harper & Brothers, 1919), 194.

2. Anon., *Madeleine* (1919), 196.
3. Anon., *Madeleine* (1919), 198.
4. William Sanger, *The History of Prostitution* (New York: Eugenics Publishing Company, 1839), 481.
5. Anon., *Madeleine* (1919), 199–200.
6. Anon., *Madeleine* (1919), 200.
7. Anon., *Madeleine* (1919), 200.
8. Norma Basch, *In the Eyes of the Law: Women, Marriage and Property in Nineteenth-Century New York* (Ithaca: Cornell University Press, 1983), 225.
9. Anon., *Madeleine* (1919), 200.
10. U. Sreelakshmi, J. Thejaswini, and T. Bharathi, "The Outcome of Septic Abortion: A Tertiary Care Hospital Experience," *Journal of Obstetrics and Gynaecology of India* 64, no. 4 (2004): 265–269.
11. Anon., *Madeleine* (1919), 201–202.
12. Anon., *Madeleine* (1919), 202.
13. Anon., *Madeleine* (1919), 203.
14. Anon., *Madeleine* (1919), 205.

Chapter 10

1. Anon., *Madeleine: An Autobiography* (New York: Harper & Brothers, 1919), 206.
2. Anon., *Madeleine* (1919), 207.

Chapter 11

1. Larry Hoffman, "The Mining History of Butte and Anaconda," Mining History Association, 12th Annual Conference, June 14–17, 2001, Montana Tech, Butte, Montana, www.mininghistoryassociation.org/ButteHistory.htm.
2. Anon., *Madeleine: An Autobiography* (New York: Harper & Brothers, 1919), 210.
3. I. Nelson Rose, "Gambling and the Law: 19th Century Games, 21st Century Players," 2015, www.//chaselaw.nku.edu/content/dam/chase/docs/lawreview/symposia/1%20Nelson%20Rose_19th%20Century%20Games.pdf.
4. Anon., *Madeleine* (1919), 212.
5. Mara Laura Keire, *For Business and Pleasure: Red-Light Districts and the Regulation of Vice in the United States, 1890–1933* (Baltimore: Johns Hopkins University Press, 2010).

6. Anon., *Madeleine* (1919), 213.
7. Anon., *Madeleine* (1919), 218.
8. Anon., *Madeleine* (1919), 219.
9. Anon., *Madeleine* (1919), 219.
10. Anon., *Madeleine* (1919), 227–228.
11. Anon., *Madeleine* (1919), 220.

Chapter 12

1. Montana Cowboy Hall of Fame, www.montanacowboyfame.org/inductees/2008/10/sheriff-henry-plummer.
2. K. Ross Toole, *Montana: An Uncommon Land* (Norman: University of Oklahoma Press, 1959), 134.
3. Michael P. Malone, Richard B. Roeder, and William L. Lang, *Montana: A History of Two Centuries* (Seattle: University of Washington Press, 1991), 221.
4. Anon., *Madeleine: An Autobiography* (New York: Harper & Brothers, 1919), 228.
5. Anon., *Madeleine* (1919), 230.
6. William Acton, *Prostitution Considered in Its Moral, Social, and Sanitary Aspects, in London and Other Large Cities and Garrison Towns: With Proposals for the Control and Prevention of Its Attendant Evils* (Kiribati: J. Churchill, 1870), 229.
7. R.K. Macalester, *Journal of Cutaneous Diseases Including Syphilis* (1896), 73.
8. Anon., *Madeleine* (1919), 231.
9. Anon., *Madeleine* (1919), 238.
10. Anon., *Madeleine* (1919), 239.

Chapter 13

1. Anon., *Madeleine: An Autobiography* (New York: Harper & Brothers, 1919), 243.
2. Anon., *Madeleine* (1919), 246–247.
3. Anon., *Madeleine* (1919), 249–250.
4. Anon., *Madeleine* (1919), 252–253.
5. Anon., *Madeleine* (1919), 254–255.
6. Anon., *Madeleine* (1919), 254–255.
7. L.K. Bertram, "The Other Little House: The Brothel as a Colonial Institution on the Canadian Prairies, 1880–93," *Journal of Social History* 56, no. 1 (2022): 58–88, muse.jhu.edu/article/865979.
8. A.A. Otter, *Civilizing the West: The Galts and the Development of Western Canada* (Edmonton: University of Alberta Press, 1986), 243.
9. Otter, *Civilizing the West*, 243.
10. Otter, *Civilizing the West*, 242.
11. Otter, *Civilizing the West*, 244.
12. R. Burton Deane, *Mounted Police Life in Canada: A Record of Thirty-One Years of Service* (Ramsey, NJ: Funk and Wagnalls, 1916), 60.
13. Deane, *Mounted Police Life in Canada*, 2.
14. Deane, *Mounted Police Life in Canada*, 4.
15. Deane, *Mounted Police Life in Canada*, 4.
16. Deane, *Mounted Police Life in Canada*, 4.
17. Deane, *Mounted Police Life in Canada*, 39.
18. Deane, *Mounted Police Life in Canada*, 42.
19. Anon., *Madeleine* (1919), 256.
20. Anon., *Madeleine* (1919), 256.
21. Anon., *Madeleine* (1919), 263.
22. Anon., *Madeleine* (1919), 264.

Chapter 14

1. Anon., *Madeleine: An Autobiography* (New York: Harper & Brothers, 1919), 277.
2. Anon., *Madeleine* (1919), 279–280.
3. Anon., *Madeleine* (1919), 283–284.
4. Anon., *Madeleine* (1919), 289.
5. S.W. Horrall, "The (Royal) North-West Mounted Police and Prostitution on the Canadian Prairies," in *Immigration and Settlement, 1870–1939*, ed. Gregory P. Marchildon (Regina: University of Regina, CPRC Press, 2000), 129–156.
6. Anon., *Madeleine* (1919), 292.
7. Anon., *Madeleine* (1919), 294.
8. Anon., *Madeleine* (1919), 296.
9. Anon., *Madeleine* (1919), 298.
10. Anon., *Madeleine* (1919), 303.
11. Anon., *Madeleine* (1919), 303.
12. Anon., *Madeleine* (1919), 304.
13. Anon., *Madeleine* (1919), 305.
14. Mara L. Keire, "The Vice Trust: A Reinterpretation of the White Slavery Scare in the United States, 1907–1917,"

Chapter Notes **183**

Journal of Social History 35, no. 1 (2001): 11.
15. Anon., *Madeleine* (1919), 315–317.

Chapter 15

1. *San Francisco Chronicle*, January 26, 1917, 5.
2. Anon., *Madeleine: An Autobiography* (Los Angeles: Hollywood Press, 1924), 334.
3. Anon., *Madeleine* (1924), 327.
4. Donald Lowrie, *My Life out of Prison* (London: Mitchell Kennerley, 1915). Time dated between newspaper and Anon., *Madeleine* (1924). *San Francisco Examiner*, Monday, January 1, 1912, 14.
5. Anon., *Madeleine* (1924), 334.
6. Anon., *Madeleine* (1924), 335.
7. Anon., *Madeleine* (1924), 321.
8. Anon., *Madeleine* (1924), 322.
9. Anon., *Madeleine: An Autobiography* (New York: Harper & Brothers, 1919), 324–325.
10. Anon., *Madeleine* (1919), 322.
11. *The Tidings* (Los Angeles), January 30, 1914, 14
12. "The Diaries of Emmeline B. Wells," www.churchhistorianspress.org/emmeline-b-wells/people/septimus-whitney-sears-jr-1874?letter=S&lang=ita#_ftnref16.
13. California State Board of Health, Bureau of Vital Statics, Local register 5902, 11,13,1926.166.
14. California State Board of Health, Bureau of Vital Statics, Local register 5902, 11,13,1926.166.
15. *Salt Lake Telegram*, Sunday, September 10, 1922, 11.
16. *Salt Lake Tribune*, Sunday, September 10, 1922, 17.
17. Emmeline B. Wells, *Diary*, February 19, February 24, and April 16, 1896, Emmeline B. Wells Papers, Church History Library, Church of Jesus Christ of Latter-day Saints, Salt Lake City, June 22 and 26, 1895.
18. Emmeline B. Wells, *Diary*, February 19 and February 24, 1896; April 16, 1896. San Francisco Co., CA, County Clerk, Great Registers, 1866–1898; Indexes, 1866, 1888–1904, vol. 4-2A, folder no. 104, Septimus Whitney Sears, district 43, voter no. 179, reg. no. 200, microfilm 977261, DGS 5030225, FHL.
19. Anon., *Madeleine* (1919), 88.

Chapter 16

1. Anon., *Madeleine: An Autobiography* (Los Angles: Hollywood Press, 1924), 331.
2. *The Bulletin* (San Francisco), Saturday, September 2, 1911, 12.
3. Anon., *Madeleine: An Autobiography* (Los Angeles: Hollywood Press, 1924), 333.
4. *The Bulletin* (San Francisco), Wednesday, June 25, 1913, 6.
5. *The Bulletin*, June 25, 1913, 6.
6. *The Bulletin*, June 25, 1913, 6.
7. *The Bulletin* (San Francisco), June 18, 1913, 11.
8. Jane Addams, *A New Conscience and an Ancient Evil* (New York: Macmillan, 1913).
9. Emma Goldman, *Anarchism and Other Essays* (New York: Mother Earth Publishing Association, 1917), 195.
10. *The Bulletin* (San Francisco), Editorial, June 25, 1913, 11.
11. *The Bulletin* (San Francisco), June 19, 1913, 11.
12. *The Bulletin*, June 19, 1913, 11.
13. Anon., epilogue to *Madeleine* (Los Angeles: Hollywood Press, 1924), 339.

Chapter 17

1. *Los Angeles Times*, Monday, February 14, 1927, 19.
2. Mary does fight the ban in court.
3. *Los Angeles Times*, Monday, February 14, 1927, 19.
4. *Brooklyn Daily Eagle*, Saturday, July 10, 1920, 4.
5. *Brooklyn Daily Eagle*, Saturday, July 10, 1920, 4.
6. *Los Angeles Record*, Friday, August 29, 1924, 1.
7. *Los Angeles Record*, Friday, August 29, 1924, 1.
8. Anon., *Madeleine: An Autobiography* (New York: Harper & Brothers, 1919), 326.
9. *Los Angeles Times*, Friday, November 16, 1934, 19.

10. *Illustrated Daily News* (Los Angeles), Friday, November 16, 1934, 4.
11. Anon., *Madeleine: An Autobiography* (Los Angeles: Hollywood Press, 1924), 338.
12. Anon., *Madeleine* (1924), 338.
13. Anon., *Madeleine* (1924), 338.
14. *California Outlook, a Progressive Weekly* (1916), 40.
15. *Stockton Daily Evening Record*, Friday, November 16, 1934, 1.
16. *Los Angeles Times*, Wednesday, December 14, 1932, 21.
17. Anon., *Madeleine* (1924), 338.
18. *Los Angeles Times*, Wednesday, December 14, 1932, 21.
19. *Sacramento Bee*, Saturday, June 5, 1920, 19.
20. John R. Adams, *Books and Authors of San Diego: A Check List* (San Diego: San Diego State College Press, 1966), 191.
21. Richard B. Yale, "The Birthplace of the San Diego Union," *Journal of San Diego History* 14, no. 4 (1968), https://sandiegohistory.org/journal/1968/october/union/.
22. *Troubadour: A Magazine of Verse* (1928), 8.
23. *Illustrated Daily News* (Los Angeles), Monday, November 12, 1934, 6.
24. *Illustrated Daily News*, Monday, November 12, 1934, 6.
25. *Los Angeles Post*, November 10, 1934.
26. Find a Grave, www.findagrave.com/memorial/6740574/vibiana.

Bibliography

Academic Papers and Articles

Bertram, L.K. "The Other Little House: The Brothel as a Colonial Institution on the Canadian Prairies, 1880–93." *Journal of Social History* 56, no. 1 (2022): 58–88. muse.jhu.edu/article/865979.

Davis, William A. "'Irréconciliables,' 'Reclaimables,' and 'First Falls': Lady Mary Jeune and the Fallen Woman in 'Tess of the d'Urbervilles.'" *Hardy Review* 10, no. 1 (2008): 69–82. http://www.jstor.org/stable/45300330.

Donovan, B. "The Sexual Basis of Racial Formation: Anti-vice Activism and the Creation of the Twentieth-Century 'Color Line." *Ethnic and Racial Studies* 26, no. 4 (2003): 707–727.

Gertzman, Jay A. "John Saxton Sumner of the New York Society for the Suppression of Vice: A Chief Smut-Eradicator." *Journal of American Culture* 17, no. 2 (1994): 41–47. doi:10.1111/j.1542-734x.1994.00041.x.

Gilliam, Philip B. "The Story of Ben B. Lindsey." *Brand Book* XXV (1969).

Goldin, Claudia. "The Work and Wages of Single Women, 1870–1920." *The Journal of Economic History* 40, no. 1 (1980): 81–88. http://www.jstor.org/stable/2120426.

Gordon, Linda. "Voluntary Motherhood: The Beginnings of Feminist Birth Control Ideas in the United States." *Feminist Studies* 1, no. 3/4 (1973): 5–22. http://www.jstor.org/stable/1566477.

Hinther, Rhonda L. "The Oldest Profession in Winnipeg: The Culture of Prostitution in the Point Douglas Segregated District, 1909–1912." *Manitoba History* 41 (Spring/Summer 2001), https://www.mhs.mb.ca/docs/mb_history/41/oldestprofession.shtml

Hornbein, Marjorie. "The Story of Judge Ben Lindsey." *Southern California Quarterly* 55, no. 4 (1973): 469–82. https://doi.org/10.2307/41170502.

Jensen, Kimberly. "The 'Open Way of Opportunity': Colorado Women Physicians and World War I." *The Western Historical Quarterly* 27, no. 3 (1996): 327–48.

Keire, Mara L. "The Vice Trust: A Reinterpretation of the White Slavery Scare in the United States, 1907–1917." *Journal of Social History* 35, no. 1 (2001): 5–41.

Kleinberg, S.J. "Children's and Mothers' Wage Labor in Three Eastern U.S. Cities, 1880–1920." *Social Science History* 29, no. 1 (2005): 45–76.

Levy, David W. "The Quest for Moral Reform." *Reviews in American History* 2, no. 1 (1974): 94–98.

Lewy, Jonathan. "The Army Disease: Drug Addiction and the Civil War." *War in History* 21, no. 1 (2014): 102–19.

Liggins, Emma. "Prostitution and Social Purity in the 1880s and 1890s." *Critical Survey* 15, no. 3 (2003): 39–55. http://www.jstor.org/stable/41557223.

MacPike, Loralee. "The New Woman, Childbearing, and the Reconstruction of Gender, 1880–1900." *NWSA Journal* 1, no. 3 (1989): 368–97.

Malone, Michael P., Richard B. Roeder, and William L. Lang. *Montana: A History of Two Centuries*. Seattle: University of Washington Press, 1991.

Rose, I. Nelson. "Gambling and the Law: 19th Century Games, 21st Century Players." 2015. www.//chaselaw.nku.edu/content/dam/chase/docs/lawreview/symposia/I%20 Nelson%20Rose_19th%20Century%20Games.pdf.
Sreelakshmi, U., Thejaswini, J., and Bharathi, T. "The Outcome of Septic Abortion: A Tertiary Care Hospital Experience." *Journal of Obstetrics and Gynaecology of India* 64, no. 4 (2014): 265–69.
Toole, Ross, K. *Montana: An Uncommon Land.* Norman: University of Oklahoma Press, 1959.
Wahab, Stephanie. "'For Their Own Good?': Sex Work, Social Control and Social Workers, a Historical Perspective." *The Journal of Sociology & Social Welfare* 29, no. 4 (2002): 39–55.
Walkowitz, Judith R. "The Politics of Prostitution." *Signs* 6, no. 1 (1980): 123–35. http://www.jstor.org/stable/3173970.

Archival Research

California Outlook, a Progressive Weekly. United States: n.p., 1916.
Canadian Encyclopedia, www.thecanadianencyclopedia.ca/en/article/american-civil-war.
Crowson, Belinda. "We Don't Talk About Those Women—Lethbridge's Red Light District 1880's to 1940." Lethbridge Historical Society, Canada (1970, repr. 2010): 46–48.
Denver Public Library, Genealogy, African American & Western History Resources, https://history.denverlibrary.org/colorado-biographies/judge-benjamin-barr-lindsey-1869-1943.
Find a Grave, www.findagrave.com/memorial/6740574/vibiana.
History of Buchanan County, Missouri, containing a history of the county, its cities, towns, etc. 1881.
Lindsey, Ben. "The 'Just' Judge." *Mc Clure's Magazine*, December 1906. The Archive of American Journalism. Lincoln Steffens Collection.
Michigan, U.S., Marriage Records, 1867–1952 (1900)—Allie E Alterauge, Grace Alterauge.
Montana Cowboy Hall of Fame, www.montanacowboyfame.org/inductees/2008/10/sheriff-henry-plummer.
National Museum of Civil War Medicine, www.civilwarmed.org/ptsd/.
Office of the State Historian. U.S. Diplomacy and Yellow Journalism 1895–1898, http://history.state.gov.
Pringle, Henry. "Comstock the Less." *American Mercury* January 1927: 56–63.
Sova, Dawn B. "Literature Suppressed on Sexual Grounds." United States: Facts on File, 2006.
Stead, W.T. (William Thomas), 1849–1912—Stead, William T. 1894. *If Christ Came to Chicago! A Plea for the Union of All Who Love in the Service of All Who Suffer.* London: Review of Reviews.
UK and Ireland, Incoming Passenger Lists, 1878–1960.
Voyant Tools used for this research: www.voyant-tools.org/docs/#!/guide/about.
Yetter, M. Susan. Inventory of Benjamin Lindsey. Collection No. 389. Colorado Historical Society, 1986.

Books and Monographs

Abbot, Karen. *Sin in the Second City, Madams, Ministers, Playboys, and the Battle for America's Soul.* New York: Random House, 2008.
Acton, William. *Prostitution Considered in Its Moral, Social, and Sanitary Aspects, in London and Other Large Cities and Garrison Towns: With Proposals for the Control and Prevention of Its Attendant Evils.* Kiribati: J. Churchill, 1870.
Adams, John R. *Books and Authors of San Diego: A Check List.* San Diego: San Diego State College Press, 1966.

Addams, Jane. *A New Conscience and an Ancient Evil.* New York: Macmillan, 1911, 1912.
Anon. *Madeleine: An Autobiography*, introductions by Ben B. Lindsey and Marcia Carlisle. New York: Harper, 1919; New York: Persea Books, 1986.
Anon. *Madeleine: An Autobiography.* Los Angeles: Hollywood Press, 1924.
Barthes, Roland. *The Pleasure of the Text.* Translated by Richard Miller. London: Jonathan Cape, 1976.
Basch, Norma. *In the Eyes of the Law: Women, Marriage and Property in Nineteenth-Century New York.* Ithaca: Cornell University Press, 1983.
Boyer, Paul S. *Purity in Print: Book Censorship in America from the Gilded Age to the Computer Age.* Madison: University of Wisconsin Press, 2002.
Boyer, Paul S. *Purity in Print. The Vice-Society Movement in America.* New York: Scribner's, 1968.
Carlisle, Marcia. Introduction. *Madeleine: An Autobiography.* New York: Persea Books, 1986.
Comstock, Anthony. *Frauds Exposed: Or, How the People Are Deceived and Robbed, and Youth Corrupted.* New York: J.H. Brown, 1880.
De Mund, Mary. *Women Physicians of Colorado.* N.p.: Range Press, 1976.
Deane, R. Burton. *Mounted Police Life in Canada: A Record of Thirty-One Years of Service.* Ramsey, NJ: Funk and Wagnalls, 1916.
Fessenden Diamond Jubilee, 1893–1968. Diamond Jubilee Book Committee, 1968.
Foucault, Michel. "What Is an Author?" In *The Foucault Reader*, edited by Paul Rabinow, 101–120. New York: Pantheon, 1984.
Goldman, Emma. *Anarchism and Other Essays.* New York: Mother Earth Publishing Association, 1917.
Halkett, Samuel, and John Laing. *Dictionary of Anonymous and Pseudonymous English Literature*, 9 vols. Edinburgh: Oliver and Boyd, 1926; London: Pickering and Chatto, 1998.
Horrall, S.W. "The (Royal) North-West Mounted Police and Prostitution on the Canadian Prairies." In *Immigration and Settlement, 1870–1939*, edited by Gregory P. Marchildon. Regina: University of Regina, CPRC Press, 2000.
Keire, Mara Laura. *For Business and Pleasure: Red-Light Districts and the Regulation of Vice in the United States, 1890–1933.* Baltimore: Johns Hopkins University Press, 2010. https://muse.jhu.edu/pub/1/oa_monograph/chapter/8676.
Laceulle, Hanne. "Authenticity." In *Aging and Self-Realization: Cultural Narratives about Later Life*, 189–218. Bielefeld: Transcript Verlag, 2018. http://www.jstor.org/stable/j.ctv8d5tp1.10.
Lindsey, Ben B. *The Companionate Marriage.* New York: Arno Press/New York Times, 1972.
Lindsey, Ben B. Introduction. *Madeleine: An Autobiography.* New York: Persea Books, 1986.
Lindsey, Ben Barr, and Harvey Jerrold O'Higgins. *The Beast.* New York: Doubleday, 1910.
Lord Byron. *The Ethical Works Vol. I.* New York: Little, Brown, 1854.
Love, Harold. *Attributing Authorship: An Introduction.* Cambridge: Cambridge University Press, 2002.
Lowrie, Donald. *My Life out of Prison.* London: Mitchell Kennerley, 1915.
Nofi, Albert A. *To Train the Fleet for War: The U.S. Navy Fleet Problems.* Newport, RI: Naval War College Press, 2010.
Otter, A.A. *Civilizing the West: The Galts and the Development of Western Canada.* Edmonton: University of Alberta Press, 1986.
Pivar, David J. *Purity Crusade: Sexual Morality and Social Control, 1868–1900.* Westport, CT: Greenwood. https://doi.org/10.2307/2701355.
Rousseau, Jean-Jacques. *Julie, or, The New Heloise: Letters of Two Lovers Who Live in a Small Town at the Foot of the Alps.* Translated by P. Stewart and J. Hanover. Lebanon, NH: University Press of New England, 1997.
Sanger, William. *The History of Prostitution.* New York: Eugenics Publishing Company, 1839.

188 Bibliography

Smith, James. *Ireland's Magdalene Laundries*. Notre Dame: University of Notre Dame Press, 2007.
Spencer, Thomas M. *The Other Missouri History: Populists, Prostitutes, and Regular Folk*. Columbia: University of Missouri Press, 2004.
Washburn, Charles. *Come into My Parlor*. New York: Knickerbocker Press, 1934. https://archive.org/details/comeintomyparlor00wash.
Watson, Julia, and Sidonie Smith. 1945. *Before They Could Vote: American Women's Autobiographical Writing, 1819–1919*. Madison: University of Wisconsin Press, 2006.
Yale, Richard B. *The Journal of San Diego History* 14, no. 4 (1968). https://sandiegohistory.org/journal/1968/october/union/.

Government Publications

California State Board of Health. Bureau of Vital Statics. Local register 5902. 11, 13, 1926.
Catalog of Copyright Entries: Pamphlets, leaflets, contributions to newspapers or periodicals, etc.; lectures, sermons, addresses for oral delivery; dramatic compositions; maps; motion pictures. Part 1, group 2. United States: U.S. Government Printing Office, 1918.55.
Catalog of Copyright Entries: Third series. United States: n.p., 1947.45.
Copyright Act of 1909.
Information Annual. United States: R.R. Bowker, 1916.
National Park Service. "6th Regiment, Missouri Infantry (Union)." *Civil War Soldiers and Sailors Database*. Accessed November 3, 2024. https://www.nps.gov/civilwar/search-battle-units-detail.htm?battleUnitCode=UMO0006RI.
New York Supreme Court appeal records of appeals, Argued by John Larkin on behalf of Harper & Brothers 1920. New York, Supreme Court, Appellate Division. 1st Division, vol. 4255, 982–1107.
Southern California Practitioner. Los Angeles: Stoll & Thayer, 1913.
The Survey, vol. LV. New York: Survey Associates, October 1925–March 1926.
U.S. Census Bureau 1923: 478; Perlmann 1988; Hunter 2001.
U.S. Copyright Office. Library of Congress. Circular 15 A 08/2022. https://www.copyright.gov/circs/circ15a.pdf.

Historic Newspapers

Alamosa Courier. Vol. XXV, no. 52, December 27, 1913.
The Atlantic. May 1997.
Brooklyn Daily Eagle. Saturday, July 10, 1920.
Catholic Record. Vol. XX, no. 1010, February 26, 1898.
Chicago Chronicle, Wednesday, September 9, 1896.
Chicago Tribune, Monday, January 7, 1935.
Chicago Tribune, Sunday, December 20, 1914.
Chicago Tribune, Wednesday, July 29, 1896.
"Cornelius Regan." *Orbit* (Bismarck, Burleigh, ND), January 4, 1905. ancestrylibrary.com.
Daily Gate City. "He Surprised Them." Sunday, December 21, 1913.
Daily Gate City. "Judge Lindsey Takes a Bride." Sunday, December 21, 1913.
Daily Gate City. "Romance Started at a Sanitarium Where Both Were Taking Treatment." Sunday, December 21, 1913.
Daily Gate City. Sunday, December 21, 1913.
Day Book (Chicago), Saturday, April 5, 1913.
Denver Weekly Post. Vol. 11, no. 630, January 3, 1914.
Harper's Weekly, 1914.
Illustrated Daily News (Los Angeles), Friday, November 16, 1934.

Illustrated Daily News (Los Angeles), Monday, November 12, 1934.
Inter Ocean (Chicago), Friday, September 2, 1892.
Inter Ocean, Monday, June 25, 1894.
Inter Ocean, October 25, 1900.
Inter Ocean, Sunday, November 25, 1900.
Literary Digest, 1913.
Los Angeles Post, November 10, 1934.
Los Angeles Record, Friday, August 29, 1924.
Los Angeles Times, Wednesday, December 14, 1932.
Los Angeles Times, Monday, February 14, 1927.
Missouri Republican (St. Louis), Tuesday, October 14, 1873.
New York Social Diary, December 11, 2020. A 2010 reissue of an interview with Adam Lewis, author of *The Great Lady Decorators: The Women Who Defined Interior Design: 1870–1955*. https://www.newyorksocialdiary.com/adam-lewis/.
New York Tribune, Friday, October 24, 1919.
Sacramento Bee, Saturday, June 5, 1920.
Salt Lake Telegram, Sunday, September 10, 1922.
Salt Lake Tribune, Sunday, September 10, 1922.
San Francisco Examiner, March 27, 1943.
Stockton Daily Evening Record, Friday, November 16, 1934.
The Tidings (Los Angeles), January 30, 1914.
Unionville Republican (Unionville, MO), Thursday, March 3, 1881.
Unionville Republican (Unionville, MO), Thursday, May 9, 1878.
Unionville Republican (Unionville, MO), Thursday, November 13, 1879.
Washington Herald, Sunday, December 21, 1913.
Washington Post, January 25, 1927.
Washington Times, "Brainard, Found Guilty of Selling Vile Book, May Get Jail Sentence," January 24, 1920. Number 11420.
Sunday News (Wilkes-Barre, PA), Sunday, January 13, 1895.

Interviews, Letters, and Pamphlets

Addams, Jane. "Jane Addams: The Sheltered Woman and the Magdalene, November 1913." *Jane Addams Digital Edition*. http://digital.janeaddams.ramapo.edu/items/show/8999.
Lindsey, Ben B. "A Secret Political League Who and What It Is: Its Anonymous Circulars Exposed and Court Cases Involving the Sex Problem; Frankly Discussed." Pamphlet, 1912.
Lindsey, Benjamin Barr. "Benjamin Barr Lindsey to Jane Addams, September 11, 1913 (fragment)." Jane Addams Digital Edition. https://digital.janeaddams.ramapo.edu/items/show/6421.
Willets, Phoebe E.H. "Phoebe E.H. Willets to Jane Addams, July 11, 1912." *Jane Addams Digital Edition*. http://digital.janeaddams.ramapo.edu/items/show/4447.

Film

Burns, K., & Novick, L. (2011). *Roots of Prohibition*. PBS. http://www.pbs.org/kenburns/prohibition/roots-of-prohibition/.

Index

abortion 4, 12–13, 22, 41, 90–92, 103–104, 106–107, 108, 124; *see also* Sanger, William
Addams, Jane 3–4, 10, 16–17, 34, 36, 142, 157
alcoholism 17, 54–56, 77, 95, 138, 140–142
Allen, Lizzie 82–84, 87, 90–91, 97; *see also* madams
American West (The West; Western Frontier) 9, 51, 76, 98
anarchism 11
anti-prostitution 157–158; *see also* Barton, Dr. R.C.
Art Institute of Chicago 80, 102
assignation house 100–101
Auburn (CA) 166

Badlands (SD) 111
Banff (Canada, AB) 129–130
Banff National Park (Canada AB) 129
Bannack (MT) 119, 121–122, 124, 125; *see also* Hotel Mead
Bannock Nation 120
Barton, Dr. R.C. 164, 165
Beach, Ann 101
Begbie, Harold 155, 170
Big Sisters 164
Blair, Madeleine 1, 5, 7, 13–14, 17, 19, 37, 48, 67, 86, 95, 141, 161, 167; *see also* Fiske, Mary Agnes; Gordon, Anita; Regan, Mary Agnes; Sears, Mary Agnes
Blake, Nona 127–129 *see also* madams
boarding house 57–58, 76, 146; *see also* brothel
Bolshevism 11
Book Censorship 161–162; *see also* Comstock Act; Copyright Act; The New York Society for the Suppression of Vice

Brainard, Clinton T. 11, 16–17, 29, 31–32, 34–35, 162, 177
brothel, bawdy house, first-class house 8, 58, 66–67, 78, 145, 165, 181; *see also* assignation house; boarding house; crib; madams; sporting house
Burton, Cpt. Deane 131–132, 182
Butte, Montana 95, 113–114, 117, 119, 122–126, 130, 150, 152

Canada 15, 48–51, 54, 97, 127–128, 131–132, 137, 187
Canadian Mounted Police 127, 129, 131–132, 134–137, 140; *see also* North West Mounted Police (NWMP)
Chicago 3, 65, 75–78, 81, 82, 86, 89; *see also* Art Institute of Chicago; Dearborn House; Everleigh Club
Christ Faith Mission 164–166
Civil War 9, 14, 21, 25, 38, 51–52, 54, 68; *see also* Confederacy; Missouri Infantry; Reconstruction
Colorado 2, 34, 42, 46
companionate marriage 59
Comstock, Anthony 21, 23, 25, 32, 40; *see also* Comstock Act; The New York Society for the Suppression of Vice
Comstock Act (laws) 21–22, 161
Confederacy 54
Copyright Act 4
Crabb, Christopher Columbus 82, 83
Crabb, Helen Bean 83
crib 66, 116; *see also* brothel
Custom House Place 78–79

Dearborn House 80–88, 94, 98, 101; *see also* Chicago; Everleigh Club
Denver (CO) 3, 13, 42–43
Double Standard 93, 105–106, 147, 155–156, 170

191

Index

drug addiction 54; *see also* reform movements; moral reform

Edmonton (Canada) 130, 138–139
Everleigh Club 80–81, 84, 86, 87
Everleigh Sisters (Minna and Ada) 80, 84, 87; *see also* madams

factory work 17, 26–27, 39, 40, 62, 64
Federal Immigration Commission 143
feminism 12, 26–27, 37, 59, 90; *see also* New Woman; purity movements; women's labor
Fiske, Mary Agnes 14, 96, 100, 150, 151; see also Blair, Madeleine; Gordon, Anita; Regan, Mary Coughlin; Sears, Mary Agnes

Gamble, Reggie 145, 146
Good Shepherd (St. Louis, MO) 64–65; *see also* Magdalene Laundries
Good Shepherd (San Francisco, CA) 164; *see also* Magdalene Laundries
Gordon, Anita 14

Hangman's Gulch (MT) 120–121
Hankins, Effie 81, 84; *see also* madams
Hastings, Mary 79–80; *see also* madams
Hearst, William Randolph 17, 29–32
Helena, Montana 15, 126, 127
Hollywood Press (CA) 162
Hotel Meade (Bannack, MT) 120–121
House of Friendship 164
Howard, Olga 88–89, 93, 94, 104, 109–110
Hull House 3

Illinois 74; *see also* Chicago; Custom House Place; Dearborn House; Everleigh Club
immigration 22, 25, 48, 71, 143, 182
Iowa 48, 51, 54
Ireland 25, 48–49, 50
Irish 48–51

Kansas City 66
Kee, Fawn 134, 135

Lake View Avenue 82, 83; *see also* Allen, Lizzie
Lethbridge, Canada (Al) 131–133, 177, 186
Linden, Cecil 157
Lindsey, Benjamin (judge) 3–4, 12–13, 15–17, 34, 36, 42–47, 59, 142, 152–153, 163

Lindsey, Henrietta Brevoort 4, 152–153
Los Angeles 150–152
Lovejoy, Laura 66–70, 73, 153; *see also* madams
Lowrie, Donald 147, 154–155, 158, 169, 172

Macleod (Fort), Canada (Al) 127
madams 58, 79, 80, 116, 139; *see also* Allen, Lizzie; Blake, Nona; Everleigh Sisters; Hankins Effie; Hastings, Mary; Lovejoy, Laura; Watson, Carrie
Magdalene Laundries 64, 68; *see also* Good Shepherd
Malta 130, 132–133, 136–137, 139
Martin, Paul 70, 94–95, 97, 104–106, 117–126, 129–130, 133, 140–142
Mckillop, the Rev. Charles 131
Medicine Hat, Canada (AB) 138–139
Midnight Mission (CA) 164
Mildred 136–137, 140, 144
miscarriage 47, 90, 107
Missouri 48, 51–54, 56, 68, 77, 100, 179, 186
Missouri Infantry (6th Regiment, Union) 52–54, 188; *see also* Civil War
modernization 37
Montana 113, 119, 120–121, 124
Monterey Diocese (Catholic) 150
moral reform (rehabilitation) 11, 158, 178, 185; *see also* anti-prostitution; reclaimables
moral standards 9, 11–12, 14, 21–27, 40, 62, 90, 93, 104, 158–159; *see also* white slavery
Morals Efficiency Commission 164; *see also* Barton, Dr. R.C.
Mormonism 151, 167

Navy 187
Nazis 16, 46
New Orleans (LA) 15, 88, 113, 146
New Orleans, Storyville 145
New Woman 26–27
New York 11, 18, 22, 28–29, 31, 33, 79, 113, 161; *see also* Hylan, John; The New York Society for the Suppression of Vice (NYSSV); Supreme Court (NY)
The New York Society for the Suppression of Vice (NYSSV) 11, 24–25, 155, 181, 185, 187; *see also* Comstock Act; Sumner, John Saxton
New York Supreme Court 16, 18, 33–36, 161; *see also* The New York Society for the Suppression of Vice (NYSSV)

Index

North Dakota 74, 180; *see also* Austin, Regan John
North West Mounted Police (NWMP) 127, 131, 132, 138, 140; *see also* Canadian Mounted Police

Obscenity Law 22, 25, 40; *see also* book censorship; Comstock Act
obscene literature 12, 16, 24, 28, 32–33

patriarch; Patriarchal Society; patriarchy 8, 18, 22, 27, 96
Pfanschmid, Emily 33
poorhouses 77
Progressive Era 13–14, 44, 46, 77, 157
prohibition 11, 44, 132
prostitution 7–18, 25–26, 37–39, 47, 57–58, 70–71, 73, 84, 91–92, 98, 100, 111, 115–116, 126, 142–145, 149, 161–163; *see also* brothels; white slavery
purity movements 9, 12, 26–27, 37; *see also* Comstock, Anthony; moral reform

reclaimables 71, 142, 158–159, 185
Reconstruction 21, 26
red light district 93, 123, 131–132
Red Scare 11
Regan, Cornelius 48–51
Regan, John 51, 75, 76
Regan, Mary Coughlin 39, 48, 51–52, 56–57, 59, 62, 77, 94
Regan, Patrick 48, 51–52, 54–55, 57, 59, 65, 76, 95, 96, 126
Richardson, (Col.) 132

St. Joseph (MO) 50, 57–58, 62, 77, 94–96
St. Louis (MO) 39, 53, 62
St. Vibiana 167
San Francisco 146, 151
Sanger, Dr. William 10, 104
Sears, Esther (Julian) 151
Sears, Gertrude Trindle 151
Sears, Laura Lucille 152
Sears, Mary Agnes (Regan) 6–7, 10–11, 17, 19, 153; *see also* Blair, Madeleine; Fiske, Mary Agnes; Regan, Mary Coughlin
Sears, Septimus Wagstaff 151
Sears, Septimus Whitney (Silas/Sep) 100, 151–152, 166–167
sex trade 12–13, 114, 123; *see also* prostitution

sexual morality 187
sexually transmitted disease 47, 66, 72–73
single motherhood (unwed) 13, 27, 65, 93, 95, 100
single women 39; *see also* unmarried women
Sixth Missouri Infantry Regiment 52, 54
Skid Row (CA) 164, 169
Smith, Alice 155–156
Smith, Dr. C.F. 139
Smith, the Rev. Paul 145
social hygiene 165
Social Purity Movement 11, 12, 25, 26; *see also* moral reform; purity movements
sporting house 133, 164, 173; *see also* brothel
stylometry 1, 47
Sumner, John Saxton 11, 24–25, 28, 29, 32–34, 162
Swann, Edward 28, 30–31, 33

Turkey Trail (Rr) 127

Unionville (Mo) 48, 51
unmarried women 26; *see also* single women

Venus Alley 114
Vicksburg (MS) 52, 53

Watson, Carrie 79, 82; *see also* madams
well-defended barrier (barrier) 164–165, 174
Wells, Emmeline B. 151, 167
Whitaker, Alma 167, 174
white slavery 3, 9–10, 12, 37, 70–71, 79, 88, 125–126, 143, 149, 156–157, 165
Windsor Club 143
women's labor 7–9, 11–12, 17, 21, 26, 37, 39, 159, 163, 166
women's suffrage 16, 27, 90, 142; *see also* Addams, Jane; feminism
working women 15, 41, 136, 162

World War I 9, 11, 14–15, 32, 54; *see also* Nazis; Reconstruction
World's Fair (Chicago) 57, 82, 87

yellow journalism 30–32
Young, Brigham 151

www.ingramcontent.com/pod-product-compliance
Lightning Source LLC
Chambersburg PA
CBHW032045300426
44117CB00009B/1196